PSL LIBRARY OF OCEAN TRAVEL

A MILLION OCEAN MILES

by

SIR EDGAR T. BRITTEN, RD RNR

WITH A NEW FOREWORD BY

JOHN H. SHAUM Jr

PATRICK STEPHENS

SIR EDGAR BRITTEN ON THE BRIDGE OF R.M.S.
QUEEN MARY

A MILLION OCEAN MILES

SIR EDGAR T. BRITTEN,
R.D., R.N.R.

Commodore of the Cunard White Star Line

With 20 Illustrations

PATRICK STEPHENS

First published in 1936 by Hutchinson & Co (Publishers) Ltd.
This edition first published 1989

I DEDICATE THIS BOOK
TO ALL MY COMRADES OF THE SEA

British Library Cataloguing in Publication Data

Britten, Sir Edgar T.
A million ocean miles.—(PSL library of
ocean travel).
1. Cruises by liners, history
I. Title
910.4'5

ISBN 1-85260-169-8

*Patrick Stephens Limited is part of the
Thorsons Publishing Group,
Wellingborough, Northamptonshire, NN8 2RQ, England*

Printed in Great Britain by The Bath Press, Bath, Avon

1   3   5   7   9   10   8   6   4   2

PUBLISHER'S PREFACE

The *PSL Library of Ocean Travel* is a collection of significant books on ships and the sea, long out-of-print but now re-issued in facsimile editions.

All the books to be included in the Library — each of which has been selected by members of a 'panel' of distinguished maritime authors and collectors — have been chosen for the rarity of their original editions, for the authoritativeness of the writer, and, above all, for their readability. Autobiographies, biographies, histories of famous ships of the past and the reminiscences of eminent mariners and sea travellers are all included, and will have a wide appeal to the thousands of present-day ship enthusiasts who have a deep interest in the maritime history of the past hundred years. For the majority of such readers, these books may be unknown and would otherwise be entirely unobtainable.

Many of the original volumes used in the production of these new editions have been supplied by Mainmast Books, of Saxmundham, Suffolk, IP17 1HZ, England, from whom all volumes in the *PSL Library of Ocean Travel* may be obtained.

A Million Ocean Miles by Sir Edgar T. Britten, originally published in 1936 by Hutchinson & Co, is the fourth volume in the *PSL Library of Ocean Travel*, and the publishers would like to thank John H. Shaum Jr for providing a foreword for this facsimile edition.

PSL LIBRARY OF OCEAN TRAVEL

Also available

Mauretania
by Humfrey Jordan

Tramps and Ladies
by Sir James Bisset

The Romance of a Modern Liner
by Captain E. G. Diggle

Other titles in preparation

The Ocean Tramp
by Frank C. Hendry

Atlantic Ferry
by Arthur J. Maginnis

Sail Ho!
by Sir James Bisset

Patrick Stephens Limited will always be pleased to hear of any titles which are felt to be worthy of consideration for possible inclusion in the *PSL Library of Ocean Travel* in the future.

FOREWORD
to this new edition by
John H. Shaum Jr

Where does one turn today in search of a hero or role model?

Today it might be a television or motion picture star. Forty years or more ago, it might have been Sir Winston Churchill or King George VI or any of the great Second World War leaders. But going back even further, the role model might very well have been a famous sea captain. Sir Edgar Britten was undeniably one of the most famous.

I have always been fascinated by the autobiographies of the famous liner captains: Sir Arthur Rostron, Sir Bertram Hayes, Sir James Bisset — Sir Edgar, of course — and many others. Perhaps it is because these autobiographies provide a look at life on the great liners in a way that no other work can. These ships were the lives of these men and little else really mattered. It does not take one very long in reading *A Million Ocean Miles* to realize that Sir Edgar Britten maintained an unabashed lifelong love affair with his ships. To read his loving descriptions of the great *Berengaria* is truly touching. One wonders what his feelings must have been for the *Queen Mary* in those few months that he was her first commander. It is a pity that these impressions, too, were not preserved for posterity.

It has been shown on countless occasions that the historian, writing from a detached point of view, can certainly do justice to the story of the great liners. But it is rare indeed to get that special *feeling* that comes from having actually experienced that awful storm at sea, that black night with enemy submarines lurking nearby, the exhilaration of bringing a great ship safely into port.

Sir Edgar's book opens with his first sight of a ship, and closes 50 years later on the eve of his retirement. In between, we are introduced to his life under sail, his introduction to the mailboats as mate aboard the *Ivernia*, the dark days of war at sea, the shipwrecks, and the many fascinating people encountered along the way. As Sir Edgar's career at sea drew to a close, so did his life. But perhaps that was the way it should have been.

As one turns the pages of this fascinating book, the feeling is of actually sitting with Sir Edgar in his quarters on the *Berengaria*, listening to him spinning his yarns over a late-night libation. It is all here — the drama, the tragedy, the humour that was part of the lives of the great ships and the men that sailed them.

Yes, we can still go to sea today, but it is not like it once was. Nothing is. But with Captain Sir Edgar Britten and *A Million Ocean Miles* we can roll back the decades and immerse ourselves in a bygone way of life at sea, as only the commander of a great ship could tell it.

JOHN H. SHAUM, JR
Baltimore, Maryland, USA

FOREWORD

THIS tale is the true romance of the sea, for it covers over forty years of ocean hazard, of storm and stress and triumphant achievement, revealing that spirit of daring which inspired our early merchant adventurers to sail uncharted oceans, and is still alive undaunted to carry the Shipping Industry through the deepest depression it has ever known.

It is the story of a great and distinguished seaman, who began his unique career as a humble ship's boy in one of the old-time windjammers, and was destined at his death to hold the proud position of Commodore of the world's largest Shipping Company.

The following chapters had been completed by Sir Edgar Britten only a short time before his sudden, brief illness at the end of October, 1936, when he was carried ashore from his beloved *Queen Mary* to die in a nursing home at Southampton. On the last day of that same month his body was taken out to sea from the *Queen Mary's* usual berth, and committed to the deep off the Isle of Wight in those waters through which he had so many times brought the *Berengaria* and *Queen Mary*.

It seemed to the Publishers that, apart from the revision of certain slight errors which had crept into the text, the narrative should be here presented exactly as the gallant Commodore wrote it.

CONTENTS

LIST OF ILLUSTRATIONS

A MILLION OCEAN MILES

CHAPTER I

MY PRESENT COMMAND

Aboard R.M.S. "Berengaria."
At Sea.

FOR many years past I have felt an urge to write my experiences covering over forty years of ocean travel, but somehow I have never been able to make a start. Now that I have actually commenced, the enormity of the task rather dismays me. Most certainly the setting is ideal. In my spacious cabin aboard the *Berengaria*, wherein I am writing these lines, with the atmosphere of the sea all around me, it should not be difficult to recall memories that have gone before. Yet, what is there to tell concerning a sailor's life which you Britishers have not read a thousand times ? Sailing over a million miles, girdling the Equator a dozen times, in far lying seas, among worlds very old, and very new, alien as Mars to your world at home. . . . Romance!

Calm seas and storm, blue skies and grey, icy winds, and winter gales. . . . Routine!

Submarines, torpedoes, mines, battered and sinking ships. . . . War!

Red-rimmed eyes, and weary brain, and a murky world of blaring sirens. . . . Fog!

Hasn't that sort of stuff been rather overdone? Would it not be more original in a yarn of the sea to stress the sunny skies, calm seas, and safe anchorage, which are the normal conditions we sailormen invariably enjoy? I think so!

Still, talking of fog . . .

The lower deck have a happy knack of finding pithy, and appropriate nicknames for their Captain. These labels are not always complimentary. As a matter of fact, the majority are quite unfit for publication. Therefore, when I went on the bridge one night during a recent voyage, determined to find out if the lower deck of the *Berengaria* had tagged me a nickname, I was simply asking for trouble. It was a most unusual thing to do, but my excuse is that it was done for a very deserving cause.

We had been discussing old sea customs at my table in the saloon at dinner earlier that evening, and it was then that someone asked me if my crew had christened me with a name of their own. I believe it was Sir Ernest Bain, a well-known figure in the Insurance world, who broached the subject.

"If they have, Sir Ernest," I told him, "I am not aware of it."

"Nor will you ever find out," he retorted. "No one would ever dare tell you, Commodore."

I weighed his words silently for a moment, and then I had an idea.

"Is that a challenge, Sir Ernest?" I asked him quietly.

"If you like," said he defiantly.

"Good! Will you wager me I don't find out . . . within the hour?"

"Done!" cried Sir Ernest. "Five pounds to the Seamen's Orphanage if you win."

Sir Ernest Bain had made a speech in the crowded lounge that day in aid of the Seamen's Charity, and had appeared for the occasion, much to Lady Bain's agitation, in a gorgeous hunting suit, all checks and spots and squares, on a yellow background. Nevertheless, that

EDGAR BRITTEN, AGED SIX

CAPTAIN TURNER, WHO WAS IN COMMAND OF THE *LUSITANIA*
WHEN SHE WAS TORPEDOED
(See Chapter V.)

wonderful creation spoke loud enough to draw a record collection for a very needy fund.

"How about including that rainbow suit of yours as well as the five pounds?" I asked him. Lady Bain fairly beamed on me as I made this suggestion. Sir Ernest agreed, somewhat reluctantly I thought.

A few minutes later I ascended the bridge.

The yarn can keep for a moment. Let me give you a brief glimpse of that Holy of Holies where, in a British merchant ship at least, the most privileged passenger may not trespass.

After over forty years at sea, and more than twenty years in command, the atmosphere of the bridge at night still fascinates me. At night, the bridge of a vessel at sea is always in inky darkness, no light must disturb the observation ahead. Even under normal conditions, in a great liner such as this, four pairs of keen, alert eyes keep their watchful vigil all through the night; one man in the crow's-nest for'ard, 150 feet above the deck, and two officers on watch, one starboard, one port. Behind, in the wheelhouse, his eyes glued to the compass, stands the quartermaster, guiding the great ship by a mere flick of the wrist, so wonderful is the machinery which controls the massive 150-ton rudder, nearly 800 feet astern of the bridge.

"Eight Bells and all's well!"

Crystal clear comes the cry, followed by the sharp clang of the bridge bell, and by the muffled echo from the bells for'ard and aft. Shadowy figures stamp on to the bridge from the bowels of the ship, the middle watch relief. Like the engineers and the stokers, working deep in the heart of the vessel, these men are seldom seen by the passengers. Their work lies in the obscure shadows . . . in the silence, unheard, unseen.

But now I've got a bet to win from Sir Ernest Bain.

My eyes have grown accustomed to the gloom of the bridge, and it is easy for me to discern the broad shoulders of the relieving quartermaster from amongst the shadowy figures of the middle watch.

"Tell me, my man! What's my nickname?"

Grand seamen, these quartermasters, all ex-naval. Reliable, efficient, perfectly disciplined, without nerves —but this fellow seems all hot and bothered for some unknown reason.

"I—I—beg your pardon, sir?" he stutters, shifting from one foot to the other.

"You heard me!"

Tense silence for a moment. Then:

"I—I'd rather not say, sir."

"So! You have got a nickname for me, eh? Well, come on, what is it?"

Damned bulldog obstinacy! He still keeps silent.

However, he told me after a little persuasion.

"Well, sir. If yer wants ter know! They calls yer 'Foggy Britten'."

Foggy Britten! I'd never heard that one before.

"And why do they call me that, my man?" I demanded.

He gulped, then did a grin.

"Because, sir, for the first three months you took over this 'ere blinking ship we had nothin' but ruddy fog."

I marched down into the lounge in search of Sir Ernest. He doled out the five pounds without demur, but he rather jibbed about handing over the suit. Lady Bain settled the argument. Overhearing that I had won the bet she suddenly disappeared, presently to return with the garments over one arm. Several hundred people were in the lounge at the time.

Allow me to digress again: the yarn about the bet can keep for a moment.

To me the great lounge of the *Berengaria* is more than just a room. It is filled with the voices of many of my friends, people whom it has been my privilege to meet on the Atlantic highway. One stands out . . . a little lady, such a small, tiny lady, all dressed in silver white. She sang to us one day, her golden voice blending in rhythm with the great, sobbing waters outside, holding a thousand passengers enthralled by its glory, stunning us into amazed silence long after the echo of that glorious cadence had been drowned by the churning seas.

Tetrazzini! The *Berengaria* was her favourite ship.

"She is a queen, Capitan. Always she inspire me!"

To get back to my course.

As I said, Sir Ernest Bain was not eager to part with his suit, so someone suggested—Sir Hewitt Skinner, I think, a director of a famous publishing house—that it be duly auctioned to give Sir Ernest a chance of buying it in. This suggestion was carried unanimously. Proceedings commenced with a ten-shilling bid. Quickly this soared until, at three pounds, Sir Ernest and Sir Hewitt were alone in the field.

"Four pounds!" hissed Sir Hewitt Skinner finally. By the nasty, baleful glint in his eye as he gazed at the suit, one could read that Sir Hewitt was determined to possess that outfit, or go broke in the attempt. Sir Ernest Bain read that look correctly. He suddenly dropped out of the bidding, and the suit was knocked down to Sir Hewitt Skinner, afterwards to be handed over to the Purser, with, of course, the whole proceeds of the bet and sale.

There was a beautiful little curtain to this amusing comedy, which further enriched the Seamen's Charity. It seems that Lady Bain, in her hurry to be rid of the suit, had omitted to empty the pockets.

The Purser found four crinkly £1 notes nestling snugly in one vest pocket.

Let me say that all these little stunts are deliberately staged in aid of some charity or another. You may be sure that Sir Ernest knew that those four notes were in a pocket of that suit. I recall the King's illness of a few years ago. Prince George was serving in the Navy at the time, and he was rushed by a destroyer from the West Indies and boarded the *Berengaria* at New York. About this time also the Welsh coal miners were having a pretty lean time, and the Prince of Wales had opened a relief fund to aid their distress. In the midst of his own anxiety and worry, Prince George found time to think of the cares of others. Off his own bat he staged a wonderful stunt aboard, which raked in several thousands of pounds for the miners. It will take much space to describe this story in detail, therefore I will leave it for another chapter.

There are other great names that cross my memory—kindly, generous Edgar Wallace, charming Evelyn Laye, Winston Churchill, Ramsay MacDonald, Sir Harry Lauder, and a host of others too numerous to mention. I have yarns to tell of each, and would far rather write of them than of myself.

However, my yarns concerning my friends must wait; for my Staff Captain, Captain Bate, tells me I am dead off my course. Not only does he declare that I am off my course, but he says that, as far as this yarn is concerned, I have no right to be on the bridge—yet. He contends that I must start as a ship's boy once again, and work my way up. Well, maybe he's right, so I will hand over the command to him without further delay, and descend to the lower deck once more, although I'm afraid it will be a dull kind of yarn until I climb up the gangway of the *Berengaria* again.

CHAPTER II

TALL SPARS AND SPIDERY CORDAGE

Aboard R.M.S. "Berengaria."
At Sea.

FIFTY years have passed since first I saw the broad waters of the Solent. I was a lad, barely six years of age at the time, a rather eager, excited little man, for was I not about to make my first sea voyage? As I walked by my mother's side towards the docks, I experienced my first real thrill in life. Above the dock buildings, tapering away up towards the skies, touching the very clouds, it seemed, I saw the tall spars and spidery cordage of many sailing vessels. Then I saw the Solent, a dream river, all dancing silver and turquoise blue. I shrieked in sheer ecstasy. Forgive this rhapsody, but I was a town bred boy, and that was my first glimpse of heaven. That was also my first impression of Southampton, and the Water I now know so well. I wonder how many times I have sailed down its broad expanse since those far-off days. I have never forgotten that memory, and I can honestly state that at that moment, at the early age of six, was born an intense desire to become a sailor.

My father was in Lima, Peru, on Government Service, and Mother and I were setting out to join him, sailing in the good ship *Don*, a 3000-ton steamer.

What a grand ship, I thought, as I made my first tour of inspection.

"I didn't know there were ships as big as this, Mother," I gasped. "Gosh! Wouldn't I like to be a sailor!"

She patted my head, but was quite grave as she answered:

"Maybe you will be some day, Edgar. And who knows, some day you may be captain of a ship as big as this one?"

Who knows! The stately Royal Mail liner *Don* might easily become mislaid on the boat deck of my present command.

My first hours at sea, enchanting days! But like all good sailormen, I had an early grouch.

I was considered far too young to sit down at table with the grown-ups. This hurt my manly dignity intensely, until I learnt that the witching hour aboard the *Don* was the very time when the big folk ate in the evening. It was during this hour that the ship's butcher slaughtered the next day's live meat, and it was sheer delight watching the poor sheep and bullocks having their heads chopped off, a recreation which would rather repel me after a lifetime at sea.

But then I was at a bloodthirsty age, as you may read before the good ship *Don* gets far on her course.

Watching the ship's log being hauled aboard at noon was another source of sheer delight. You may be sure I soon learnt all there was to know about this old method of checking the number of nautical miles covered by the vessel each day. The profound knowledge which I gained of this intricate instrument after two days of study was the cause of my first scrap.

In the ship was another youngster about my own age —Tony Bellamy.

I believe he was bigger than I was—much bigger; we'll say so, anyway. I have never forgotten Tony, and if he is still alive, and happens to read this yarn, I'd like to thank him for helping me towards my ambition. Without exaggeration, he was actually one of those little pawns of Fate, or Chance, which make or mar careers; he and a silver shilling.

It came about in this way:

I never saw anything of Tony during the first three days at sea—he was probably down in his cabin seasick—

but when, on the fourth day out, I saw him examining the log aft, I quite naturally approached and entered into an explanation of its functions and mechanisms.

Tony snorted!

I may have been a little boastful; naturally, I had a right to be, and I might have puffed out my little chest more than I should; but still, I was only trying to be chummy.

"You see, Tony," I told him, "without this thing we'd never get to Lima."

Tony snorted again, rather rudely, I thought.

"The ship might even sink without it, Tony."

That did it. Tony voiced his disgust.

"Garn!" he sneered. "It's nothing more than a bloomin' fishing-line."

The ungrateful, disbelieving, little beast, I thought indignantly. Now I ask you, could two feet of flesh and blood be expected to stand an insult of this nature? Of course not, so I promptly walloped him on the chin.

Just as promptly he walloped me back, and the fight was on. As we circled round and round, feinting for an opening, I remember turning one eye for a moment searching to see if Mother was about. Tony filled that eye. I forgot all about Mother after that.

There was one, Captain Joste, who had overheard my lecture and had witnessed the commencement of the hostilities. He let us scrap for a few minutes, and then he parted us.

"Shake hands, boys, that's enough," he commanded.

"Not till Tony apologizes," I breathed belligerently.

Tony refused to apologize.

Peaceful arbitration being thus scorned by both of us, Captain Joste formed a ring of passengers, and offered a shilling to the victor. Captain Joste had to answer to Mother later for this, but I won that shilling.

I've still got it tucked away in my locker, the first money I ever earned at sea, or anywhere else. The date on that precious coin is 1875. It was to play its part in leading me to my present position.

I want my readers to remember the name of the donor —Captain Joste. We will meet him again.

Nearly ten years passed. My parents had returned from Lima, and my home was then in Birmingham. I am a "Tyke," a Yorkshireman by birth and breeding, but my school-days were spent at the King Edward VI Grammar School in Birmingham.

About the time the next episode of this yarn takes place I had left school a few months previously, and was working between four hateful office walls. How I loathed that job, my mind and memory for ever picturing the vision of those "tall spars and spidery cordage," and that glorious voyage on the good ship *Don!* At least once a week I pleaded with my parents for permission to follow my heart's desire. The longing was intense, unbearable. But my parents were dead against it, turning a deaf ear to all my entreaties, my father particularly. With true boy-like perversity, this increased my determination to follow my ambition, and so, one day, I ran away from home. I had little money, but eventually I managed to reach Liverpool. With a tight belt, and empty pockets, I haunted the docks in search of a ship, but without success.

Then, one day I met him again.

He was walking past me when I got just one quick glance at his face, and then he was hurrying away. I followed hard in his wake. Could I be mistaken? I was so young and small, and it was so long ago. Would he remember me?

"Captain Joste," I whispered meekly.

He whipped round like a flash, his eyes searching my face.

"Don't you remember me, Captain Joste? Edgar Britten . . . the *Don* . . . and I've still got your shilling," I said eagerly.

He grabbed both my hands, and his face beamed in recognition.

"Well, well," his deep voice boomed. "I should say I do remember you. And you've still got that shilling?" he added absently.

"Yes, sir. I've still got it," I said proudly.

He paused for a moment, eyeing me keenly from crown to toe.

"Why have you kept it all these years? Have you never felt the urge to spend it?"

"No, sir . . . somehow I felt I would meet you again one day, and—and——" I paused, stammering confusedly, for the keen gaze of the old mariner disconcerted me.

"Go on, lad . . . and what?"

"I thought, maybe, sir, you might help me."

"Help you, lad? Why, if there is anything in the world I can do for you let me hear what it is, and for the sake of the good ship *Don*, and the silver shilling and . . ." here he chuckled delightedly, "and that glorious scrap you put up that day, you can count on me, Edgar."

"I want to be a sailor, sir," I blurted eagerly.

Again the keen eyes searched mine.

"How long have you had that ambition, lad?" he asked me quietly.

"From the first moment I stepped aboard the *Don*, sir. I've never forgotten the ship, sir, nor that voyage."

"What do your parents—what does your father think about it?" he queried sharply.

Shamefacedly, I confessed that they were dead against it, and that I had run away from home.

He stood silent a moment after I had told him, deeply pondering. Then:

"Tell me, lad," he asked me earnestly. "Is your mind absolutely set on this thing? D'you realize the kind of life, the hardships and dangers, you'll be called upon to face? Another thing, if you go to sea without the consent of your parents, you'll have to start right at the bottom, lad. Are you prepared to do that?"

"Yes, sir," I declared eagerly. Then I added impulsively: "Oh, sir, it cannot be worse than sitting day in, year out, on a hard wooden stool, pushing a pen over reams and reams of paper."

The old man smiled. "No, lad, no!" he muttered, and his next remarks were delivered in a far-away tone, as if he was recalling some long-forgotten memory.

"I said the same words fifty years ago . . . but, come on, Edgar," he added briskly, "follow me, my lad, and we'll see what can be done for you."

That was the beginning of the end for me. Thanks to Captain Joste, I was able to obtain a berth as a ship's boy in a sailing ship at the princely salary of five shillings per month. Thus, I actually commenced my career from the humblest possible position which the sea had to offer, and without the advantage of an articled apprenticeship.

On the 1st day of January, 1896, I joined the sailing ship *Jessie Osborne*, and as I entered the dank, dark fo'c'sle, with its atmosphere of tar and bilge water, and learnt that this was the palatial quarters of the crew, I confess my thoughts turned to Mother and my comfortable bedroom back at Birmingham.

The first gentleman I met aboard was one Micky Donovan, an Irish giant of tremendous strength, and a typical shellback of sailing ship days. Micky was the Bos'un of the *Jessie Osborne*, and I was quickly to learn of his exalted rank.

It was late afternoon when we sailed out of South Shields, with half a gale blowing and bitterly cold. The *Jessie Osborne* was a frail little vessel, and did she roll, and did she heave? She was not alone in the heaving! I had been warned of the heaving, and before we sailed that day I had managed to sneak ashore to a tuck shop and had enjoyed one last, slap-up dinner. Pork sausages

and mashed potatoes were one of the items on the menu.
For years afterwards the sight and smell of a sausage made
me feel seasick, and all I can remember of my first hours
at sea are wet clothes, evil smells, the eternal rolling and
pitching of the ship, and seasickness.

"All hands on deck!"

That night, the stentorian blare of the Mate reached
me as I lay curled up like a dying duck in the darkest
corner of the fo'c'sle, but I felt so damnably sick that I
took not the slightest notice.

" Hi, you, ship's boy, get up!"

Someone dug me fiercely in the ribs, which somewhat
eased my quivering frame, and wearily I felt my way on
deck.

As I slithered along the heaving, sea-washed decks,
clawing my way through impenetrable darkness, I heard
the order given to shorten sail. But I didn't know what
the devil to do, nor where to go, and as there was no one
to guide me I just stood shivering near the cook's galley
with the cold water swirling about my knees.

I hadn't been long there, however, when a great shadow
loomed over me, increasing the darkness of the night.

"Who the blue blazes are you?" a fog-horn voice
boomed in my ear, and I recognized the dulcet tones of
the Mate.

"P-p-please, sir, the ship's b-b-boy," I meekly explained, my teeth chattering like castanets, for I was
frozen stiff.

"What the hell are you doing down here?" he
demanded fiercely.

"I—I don't know, sir!"

"You don't know, heh!   Well, d'you know where you
ought to be?"

"N-no, sir, I don't."

The huge shadow waved to the great dizzy spars
reaching away up into the blackness of the night.

"Up that darned yard!   Get!"

I felt the wind of his great paw as it whizzed passed

one of my ears, and although I had never previously been up aloft, there seemed little room for argument. I "got." Nor did I tarry by the way.

It was dark; inky dark, easily the darkest night I had ever experienced, and that rigging! I had never felt anything so cold and slimy. Half-way up I paused for breath, hanging on with my eyebrows. So! These were the tall spars of my dreams, and this darned, slippery rigging, the spidery cordage which had inspired me to become a sailor. They seemed much higher than those I had seen on the ships at Southampton, and ten times higher than those on the good ship *Don*. However, I managed to claw my way up on the topsail at last, there to receive a cheerful greeting from Micky, the Bos'un. As he perceived my dim shadow at the end of the spar, his raucous howl rose high above the wind.

"Who the blue blazes are you?" he yelled, after the approved manner of the Mate below.

Again I meekly explained my identity and was greeted by the most horrible flow of profanity which I have never heard eclipsed during the whole of my career at sea.

The Bos'un never forgave me for arriving late aloft on my first night at sea. My plea that I knew no better was not accepted, and only seemed to make matters worse. He seemed to make a dead set at me, and never tired of boosting me around.

Life under him was hell, sheer hell! Strangely enough, looking back through the mist of years, I know now that Micky did not mean to be unkind. His manner was really a form of kind-heartedness at sea.

I recall the day we parted.

"I suppose you think I've been very hard on you, Britten, don't you?" he growled.

"Yes, you have," I retorted fiercely. "Darned hard. And I only hope that some day you'll be in a ship under my command, then I'll teach you better manners."

He laughed loud and derisively at that.

"Why, you young swab, you'll thank me then, if ever

that happens," he roared.   His great bulk loomed over me, and he grabbed my shoulders roughly.   "D'you think I haven't been watching you studying them books every chance you got."   He held out his hand.   "Don't bear malice, Britten," he muttered gruffly.   "The boosting I gave you was for your benefit, lad: you'll profit from the discipline and training later on."

I gripped his hand in return, beginning to see light.

"Go right ahead and get your command," he added kindly.   "And in the years to come maybe you'll bless Micky Donovan."

I have done so, scores of times, since that day, and I take this opportunity of paying a tribute to a fine sailor-man.   Micky Donovan was, indeed, one of the old school of shellbacks who helped to make the British Merchant Service the envy of the world.

CHAPTER III

THE SHIP'S BOY TAKES COMMAND

Aboard R.M.S. "Berengaria."
At Sea.

WE are back again aboard the *Berengaria*.
"Seven bells, sir! Your coffee."
" Aye! Aye! Croughan."
Croughan is my "Tiger," as the Captain's steward is
called at sea. He is rather perturbed about this writing
business. Croughan has been with me for several years
now, but he has never seen me on this course before. I
don't think he can quite make it out.

From the port-holes of my cabin I can see away for'ard.
The Atlantic is in a turbulent mood this morning, the
skies o'ercast, but I see by the glass that we're in for a
spell of good weather.

Follow me up on to the bridge; we'll get a better view
of this mighty ocean from there.

"Course 265°, sir. All's well!"

Not another ship in sight. We have the Great Waters
to ourselves.

I have heard say that with the passing of the sailing
ship so passed the romance of the sea. I wonder ? Have
a look at the *Berengaria* from the dizzy height of the
bridge.

Look back! See the black smoke belching from her
three gigantic funnels. Down each two railway trains
might easily pass. Look down! Down at her great
broad decks gleaming white nearly 100 feet below. Gaze
on the massive hull of her, black as the night. Watch

her razor-edged bows cleaving the mighty waters, an inspiring sight.   See the white-capped waves racing along her 900 foot length, lashing the seas into white foam far behind in the wake.   Feel the mighty power of her, this great hulk of steel and woodwork, crashing across the vast Atlantic at 30 land miles an hour; and although all alone on this great sea, with no vestige of land in sight, the whole world knows just exactly where we are.

"*Berengaria* 1500 miles West Bishop's Rock."

By that one short paragraph in your morning papers, my readers, and a quick glance at a map, you may place your forefinger on our exact location.

Is not that Romance?

Fifteen hundred miles astern lies Southampton.   At a similar distance lies New York, and down below, tucked snugly in their beds at this early hour, 2000 human souls are resting in this strange world of living steel.

Is that not Romance?

But greatest wonder of all, to my way of thinking, although we are almost in mid-Atlantic, my passengers at a moment's notice, if they can afford it, may telephone their relatives at home and wish them "good morning."

Is that not a fairy-tale?

As my yarn progresses, and space permits, I will describe some of the wonders of our big ships and, by way of comparison, we will examine some of the marvels of the *Queen Mary*, that we may judge how far we have advanced in the art of ship-building during the last twenty years.

But here comes Captain Bate, my Staff Captain, to remind me that I must become a humble ship's boy again.

I have never forgotten my first ship, the *Jessie Osborne*. She was a barque, and to me a thing of beauty, and under full sail a rhapsody in white.   Tall and graceful, with the symmetrical lines of a Greek goddess, my whole boyish heart went out to her.   Fast on occasion, often capricious, after the way of her sex, but always trim and neat. I never once saw her dowdy. My wife has often asked why we sailors allude to a ship as "she," and sometimes "sweetheart." There are many reasons. Don't we learn to love them? Do we not invariably christen them with feminine names? Are they not woman-like in their ways? One never knows what the darned things will do on occasions. Have they not their whims and their fancies, their virtues and their weaknesses? Don't they moan and groan when there's dirty weather around? But see them romp along full of pep and vim, and dressed in all their pretty finery, when the sun is shining.

Why do we call them "she" and sometimes "sweetheart?" Indeed, I could fill several pages in explanation. Why, often I've seen a hairy old shellback, dirt-grimed and blue-patched, clawing on to the great wheel aft, while great seas crashed and pounded aboard, solemnly beseeching his beloved sweetheart to watch her step.

"Take it easy, Jessie, take it easy! Steady, old girl, steady!"

He never knew whether Jessie would kiss him or kick him on these occasions, and the capricious wench was capable of doing both within the space of as many seconds.

That is one of the reasons why we christened the old windjammers with feminine names.

The *Jessie Osborne* was commanded by Captain Hugh Thomas, a Welshman. This grand old mariner is still alive, and I certainly owe him a debt of gratitude which I can never hope to pay in full.

I remember him as a kindly old gentleman ; patient, long-suffering (in my case particularly), who gave me my first training in seamanship. I was merely a ship's boy, and not an articled apprentice. I was therefore not entitled to any tuition. But the "old man" spent long hours on end counselling, advising, and teaching me all the arts of his trade.

Long years afterwards, in the first year of the war, as a matter of fact, I met him by chance in a Liverpool street.

The "old man" had fallen on lean times, and was out of a ship.

A few more months passed by and I was appointed to the command of the *Ascania*. As I stepped aboard my new ship one of my junior officers saluted me. "He's very old," I murmured to myself, and then I started back in amazement.

That junior officer was my first Commander, Captain Hugh Thomas.

Truly the boy was indeed Master of the man.

For two happy and more or less uneventful years I served in the *Jessie Osborne*, rising from ship's boy to the exalted position of "Ordinary Seaman." One learnt seamanship by seeing things done, and to avoid the rope's end wielded by the lusty Micky Donovan.

There were other forms of correction besides the rope. An hour's perch on the dizzy heights of the royal yard, or greasing the same mast with slush from top to bottom in dirty weather, were forms of recreation which brought a due respect for discipline and authority. As for the food in the old days, we waxed fat on salt junk and "Liverpool Pantiles," as the hard ship's biscuits were termed. The "pantiles" shipped at Liverpool always seemed to be harder than any shipped from any other port. Bristol "Pantiles" were the favourites, and I believe the firm who used to supply this commodity entirely to sailors now concentrate a large part of their efforts on the manufacture of dog biscuits. Lucky dogs!

Enough has been written of the terrible hardships experienced in windjammer days, and I do not intend to stress this point.

I do not think I would, even if I could, for strangely enough I remember all that was best in this phase of my career.

Long, lazy days of unending sunshine, sailing along with flapping sails, and scarcely a breeze to ruffle the placid seas. It was during these enchanting spells that the ship's orchestra came into its own. A comb wrapped round with paper, a sea-kettle, and a frying-pan can produce an enchanting rhythm when blended with the soft hiss of flying spindrift, and the hum of straining cordage.

Sometimes in the dog-watches, Micky would bring out his concertina and squat in the starlight, ringing out old sea-chanties, wild, ferocious, triumphant, then of a sudden ghastly with despair. My pleasantest memory of him belonged to those night watches when, the music over, he would tell stories of the sea, the saga of windjammer days.

Like all seamen, of course, who have served under sail, I have been round the Horn, and I can honestly say that nothing has been written concerning this latitude which is in any way an exaggeration.

Sometimes the battle to sail a ship around this point lasted for weeks, and sometimes months on end. The terrific storms, the devastating velocity of the winds, the awful power of the crashing mountains of water, sometimes makes me wonder how on earth it was ever possible to sail a frail craft of wood and canvas in these regions at all.

Only the strongest and the fittest survived a voyage round the Horn. Weeks and weeks on end with only a few hours of rest from the eternal rolling and pitching of the vessel, hot food was unknown, dry clothes a dream of calm seas far astern. Eternally, every hour of night and day, we were furling or unfurling canvas, and the herculean efforts required to handle the billowing, frozen canvas, high on the dizzy, lurching yards, beggars description. Even on deck it required muscles of steel to hang on to the life-lines, which stretched from one end of the ship to the other, to prevent the great combers from washing one overboard.

Naturally, these conditions did not tend to soften, and it is not to be wondered that many of the officers in sailing ship days had the reputation of being callous and hard. Maybe, I was fortunate, therefore, that my first commander was a kindly old man who did everything in his power to teach me his trade.

Sailing ships are now few and far between on the Atlantic highway, but whenever one does cross my course I picture again the *Jessie Osborne*, and in imagination I see dear old Hugh Thomas bending low over a little boy seated on the poop, his nose buried deep in some manual of the sea.

CHAPTER IV

DISASTER

Aboard R.M.S. "Berengaria."
At Sea.

AFTER leaving the *Jessie Osborne* I obtained a berth as A.B. (able-bodied seaman) in the full-rigged ship, the *British Merchant*. This was a further step up the ladder.

My duties as a seaman left me very little time for study, especially in stormy weather, and I was therefore five years at sea, which was twelve months longer than the prescribed time required by the Board of Trade, before I felt that I had learnt sufficient to enable me to pass the examiners.

I emerged from the examination triumphant, with my Second Mate's ticket tucked deep in a pocket of my blue-reefer coat.

I was now a member of the "after-guard."

Then came a voyage which lasted for over fourteen months, as Second Mate on the Dundee ship *Kinfauns*. She was a beautiful barque under the command of Captain Alex Crighton, a typical Scot. Crighton was another splendid seaman, and I quickly made him aware that I was as keen as mustard to learn all he knew.

Calm or storm, rain or sunshine, I still kept hard at my studies. I was determined to catch up with those twelve months I had lost through being obliged to commence my career from the lower deck.

At the end of my first voyage in the *Kinfauns* the

heavens fairly opened and all the Gods of Fortune beamed on me. They say there is only one God of Fortune. Don't believe it. There's a million of them. The whole outfit were waiting for me at the gang-plank as the *Kinfauns* berthed.

Promotion is slow to-day, but even in my younger days one might sail for years as a second mate, although carrying a master's certificate in one's locker. When, therefore, the *Kinfauns* docked at the end of her long voyage, I had only completed fourteen months as a Second Mate, and had no hope of promotion for some time to come. It was then that those million gods trooped aboard.

Captain Alex Crighton sent for me as I was packing up dunnage before going ashore.

"Britten," said he, "we sail again in fourteen days."

"Yes, sir!" said I, expectantly.

He paused for a moment, then literally, he took my breath away.

"If you can obtain your Mate's ticket before we sail, you can come back as Mate in this ship."

Good Lord!

"D'you mind repeating that, sir?" I gasped, not daring to believe my ears.

He repeated the sentence, slowly and deliberately, smiling encouragement. Then:

"D'you think you can make it, Britten?"

Could I do it! By heck! I'd have a darned good try. What an incentive! What a chance! One of those million to one chances that come once only in a man's lifetime. And what a prize!

Could I do it? I must! There was no argument! It had to be done! Still, fourteen days was a darned short time. Thus raced my mind. But my legs raced quicker, as they bore my excited frame towards the Nautical School at Liverpool.

Mr. Merryfield was the Head of the Nautical School in Liverpool, a name which all sailormen of my generation will remember with gratitude. I wonder if he is still alive? He must be very, very old if he is.

"Impossible, Britten!" he declared emphatically, when I informed him of the wonderful opportunity offered me.

"I can do it, sir," I insisted eagerly. He shook his head decisively.

"You can't, lad. I can't possibly prepare you in fourteen days," he declared emphatically.

"Try, sir, try. Do try! I'll work night and day to get through."

He hesitated for a moment. Then:

"Oh, all right, but I don't think you've got a dog's chance of winning through."

I squared my shoulders. "I'll take *that* chance, sir," I said determinedly.

I burned a lot of midnight oil during those fourteen hectic days. I felt very much like a ship at sea, riding away up on the crest of the waves of Hope one moment, and wallowing in the Sea of Despair the next.

I was all excitement on my first day under Mr. Merryfield, trying to cram a year's study within the space of a few hours. This was facing the gale with all canvas set, and I had enough sense to shorten sail.

On the second day I forgot the prize and tackled my papers as if victory was assured. At the end of the first fateful week I felt that I could not possibly succeed. By the middle of the second week, when I had only a few days to spare, I thought I had just a chance of winning through. So it went on, hope and despair, but always the determination to succeed. Then came the eve of the thirteenth day, on the morrow I would sit for an examination the outcome of which might make or mar my whole career. I felt that I knew sufficient to see me through, but there is a wide line of demarcation between theory and practice, and I was somewhat afraid of copy-book navigation. The momentous day dawned. . . .

Captain Alex Crighton met me as I walked wearily

across the gang-plank of the *Kinfauns* on the morning
of the fourteenth day. She was due to sail with the next
tide. I was all in, and rather tired.

"You've failed, lad?" he greeted me anxiously.

But I shook my head, and I think I managed a smile.

"No, sir, I haven't failed," I said humbly.

Then I fumbled in my pocket and produced the
precious document, and then—well, I just turned in for
a spell.

I set off on my second voyage on the *Kinfauns*, and
only the Captain himself was above me in command.
Barely twenty-two years of age, I had already been seven
years under sail, and had been around the world several
times. Naturally, I felt rather proud of myself. I was
very young. Maybe I swanked a little. I think I must
have done, for it was during this voyage that those million
gods deserted me.

We loaded a general cargo in London for Honolulu,
a voyage which under normal conditions would have
taken us well under four months. Under normal conditions . . . it took us exactly eleven months to reach our
port of destination.

As we were towed down the river I can distinctly
remember thinking that I was the luckiest man afloat.
Merely a boy, yet here was I second-in-command of this
great stately ship. Why, if anything happened to the
"Old Man" (Heaven forbid), the responsibility of taking
men, cargo and vessel into safe harbourage would be
mine alone.

My seven years under sail, too, had been remarkably
free from disaster. There was one coming along, just
over the horizon.

We let go our tug off the Nore and, being mid-winter,
we received a rare old buffeting in the Bay of Biscay. All
went well, however, until we reached a point about a
hundred miles west of Lisbon, off the Portuguese coast.

And then—Whew!

It happened about 2 a.m. one pitch-black night. We were scudding along with the North-east Trades, and making fair way. I was on watch and had joined the look-out for'ard.

Suddenly, coming towards us, I observed the dark hulk of some great steamer on our starboard bow. In the darkness, against the black loom of the horizon he appeared of gigantic size, bigger than any vessel I had seen on the Seven Seas. I expected him to keep on his way. Judge then my feelings when I saw the great bows swing round towards us.

By heavens! He meant to run us down.

"Hard aport!" I yelled to the helmsman. My frantic cry brought all hands tumbling hurriedly on deck.

But his speed was twice as great as ours.

There was no escape.

On, on he came!

I shall never forget those few pregnant moments as we watched the loom of the great ship bearing relentlessly down on us.

There was nothing to do but wait—just wait!

I remember an awful feeling of helplessness—a dull, dumb wonderment as to what would happen.

"You murderous hounds!"

Just before he struck I heard a man scream, but the hands for the most part were silent.

Then he hit us!

Crashing straight across our bows, shearing clean through the bowsprit and boom, he cut off half the fo'c'sle-head as if it had been made of cheese.

With the loss of the boom stays the great foremast of the *Kinfauns* snapped six feet above the deck, falling aft and landing against the main yard. The tremendous weight of this wreckage brought down the main top-gallant mast, and the vessel, rolling in the trough of the seas, with first the starboard rail completely under water and then the port, completed the disaster. The inferno of that crashing mass of spars and cordage, the yelling of frenzied men, the hopeless, awful blackness of the night, the sudden, unexpected shock of it all are still very vivid memories. Strangely enough, although every man was on deck at the actual moment of impact, not one was hurt by the mass of falling spars.

As soon as the steamer hit us he sheered off, but we could just discern the great black hulk standing by in the distance. It wanted two hours until dawn, but we could do nothing in the darkness, only wait until daylight, rolling helplessly in the trough of the sea. When dawn broke we discerned that the other vessel was a Portuguese man-of-war, but why he was steaming without lights, and why he altered his course, was not explained at the subsequent enquiry. A few minutes after daybreak he lowered a boat and presently I received a gorgeously dressed Portuguese naval officer aboard. This was actually the first man I had seen in uniform since I had been at sea. I was rather impressed with the gold braid and dangling sword. But when, on closer inspection, I observed that the somewhat smoky-coloured shirt of the officer was showing conspicuously through the busted seams of his armpits, the effect was rather lost.

You may be sure that Captain Crighton was broken-hearted because of the damage done to his beautiful ship. It was left to me to show the officer the extent of the damage. He had landed aft and I could not persuade him to go beyond the mainmast.

"Ah! Feenish! Feenish! No good, no good, Señor," was all he would say, waving his hands towards the wreckage. He wanted to leave it at that, but I heralded him below for an interview with the "Old Man."

Captain Crighton could not speak Portuguese. He did most of the talking in good, broad Scotch, but the officer must have understood a little of what was said, for towards the end of the interview he seemed in a hurry to get back to his warship. He promised to send off a squad of naval men to help us clear away the wreckage,

but a few minutes after boarding his own vessel the battleship cleared over the horizon, leaving us the whole of the
sea.

It was then that I received my first big lesson in seamanship, an experience which has been of benefit right
throughout my career, and which was of tremendous
assistance when the time came for me to sit for my
Master's Certificate.

Under the able direction of the "Old Man" we set to
work clearing that bewildering mass of twisted cords and
splintered spars, a herculean task. Luckily the weather
held, otherwise no power on earth could have saved the
vessel from complete disaster.

Toiling like fiends we cleared the mess under two days,
and then managed to rig a jury mast and set sufficient
sail to take us to St. Michael's, in the Azores.

This was really a brilliant piece of navigation—I take
little credit for it—for to control a vessel of the size of the
Kinfauns with a veritable postage stamp for a sail, and
thus bring her over 800 miles of open sea was indeed
seamanship of the highest order.

Arriving safely at the Azores, another record was
established in connection with this disaster. We at once
cabled details to the owners in Dundee, and about a month
later the Liverpool tug *Blazer* appeared on the scene.
This little beggar towed us all the way back to Cardiff.
I may be wrong, but I believe that this still stands as a
record tow.

That month of waiting at St. Michael's was not spent
in idleness, for before the tug had arrived we managed
to fit a more substantial jury mast, and a temporary
wooden bow, another creditable piece of seamanship.
As a matter of fact, we might well have done without the
service of the perky *Blazer*, for, a good wind favouring us,
the tow-rope was slack right up to the moment we
anchored off Cardiff.

This proved my last voyage under sail, and I now
decided to enter steam.

Do any of my readers believe in luck ? We sailors are supposed to be very superstitious, and I could fill many pages were I to describe all the "signs" and "warnings" which we old shellbacks accepted with simple faith in sailing ship days.

Certainly, the first day of the year stands out very prominently in my life, and my lucky star must be at its zenith about this time. Examine the following amazing sequence of events, the most important factors of my whole career.

1. On January the first I joined my first ship, the *Jessie Osborne*.
2. On January the first, 1901, I first joined the Cunard Company.
3. On January the first, 1934, my name appeared in the New Year's Honours List, when His Majesty graced me with the order of Knighthood.
4. In the year 1935 on January the first, the Directors of the two great shipping companies, the Cunard and White Star, paid me the honour of appointing me as the first Commodore of the new merger.
5. Again it was on a New Year's Day—I mustn't tell you how long ago—that I first met my dear wife, Lady Britten.

Coincidence! Sheer coincidence!

Ah, well, have it that way if you like, but I'll still sit up listening to the bells of New Year's Eve—hoping —and expecting.

On New Year's Eve, 1900, I left home to seek my first job under steam. I had gained my Master's Certificate, and I felt that success was now assured. My mother was still alive, and as I had recently returned from a long voyage, mother-like, she was anxious to keep me at home as long as she could.

"Why leave home on New Year's Eve, Edgar?" she pleaded, "why not wait until after the holidays?"

"No, Mother," I said firmly. "I am starting a new career. What better time than to start with the first day of the year?"

This little conversation, and that resolution of mine may seem almost insignificant, but, as events proved, I might have missed the great opportunity of joining the Cunard Company had I postponed my search for work.

Arriving at Liverpool I first decided to try my luck with the White Star Company.

Again Fate, or luck, or chance—what you will, took a hand in shaping my destiny. When I called at the offices of the White Star the Marine Superintendent was out.

"He'll be back in twenty minutes. Won't you take a seat?" a clerk invited.

No! I wouldn't take a seat! I'd call back within that time. I went for a stroll and got back again about half an hour later.

"Oh, you've just missed him," the clerk exclaimed. "Better sit down and wait this time. He'll be back any minute."

I sat down and waited. Five—ten—twenty minutes went by. To the deuce with this, I thought! Why waste time waiting for him? Might as well wander over to the Cunard and try my luck there meantime. I hadn't much hope of landing a job on the spot, but I wanted to get my name on the books of at least one of the big companies. The Marine Superintendent of the Cunard was in, and saw me at once.

"Got your ticket?" he asked, the preliminaries over.

I produced my ticket.

"We want a fourth officer for the *Ivernia*. Get ready to sail at once!"

Now was that luck, or was it not? Young officers were calling every hour on these companies. Had I put off until to-morrow, somebody else might have snapped up that job. Again, had the White Star man been in his office when I called, I might have gone home, content to await a vacancy with that company. It seemed a strange twist of Fate, that thirty-four years later I was to be the first Commodore when the two great companies combined. But now that I have reached a new phase in this log, I think I will smoke a pipe and turn in for a spell. In the next chapter I will describe life aboard the Cunarders. I have served in practically every vessel in the fleet, including such famous ships as the *Lusitania*, *Mauretania* and *Aquitania*, right up to my present command.

CHAPTER V

DRAMA OF THE HIGH SEAS

Aboard R.M.S. "Berengaria."
At Sea.

"THE *Majestic* approaching, sir, on our port beam!"

"Aye! Aye! Croughan."

We must go up on the bridge to see the two great sisters pass.

The Atlantic is in one of her best moods this morning; calm, lazy sea, and sky-blue merging on a sunlit horizon. It feels grand to be alive on a morning like this, and grander still to be a sailorman. I shall hate, like the dickens, to bid good-bye to the Great Waters, and that time is not afar off.

Two miles on our port beam, clear-cut as a cameo, the *Majestic* draws abreast, homeward bound. As she passes, her stern flag flutters slowly down from the masthead. That is a compliment to me—she is raising her hat to her Commodore. We return the salute.

From the sun-deck beneath a clear feminine voice reaches the bridge.

"Look, George darling, she's pulling down her flag. Why has she done that?"

"I dunno!" a gruff voice answers. "In for a spell of dirty weather, I guess. She's pulling it in before it gets wet."

Somewhere on the bridge a bell tinkles warningly.

"Crows-nest look-out reports, sir! Strange object on our starboard bow."

Many glasses are levelled on the distant horizon, but from the bridge no object is yet discernible. By virtue of his great height from the deck, the look-out in the crow's-nest can see far beyond the horizon of the bridge, a convincing factor which establishes that the world is round. I often wonder why it took our ancient mariners so many ages to solve this simple problem.

The bell tinkles again!

"Look-out reports, sir! Ship's life-boat six miles off our starboard bow."

Again all eyes are glued to glasses, and there is a tense silence on the bridge as the minutes tick past. The keen eyes of Mr. Cove, the senior officer on watch, are the first to sight her.

"There she is, sir—away starboard!"

Far away, on the distant horizon, almost at right-angles to our bows, a tiny black speck slowly merges into sight.

"Anyone in her, Mr. Cove?"

"Can't see yet, sir. No signals! Shall I alter course, sir?"

I nod assent. Slowly the great bows of the *Berengaria* swing round, pointing dead for the black object ahead. Like a tiny cork, dancing perkily towards us, the frail craft takes shape.

"Empty, sir! No one in her!" Mr. Cove's voice is sharp, decisive. A minute later we swing back again upon our course, leaving the little boat to her fate.

"Any name on her, Mr. Cove?"

"Can't make one out, sir. She looks as if she's been adrift for months."

Adrift for months! It seems hardly credible that a frail ship's boat should ride the winter gales of the Atlantic for several long months and still keep afloat. Later that day a little old lady reproached me:

"Oh, Captain, why didn't you stop to pick the poor thing up," she exclaimed tremulously.

I was quite grave as I answered: "Because we are a

mail-boat, madam.   We only stop to save life," I told her gently.

Quietly musing, as I puff my pipe in the quiet seclusion of my cabin to-night, that derelict ship's boat reminds me of my first real thrill under steam.   It is a yarn concerning one of those grim little dramas of the high seas which might have cost twenty-three men their lives but for the uncanny judgment of Captain Turner, a famous Cunarder.   Associated with this yarn is that wonder invention, wireless telegraphy, and, of all the marvellous appliances which have helped to make life safe for those who go down to the sea in ships, I give pride of place to this apparatus.   To me there is something uncanny allied to that mysterious message which is flashed through space between vessel and vessel riding, maybe, a thousand miles apart.   Even to-day, although I have received many countless calls for help, they never fail to affect me deeply.   I recall only a little more than a year ago my desperate efforts to reach the ill-fated *Saxilby*.

"*Berengaria! Berengaria!*   Forward hatch stove in, we are sinking fast!"

Three hundred miles of terrible seas were between us and the crippled vessel.   Many other ships were nearer than we, but were themselves hove-to for safety.   Only a ship of our great size had the power to drive safely through those seas.

"Hang on, *Saxilby!*   We are coming to your rescue!"

My engineers and stokers toiled like fiends to drive the great ship along.   Steady as a rock, haughtily defiant of the great waves rushing and pounding on her stately bows, snorting her defiance at the howling winds, she swept towards her small, stricken sister at far above her normal speed. . . .

"Steady as you go, sir?"

"Aye! Aye! Quartermaster.   Stick to the course."

My yarn concerning the *Saxilby* must wait another chapter.

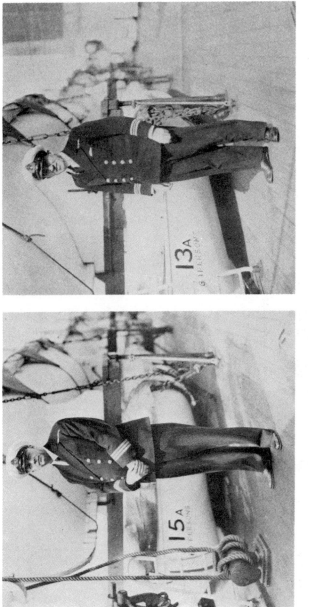

DOCTOR O'BRIEN

CHIEF WIRELESS OFFICER DUNCAN CRAGG

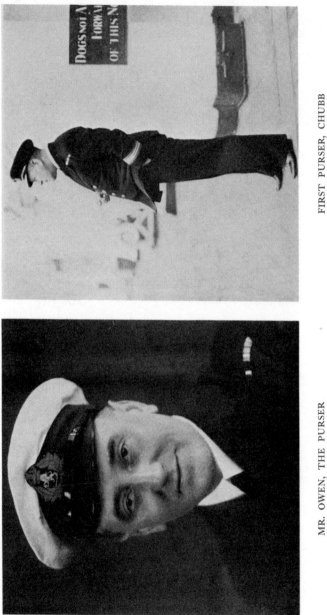

MR. OWEN, THE PURSER

FIRST PURSER, CHUBB

(See Chapter VI.)

As in sail, my life under steam has been extraordinarily even and free from thrills, if we except the war years.

My promotion also, from small steamships to the giant Cunarders, has been steady and fairly rapid. Naturally, I feel exceptionally proud of the Company under whose flag I have sailed for more years than I care to remember. The fact that we have held the Blue Riband of the Atlantic against all comers for some fifty of the last ninety-five years, and that I have played a small and humble part in maintaining this great record, is something in which one can justly feel pride.

To maintain this proud record required ceaseless effort, and the building of bigger and yet bigger and faster ships. Thus was born the *Lusitania* in 1907, to be followed later by her giant sister, the *Mauretania*. The amazing size and speed of those two leviathans of the deep were the wonder and envy of the world. For sheer daring and ship-building enterprise, as regards bulk of tonnage, no vessel ever built could compare with them. With their birth the era of Big Ships was established in Maritime History. I shall never forget the day I crossed the gang-plank of the *Mauretania*. As I stepped upon the bridge of the world-famous ship and gazed down on her great hull, her tremendous bulk held me in speechless amazement. I felt that my efforts to win promotion had indeed been crowned with a success far beyond my wildest imagination. Was I really second-in-command of this wonder of metal and woodwork? It seemed only yesterday that I was a humble ship's boy in the *Jessie Osborne*. Could this great thing of living steel be allied to that toy ship of wood and canvas?

Impossible! Impossible!

Yet hoary old Neptune was the father of both. To me that will always be the world's most entrancing fairy-tale.

One afternoon, about three days out from New York, homeward bound, or on what we term our Eastern run,

the *Mauretania* received a wireless message from a
Leyland steamer:

> "Have picked up boat's crew belonging S.S.
> *Westpoint*. Captain and 22 men missing in second
> boat. Last seen six days ago, heading East-bound
> Track."

Further wireless messages informed us that the *Westpoint*, an English cargo vessel, had caught fire in mid-
Atlantic and had been abandoned.

Her crew had left in two boats. One had been rescued,
but the missing boat had been sailing for six days exposed
to the winter gales of the Atlantic. The month was
January, and one can imagine the conditions which these
men were facing. As I have said, Captain Turner was in
command of the *Mauretania* at the time. We were both
in the chart-room on the bridge when the full details of
the tragedy reached us.

"Poor devils!" I heard him mutter compassionately.
Then his gaze wandered absently across the mighty
waters.

"Six days adrift in an open boat in this weather,
Britten!" he murmured half to himself. "They can't
possibly be alive, Chief." Again he was silent.

"Their plight must be terrible if they are, sir," I
murmured.

But he didn't hear me. The absent manner had
changed. He was again that cool, unruffled seaman that
I remember so well. Quick in decision, brilliantly
accurate in navigation, marvellous in judgment, as my
readers will probably agree before this yarn concludes.

"Double all look-outs, Britten. Post every available
man, and instruct all hands to keep their eyes skinned for
the missing boat!"

"Aye! Aye! sir."

His instructions carried out, Captain Turner was bent
low over the chart when I returned to the bridge.

"I think we had better alter course, Britten," he said,

without looking up. He picked up the latest wireless message and continued. "According to the position when the two boats parted six days ago, Chief, the missing boat can't possibly have had time yet to make the East-bound Track."

"You think not, sir?"

His forefinger moved across the chart and came to rest. "I make them out to be about there, Britten."

"Yes, sir."

He remained silent for another moment, pondering, his eye still glued to the chart. Then he stood erect and snapped out an order.

"Alter course, Britten: 25 miles North."

There was no indecision about that order. The "Old Man's" mind was fully made up, and he knew the Great Waters as a farm duck knows its local pond.

"What time d'you reckon we should pick them up, sir, if they are still afloat?" I asked.

"Midnight!" he snapped, then added laconically, "if they are still afloat."

Midnight! Eight bells!

"Eight bells! And all's well!"

Clear through the darkness came the cry of the look-out for'ard, eerily breaking the stillness of an exceptionally black night. From the bridge one could hardly discern the black hull of the mighty vessel as she ploughed her way through the seas. Midnight had just struck. My mind was centred on the little boat. Small chance of seeing her on a night like this, I thought, my eyes vainly searching the inky blackness around. Not a hope. Not a dog's chance . . . not . . . !

With one quick spring I had grabbed the signal lever leading down to the engine-room.

Clang!

"Full speed astern!"

Right dead ahead in our tracks I had seen a tiny blue flame flutter. One split second flicker, and then swallowed by the darkness. That was all. Quickly our searchlights were ablaze. There, almost beneath us, was the missing boat.

The *Mauretania* had a full complement of passengers, nearly 2000 strong. Every soul aboard knew we were searching for the shipwrecked men and the decks were crowded as we slowly circled the little craft. From the bridge, in the glare of our searchlights, we could see that the unfortunate men were in a pitiable condition. One man waved a feeble arm to the cries of the encouragement from our cheering passengers. But most of the poor fellows were lying huddled and still in the bottom of the boat. Within minutes we had them aboard. Hot stimulants and blankets were quickly forthcoming. Every woman on that boat clamoured to be a nurse that night. Sailors are tough! Within hours every man had recovered, and before the night was far advanced the whole ship was rocking with laughter over a remark reputed to have been passed by one of the rescued sailors to his Captain a few minutes before we picked them up.

"We were past caring, beyond all hope before we saw your lights to-night," said the Captain of the *Westpoint* to a group of passengers.

"Luckily, I had saved one last blue flare. Had I not done so, you would probably have passed us in the darkness.

"We had used up all our other lights during the first three nights we were adrift. Since then, time and time again, I was sorely tempted to light this one also, but something told me to keep it back. It was our last despairing hope. Even to-night, when darkness fell, many hours before we saw you, I again felt the urge to use it. But the impulse to preserve it proved predominant. So I nursed it next to my bare skin to keep it dry until we saw you bearing down on us."

Then the Captain told the yarn which turned this drama into comedy, and sent everybody to bed hysterical.

It appears that one of the *Westpoint's* firemen, a New York Irish-American, had not previously seen a ship of the size of the *Mauretania* at sea. Thus, as we swept over the black horizon in a blaze of lights, this fireman, partly delirious from terrible exposure, thought he was seeing a favourite home spot adrift on the Atlantic.

The Captain of the *Westpoint* continued:

"For several hours to-night no one in the boat had spoken. Irish Mike, one of my firemen, was sitting aft beside me with his head lying on my shoulder. The rest were more or less unconscious. I was fighting desperately hard to keep awake. I knew that another day must mean the end. But I must have dozed off. Mike stirred and awoke me. I felt him start. Then I heard him mutter beneath his breath. I felt his arms move. Somehow I knew he was rubbing his eyes.

"What's up, Mike?" I asked him. "Can you see something?"

" 'See som ethin'?' he muttered. 'Holy Smoke!'

"Then he let out a frenzied howl and flung his arms around my neck.

" 'Look! Captain—look!' he yelled. 'Them lights! Them lights! Holy jabbers, here comes Coney Island!' "

At sea we have another use for wireless telegraphy little known to the general public, but as this part of my yarn chiefly concerns the ship's surgeon we will switch back to the *Berengaria* for a brief spell, that I may introduce the Medico at present serving under my command.

Out in mid-Atlantic we receive frequent wireless messages from captains of small cargo vessels, seeking medical advice.

"Have man very ill. High temperature. Pulse falling. Acute abdominal pains. Please advise."

This cryptic message, tense with romance and drama, may come across the ether from a vessel a thousand miles away.

Most captains, even on the small vessels, have a knowledge of medicine and first aid, and Board of Trade regulations require that all ships under the British flag, at least, shall carry medical comforts, and surgical dressings. It will, therefore, be appreciated that only in the most serious cases will captains resort to wireless to seek advice. One can therefore picture the scene which the above message conjures . . . the frail cargo vessel pitching and rolling in the ceaseless swell of the mighty Atlantic, the Captain down in the dim-lit fo'c'sle battling grimly for the life of some poor seaman, dependent on that mysterious message of advice which seems to come out of the very heavens.

"Advise you do so-and-so.   Report if no improvement."

Back in the *Berengaria* the tall, impassive Doctor O'Brien awaits, with his calm, inscrutable smile, the result of his advice.

All through the long night messages may flash between him and his unseen patient.   He may save the life of the man, yet may never meet him, may never even learn his name.   I have known these weird battles to last for days on end.   Yet the Doctor will ask no fees, nor will he expect any wasteful message of thanks.   This is just one example from the unwritten code of the sea—a code which holds all sailormen together, no matter creed or flag, in a bond of good-fellowship which has no equal on land.   Sometimes those dramatic messages are spiced with humour, so typical of the breed concerned.   For example, Doctor O'Brien will tell you of a " case " he had in an American cargo vessel a few years ago.   His wirelessed advice on this occasion had dire results for the Captain who tried to put that advice into practice.   It appears that one of the firemen in the American ship had fallen down a hatchway and had sustained a gash on his scalp which required to be sutured, or sewn up.

"Thinking," said Doctor O'Brien, "that it would be

unwise to advise the Captain of the American ship to sew the wound in the ordinary way, I wirelessed him:

> " 'Draw flesh firmly together and secure with sticking-plaster.' "

About half an hour afterwards the American wirelessed:

> "Carried out instructions, but can't stop wound from bleeding."

To this message the Doctor replied:

> "Stitch flesh together with common straight sewing needle and ordinary thread. That is only way to stop bleeding."

"I turned in after sending that last message," said the Doctor; "I didn't expect to hear any more word concerning my distant patient.   Shortly afterwards, however, I received another communication.   This read:

> " 'Patient strongly objects to last advised treatment.   Wound still bleeding freely.   Is there any other method?' "

The Doctor's answer was terse and to the point:

> "Secure him.   Use force if necessary."

After the Doctor had sent that last drastic message, which, of course, was the only possible advice under the circumstances when it is remembered that a disabled man on a small cargo vessel might cripple the efficiency of the whole unit, there was complete silence for nearly an hour.

"Then I received a final message," said the Doctor, with a chuckle. "It read:

> " 'Man still objects to treatment.   Very violent. But thanks for advice. Now sewing up Captain's head.' "

It does not require a very vivid imagination to picture the scene which that message conveys. I can see that blood-spattered fireman struggling fiercely to free himself from his comrades, strongly objecting to having his head sewn up like an old sock, and finally, breaking loose, cracking the "Old Man" over the head with the first weapon to hand—while over a thousand miles away sits the inscrutable O'Brien, the innocent cause of that comedy-drama of the high seas.

During the voyage passengers are, of course, entitled to the full use of the wireless and radio telephone on the payment of certain prescribed fees. Mr. Duncan Cragg, my Chief Wireless Officer, tells me that strange indeed are some of the messages which are privately flashed across space. Naturally, such messages are strictly private and confidential. They must not even be discussed amongst my staff of operators. I have persuaded Cragg, however, to give two harmless examples which I think may be safely published without infringing any code.

"On quite a recent voyage," Cragg tells me, "a gentleman came aboard at New York, and as we didn't sail until 2 a.m., he rather delayed going to bed. About 3 a.m. he came up into the wireless-room looking in the worst of tempers.

" 'I want to wireless my wife, urgent,' he said. 'Can I send a message now?'

" 'Why, yes, sir!' I said. Then I added: 'Trust there's nothing wrong, sir?'

" 'Plenty!' he snapped savagely. 'I can't find my silk pyjamas. I've turned my trunks outside in and can't locate the darned things anywhere.'

" 'Why not call the night steward, sir?'

" 'I have done so. He can't find them either.'

"I handed him a wireless form and he wirelessed his wife:

" 'Where are my pyjamas!'

"Then he went to bed. At dawn next morning back came the answer:

" 'In one of your night socks!' "

It would appear that the silk pyjamas were so fine in texture that they could be rolled into a sock, a hiding-place that proved somewhat costly to their owner.

During the war the demand for wireless operators was so great that many youngsters were employed of little experience. One night at sea one of these greenhorns got in touch with a coastal station at St. Miguel, Newfoundland. This station was always sparking away with tremendous power, and most of the operators were of French extraction. The youngster, under the impression he was in touch with another ship at sea, immediately wirelessed the station:

"Q.R.D.?" which means, "Whither are you bound?"

To this there was no reply, the Frenchmen at St. Miguel probably being unable to understand the meaning of the code.

"Q.R.D.? . . . Q.R.D.?"

The youngster was insistent, but failing to get a reply, he sent the message in full.

"Whither are you bound?"

Back came the answer, which did not help matters:

"We no move some. We stay sit still!"

CHAPTER VI

A BRUSH WITH CARD SHARPERS

Aboard R.M.S. "Berengaria."
At Sea.

SOUTHAMPTON three days astern and the weather still holds. I'm beginning to think a cargo of ink must be lucky freight. Of course, even the worst of weather has little effect on a ship the size of the *Berengaria*. The "Old Girl" wants a lot of rocking when she's showing her heels. Mr. Frank Owen, my Chief Purser, and I have just had a long yarn. We were discussing card-sharpers, and a brush I had with an infamous gang a few years ago. As Owen was concerned in that little fracas, I think he ought to be formally introduced. It is difficult to reproduce Mr. Owen in ink. Bland, persuasive, the soul of tact and discretion, he is a master diplomat indeed. He needs to be, if it is appreciated that he has to handle thirty different nationalities on occasion, and keep about two thousand people happy, comfortable and contented, throughout the voyage. His duties form an incredible complexity. It would require the remaining pages of these memoirs to enumerate them in detail. I won't attempt that task, indeed, I haven't enough ink aboard if I was so minded. Before we get on to the subject of card-sharpers, however, here is one yarn which may give some idea of the problem with which my purser is faced almost every hour of his very busy day. Mr. Owen reads out the lesson at the Church Service every Sunday at sea. His delivery is exceptionally good. Thus thought a dear old lady on a recent voyage. She called on the Purser immediately after the service.

"My dear Mr. Owen, what a beautiful delivery," she exclaimed earnestly. "How divinely . . . how exquisitely you read that lesson."

"Ahum!" gently coughed the Purser politely. Owen has acquired that little cough from long and bitter experience. It sort of gives him time to think, to turn over in his mind what infernal problem is coming along next. Had the dear old girl met him casually and delivered her praises in passing, he might have been caught off guard. But to jump on him in his office, before he had time to put away his Bible, kept our Prime Minister immediately on guard. He knew there was some sinister meaning behind that little bit of blarney. He was not mistaken.

"I wonder if you would do something for me, dear Mr. Owen?"

"Ahum!"

Mr. Owen has never been known to commit himself, even to dear old ladies, although he tries to be all things to all women.

"You see, Mr. Owen, my dear husband passed away quite recently, such a peaceful end he had, and . . . Oh! I wonder if you would . . .?" the old lady clasped her hands in pious supplication. But Owen is granite-hard behind that whimsical, winning smile of his.

"Ahum!" he coughed, still waiting.

It came at last, a request which stumped the good Owen for once.

"I wonder if you'd be so kind, dear Mr. Owen, to write a—a verse . . . an epitaph for my dear husband's tombstone?"

I'll wager my Purser did a lot of dry coughing before he found the answer to that one.

In the days before the war card-sharpers were as naturally attracted to the great liners as moths to a candle. This was only to be expected when it is remembered that we carried some of the world's wealthiest people, as we do at present, of course. It became a habit to expect these gentry aboard, and I got to know many of the leading gangs by sight. Why, then, it might be asked, did we allow these undesirables aboard ? We did not, if we were absolutely sure that they were "crooks." But it was the hardest thing in the world to produce proof that they were card-sharpers. Why, I heard of a case where a private and very astute detective closely watched a game where a "pigeon" was plumed of a fortune, and so fiendishly clever were the cards manipulated that even the eagle eye of the trained sleuth could detect no flaw. Again, the majority of the victims, astute business men as a rule, probably ashamed to admit their folly, or considering the lesson well worth the price, preferred to keep their losses secret, and their suspicions to themselves. It will be appreciated, therefore, that the big shipping companies were faced with a problem which required the most tactful handling. There was only one possible method to adopt to drive these parasites from the high seas, and so make ocean travel safe for the most simple-minded of passengers. I am thankful to say that it has succeeded. It took us a long time, but for the last six years I have not had one single complaint in this direction. I have said that we adopted one method: this is not literally correct, for the methods we adopted were many and varied. For instance, in all the public rooms we hang conspicuous notices, warning passengers of the risk of entering into card games with strangers. These notices are everywhere. The least observant cannot fail to see them. But there are people in this world who read yet do not learn or digest, as the following yarn from my Staff Purser, Mr. Chubb, will prove. Mr. Chubb tells me that on a voyage several years ago he walked casually into the smoke-room one night, and there he saw an old gang at work. They were playing poker, the stakes were high, and the pigeon was a wealthy New York stock-broker.

Mr. Chubb says: "I stood and watched the game for a moment, trying to catch the victim's eye. The stockbroker looked up at me at the end of one hand, and I warned him by a shake of the head and a significant look as plainly as I could have done by word of mouth that he was in the hands of card-sharpers. The leader of the gang saw my warning glance and his lips curled sardonically as I turned away. I hurried down to the Purser's office, procured a big square of white cardboard and wrote on it with a blue pencil, in large conspicuous letters:

"It is known that a well-known gang of card-sharpers are on board. Passengers are warned to be on their guard."

"I marched back into the smoke-room with the card in my hand. The stockbroker was sitting in a chair facing one of the walls of the room and I hung the card, literally under his nose, and in a line with his eyes. They all saw it, and as I paused to look at my handiwork I read the last line aloud:

"Passengers are warned to be on their guard."

"One of the gang laughed in my face.

" 'Say, Chubby!' he drawled. 'Wouldn't it just be too bad if you caught them guys!'

"I fixed him with an icy stare: 'Yes, it would just be too bad. But maybe we will some day. I've known clever guys to come unstuck sometimes."

"But these fellows know every move of the game. When I first left the room the stockbroker was being well plucked, he had only a few winning chips at his elbow. During my absence the gang had let him win. To his hand was a pile of dollar chips. They knew that I had gone to stage some move to further warn their victim. That was their counter move. The lust to win easy money proved far stronger than the warning card. They played all night and the stockbroker lost a fortune."

From the above statement it will be realized that Mr. Chubb, short of getting hold of the passenger concerned by the scruff of the neck and pulling him away from the table, had done everything that was humanly possible to save the man.

"We had no definite proof that these fellows were card-sharpers, sir," Mr. Chubb concluded. "As far as I was concerned they were ordinary first-class passengers who had paid their fare and were otherwise behaving like gentlemen."

That was the snag! He had no definite proof that these men were card cheats.

The precautions we take to-day are manifold and, as I have said, they have succeeded in stamping out these pests. In the *Berengaria*, for instance, we carry eight policemen, called "Masters-at-Arms." These men are ex-officers of the police force of long experience, and although they are most inconspicuous, they are on duty night and day when we are at sea. Our public room waiters and stewards are also specially picked men, trained in observation. These fellows never forget a face, and as they generally hold these coveted posts over long years they soon learn all there is to know concerning our regular passengers. On the gangway, too, at both New York and Southampton special men are posted . . . and to sum up briefly, we have made it so hot, and the game so unprofitable, for these slick-fingered gentry that they don't like us any more.

A few months ago I was with a friend in the Maritime Exchange in New York. I was introduced to a group of members, and towards the end of the evening one of the latter, an American, button-holed me and drew me on one side.

"I'm not sure if I got your name right, Captain," he said. "Did you say it was Britten?"

"Yes," I said. "My name is Britten."

He thrust out his hand.

"Put it there, Cap!" he cried joyously. "You did me a darned good turn in the *Lusitania* a few years ago."

I stared at him rather quizzingly, searching my

memory, but I could not recall ever having met him before. He was quick to note the meaning of my glance.

"No, we've never met before, Cap," he exclaimed. "But you did me a good turn just the same. I heard all about it from the Purser."

He then refreshed my memory, and I had little difficulty in recalling the circumstances to mind. I was Staff Captain of the *Lusitania* at the time, and a message reached me as I was dressing for dinner one night that several men were squabbling in the smoke-room over a game of cards. It appears that two had been openly accused of card-sharping. In those days the smoke-rooms were exclusively reserved for men. The late Commodore Sir James Charles was in command, and as I didn't know quite how to handle the situation, I sought his advice. Allow me to digress that I may say a word concerning my old comrade.

Sir James Charles' last command was the *Aquitania*, and the whole shipping world was shocked by the tragic poignancy of his death. All his life he had sailed the Great Waters, winning the respect and admiration of all those privileged to serve under his command. I remember him as a quiet, dignified gentleman, powerful in command, unruffled in judgment, stamped as a leader of men in every line of his strong, rugged face. Looking into those calm, steadfast blue eyes of his, one felt a sense of trust and security which inspired the feeling that this man could do no wrong. At one time the *Aquitania* and Sir James Charles were synonymous terms, but the years were passing. Both were growing old in the service of the sea. There came the last time when Sir James was to guide her, homeward bound, across the broad Atlantic. It was his final voyage before retirement. In New York, before the great ship sailed, the docks were gay with bunting and the vessel was invaded by the leading citizens of America who had come to wish the grand old seaman good-bye. The *Aquitania* sailed at midnight, and as she nosed her way down the mighty Hudson, to the blaring of sirens and the clanging of ship's bells, I can picture Sir James gazing pensively back at the myriad lights of the giant skyscrapers slowly receding astern, gradually dimming and finally flickering out, leaving only the darkness of the Great Waters ahead.

Six days later the fussy little tugs were caressing the great vessel as she steamed slowly up Southampton Water. Safely berthed, Sir James slowly descended from the bridge and entered his cabin. Wearily he removed his muffler and bridge coat and sat down at his desk for the last time. There were many documents to sign before he could say good-bye to all this. His steward entered the room a few moments later. The figure at the desk was strangely still.

"Sir James!"

But there was no answer. His job was done.

As I have said, I was in the middle of dressing for dinner when news reached me of the commotion in the smoke-room, and partly dressed I hastened to Sir Charles' cabin.

"What would you advise me to do, sir?" I asked him, after furnishing the details. His calm eyes searched mine for a moment in silence. Then he murmured gently:

"Carry on with your dressing, Britten. Then have your dinner. Don't hurry over it. After you've had your dinner go and see what the little fuss is all about."

I stared at him hesitatingly.

"Carry on, Britten," he said, even more gently.

"But, sir . . .!"

He held up his hand reprovingly.

"Just do as I tell you, Britten. You'll find that by the time you have had your dinner, and enjoyed it, I hope, the little affair will have settled itself and the ship will still be safely afloat."

That sterling advice has proved useful to me on many an occasion since. Had I gone up to the smoke-room during the heat of the quarrel, drastic action might have been required, probably leading to all sorts of complications. As it happened, when I did go up about two hours afterwards and enquired of the smoke-room steward what it was all about, he said:

"Oh! It's all over now, sir. They're all down in the bar, the best of pals."

The good turn referred to by my American friend, although we had not even met over this little affair, was the fact that I had kept out of it, thanks to the excellent counsel of my late friend, Sir James Charles.

My last serious case of card-sharping happened as far back as 1929. I was sitting in my cabin one day on the east-bound run from New York when a steward brought a message from a passenger asking permission to see me on a matter of grave urgency. It was the last day of the voyage, and I wish my readers to take particular note of this fact. I never refuse to see a passenger, but when I sense trouble I try to obtain as much information as I can beforehand the better to enable me to handle the situation. I sensed trouble in this case, so I at once sent for Mr. Owen, whom you have already met. If there was any little trouble aboard, my Purser would know all about it. I was not mistaken.

"D'you know anything about this, Mr. Owen?" I asked, tossing him the letter.

He merely glanced at the passenger's signature.

"Yes, sir . . . card-sharping!" he answered tersely.

I asked for details.

"There are three in the gang, sir, all presumably strangers to each other. All three are booked on different decks. One has a private suite on 'A' deck, with a sitting-room, the other two have single cabins, one on 'B,' and one on 'C' decks, sir."

"The usual method, Mr. Owen?"

"Yes, sir! I received reports from different stewards that these men were suspected card-sharpers almost as soon as they stepped aboard.

'No definite proof that they are cheats? Any previous complaints against any of them?"

"Absolutely none, sir. But the one on 'B' deck travelled with us about six months ago, and won a large sum of money."

"Did the victim squeal on that occasion?"

"No, sir. One of the lounge stewards found out only by accident."

"Then what makes you suspect that they are sharpers Mr. Owen?"

"The fact that they pretended they were strangers to each other, sir, and that they only play in the private sitting-room occupied by the one on 'A' deck, instead, as is usual, of playing in one of the public rooms."

I again picked up the passenger's letter.

"How soon did you discover that this man had fallen into their clutches, Mr. Owen?"

"One of the Masters-at-Arms saw the four of them repair to the private suite one night, and a little later he sent the bedroom steward into the cabin on some imaginary pretext. It was then reported to me that they were playing poker for high stakes."

"Did you warn the man?"

"Yes, sir. Next morning I drew his attention to one of the notices warning passengers to be on their guard against card-sharpers, and I asked him to read it.

" 'That's all right, Purser,' he said, off-handedly. 'I'd recognize the type at a glance. No need to warn me specially.'

"I removed the card from the wall, sir, and I actually thrust it in his face.

" 'Read that notice again,' I insisted politely.

" 'Why? What's the big idea, Purser?' he exclaimed rather peevishly. 'What's on your mind?'

" 'You were playing cards last night, were you not?' I next asked him.

" 'Yes, I was!' he said. Then he laughed happily.

'And what's more, I won seven hundred dollars, my lad,' he added."

Mr. Owen waved his hands despairingly.

"There was nothing else for it, sir. He wouldn't take a veiled warning, so I told him bluntly that his new-found companions of the night before were suspected of being a gang of notorious card-sharpers."

"Did he believe you?"

"He laughed at me, sir!"

"And now he's squealing. All right, send him up, Mr. Owen."

As the Purser turned to leave my cabin, I again glanced at the signature on the letter, and fired another question.

"Who is our friend, Mr. Owen ; d'you know his business?"

"Yes, sir. A soap manufacturer, reputed to be very wealthy. He travelled with us three and a half years ago."

I now had all the information required, and a few minutes later the passenger was shown into my cabin.

He was a gentleman well over middle age, and looked just what he was, a very keen and astute business man.

"How did you come to meet these fellows?" I asked him, after he told me what I already knew. "Did you know any of them prior to coming aboard?" I added.

"No, Captain, I didn't," he answered. Then went on: "I was leaning over the rail having a quiet smoke on the first night out, when one of them came and stood by my side, and entered into casual conversation. He then told me he was a lumber king from Canada. I met him again in the smoking room just before dinner, and he invited me to have a cocktail. There was another fellow with him, and he said:

" 'Meet my friend. We've actually been neighbours for years out West, he owns a copper mine near my lumber camp, and yet we've never met until this moment.' "

"You believed him?" I asked.

"Why, yes, Cap!" he exclaimed. "I had no reason to do otherwise. They looked like gentlemen."

"They always do," I said drily. "But go on with your story."

Incidentally, before our passenger continues, we will call the gang-leader Mr. Smith, and the other two, Jones and Robinson—fictitious names, I hasten to add. We haven't met Robinson yet, only Smith and Jones.

"After dinner that night," the passenger continued, "Smith, Jones and myself sort of drifted together, and the latter casually mentioned a game of cards."

" 'A three-handed game isn't much good,' said Smith. 'I wonder if we can get a fourth.'

"There was another gentleman sitting at an adjoining table, apparently deeply engrossed in a book, and Smith, leaning towards him said:

" 'Excuse me, sir! I don't know if you play cards or not, but we are anxious to make up a four-handed game. Would you care to join us?' "

Again I interrupted his tale.

"He wasn't anxious to join?" I grunted.

"Why no, Cap! He wasn't," the passenger agreed, looking at me as much as to say, 'How the deuce did you know that?'

"But he agreed, after a lot of persuasion?" I added.

"That's right, Cap."

"And Mr. Smith suggested that it would be far more comfortable to play in the privacy of his suite than in the smoke-room?"

The passenger nodded: "You know all the answers, Captain," he said grudgingly.

"Carry on with your story," I said sharply, for to be frank, I had little sympathy for the man. We would have stamped out these sea-parasites years before we did but for the amazing folly and credulity of some people.

"We played until the small hours of the morning," he continued, "and when I reckoned up I found that I was about seven hundred dollars to the good."

I interrupted him again.

"What game were you playing?" I asked him quietly.

He stared at me confusedly for a moment, then he drawled:

"Wal, to tell you the truth, Cap. I'm darned if I can tell you," he exclaimed.

I sat up in my seat in amazement.

"D'you mean to tell me you were playing for high stakes and didn't even know the name and nature of the game you were playing?" I demanded sharply. He remained silent a moment. Then:

"Wal, you see, Cap," he explained somewhat sheepishly. "I don't play cards very much." Then he blurted out. "Why, I've never played a game in my life before I came on this ship."

This astounding statement nearly took my breath away. Here was a pigeon, indeed, which required little plucking.

He continued his story:

"Each night after dinner the four of us all seemed to casually assemble together, without previous arrangement, and so the game went on.

"For four nights this continued and at the end of that time I found I had won something like seven thousand dollars. Then came the last night of the voyage, Cap. In our previous games the play had been rather quiet and dull, and my three friends always seemed half asleep long before the games ended." He suddenly broke off his story, leaned forward in his chair, and I heard him draw in his breath. He was living the last game over again. Then he gasped: "By gad! Cap'n!" he exclaimed savagely. "They were wide awake last night. The play was so darned fast and furious that I was simply swept clean off my feet. When I lost a hand the gang didn't take time to count the chips. They simply swept them aside, and another hand was on. They skinned me of a fortune in less than fifteen minutes."

There was a tense silence for a moment. Then:

"How much did you lose?" I asked him quietly.

"Thirty-three thousand dollars!" he told me bitterly.

A fortune indeed! Approximately £8000 in English money!

"What are you going to do about it, Captain?" he went on anxiously. "I want that money back."

I sat back in my chair, eyeing him silently. Then:

"I am very sorry," I told him politely. "But I might as well be blunt and tell you that I have very little sympathy for you. My company do everything to protect you. There are warning notices posted in every public room on the ship, and my Purser informed me that he strongly advised you not to play with these men. As a matter of fact, since we have no proof that these men are cheats, Mr. Owen stretched his duty in an effort to save you."

He was inclined to argue the matter, and was at first somewhat taken aback by my bluntness. But when he discovered that I was in possession of all the facts, and in face of his amazing confession that he did not even know the name of the game he was playing, he agreed that he had no kick against anyone but himself.

"I am glad you admit that," I told him, as we shook hands. "But at the same time I will see if anything can be done to get that money back, although I have little hope."

After he had left me I sent for the passenger occupying the private suite, and whom I suspected was the leader of the gang. A few minutes later he entered my cabin, and I can remember him to this day. There is something, a fascinating attractiveness about this type of "crook" which stamps them indelibly on one's mind. Big and handsome, well over the six-foot mark, with a frank, open face, he entered my cabin with a swinging jauntiness, and an air of calm assurance which rather intrigued me.

"Yuh wanna see me, Cap?" he grinned, coolly selecting a seat, uninvited.

I was immediately struck with the keenness, the tense quickness of a pair of keen, penetrating eyes which appraised every article in my cabin, myself included, in one flashing glance. Here, indeed, was the master card-sharper—keen-witted, cool, confident, self-assured, with nerve-tensed, restless fingers—fingers that could never keep still unless a deck of cards were between. Nothing on earth could call this man's bluff. So I proved very early in our conversation. Towards the end of the interview he said:

"If that gink can prove that I am not a bona-fide business man, Cap, I'll hand over the thirty grand without a kick. . . . Why, Cap, I've been at this game for twenty years," he continued with a grin. "But I'm not a 'Crook,' and I defy any man to prove that I am. I play a good game of cards, and I generally win, Cap."

He leaned forward and deliberately winked at me.

"Can I help it if a 'mug' wants to play with me, Cap?" he leered.

I looked as stern as I could.

"That's all very well, my friend," I said severely. "But the mug in this instance is a simple old man. Don't you think you were a little too hard on him?"

"Simple nuthin'!" he exclaimed derisively. "Didn't he take seven thousand bucks off us? He didn't squeal then, did he?"

"Then you won't give him any of his money back?" I asked.

"Not a darned cent, Cap. He was after our dough. We got his, instead. Would he have given us any of our money back? I'll say he wouldn't."

I could do nothing more, but as he was leaving my cabin, I asked him:

"Tell me, have you ever been reported before?"

The big fellow laughed hilariously.

"Sure I have, Cap! Why, I've been before every go-darned skipper that sails the Atlantic . . . and I'll say you're good guys."

CHAPTER VII

THE *AQUITANIA* SHOWS HER SPEED

Aboard R.M.S. "Berengaria."
At Sea.

IN this chapter I will tell you a little of war. Firstly, let me explain that many years before the Great War the Admiralty had taken measures to prepare the Mercantile Marine for war service. Practically every officer underwent a course of naval training, and a large number of our fastest liners were constructed so as to be capable of rapid conversion into armed cruisers if the need arose. On the outbreak of hostilities one of the first vessels to be so converted was the *Aquitania*. This meant the ruthless stripping of all her luxurious fittings and splendid appointments. No less than 5000 men were employed on the immense task, and it required more than 2000 wagons to remove her fittings to the shore.

The famous vessel certainly did her bit during the years that followed.

After being converted into an armed cruiser carrying a complement of eight 6-inch guns, she left the river Mersey for patrol duty on August 8th, 1914, exactly four days after the declaration of war . . . a marvellous achievement, considering the immense alterations made.

In May, 1915, she was converted to a transport, and between that date and August of the same year carried some 30,000 troops to the Dardanelles.

She then became a hospital ship until the end of 1916, and carried a total of no fewer than 25,000 wounded troops.

Early in 1918 she was again requisitioned as a transport, and made nine trips across the Atlantic, carrying over 60,000 American troops to Europe.

Upwards of 120,000 troops were, in fact, carried by the gallant *Aquitania* during her war service, and her story is the story of all her sisters of the Cunard Fleet, with the exception of those, of course, less fortunate, who were destroyed by enemy action.

I joined her as Staff Captain early in 1915, and at Liverpool, one day in July of the same year, we embarked no less than 6000 troops aboard, all bound for the Dardanelles. They were mostly Yorkshire coal-miners belonging to Kitchener's Army. From the bridge I watched them stream up the gangways. What fine fellows they were . . . the cream of England's young manhood, leaving their homes for the first time, many never to return.

"Don't forget your war-babies, lads!"

"War-babies" was the name bestowed by Tommy on the life-belts which they had to carry about with them at all times after Germany had declared her U-boat campaign.

It took some time to divide that vast army of men into boat units and to show them their respective boat stations, and hours before we sailed every man had disappeared below decks, each hugging his precious war-baby.

We were under sealed orders, and sailed down the river about ten o'clock at night, under cover of darkness, with an escort of two destroyers. Towards dawn our two destroyers signalled their message of farewell and God-speed and disappeared into the grey light of the horizon. Shortly afterwards, as dawn was breaking, the alarm bell on the bridge tinkled sharply. It was a message from the look-out aft

"Torpedo, sir. Passed within 50 feet of our stern."

What a prize to miss by a bare fifty feet, the finest ship afloat, with an army aboard. Even now I can picture that U-boat Commander, his eye glued to the periscope, gazing in consternation as he saw the wake of his torpedo swirling harmlessly past our stern. But he would be after us. Come, old lady, that extra burst of speed for which you are famous, for on that alone depends the lives of 6000 men.

The *Aquitania* did not fail.

With the coming of clear daylight there was no sign of the submarine, but it was more than likely that others might be lurking ahead. I sent for the Orderly Officer.

"Get out your buglers and sound the alarm!" I ordered tersely.

The officer quickly found his bugler, but the man could not find his bugle. I slated them both unmercifully, then personally went in search of the General Officer commanding. My mind was centred on that vast army of men below. Before I found the G.O.C. ten precious minutes were lost before the general alarm was sounded. The *Aquitania* is still one of the world's largest vessels. There are nine decks and eight main staircases leading from below to the upper decks. But the vast majority of the men had been marched down the main staircase, and when the alarm was eventually sounded the entire crowd made a rush for the only outlet they knew, following each other like a flock of sheep. Therefore, two long hours elapsed before every man was safely above deck and standing before his boat station. This was a very grave matter indeed.

"See that every man knows the exact location of the staircase nearest his quarters," I instructed before the men were dismissed.

"How many buglers on duty at the same time?" I next demanded.

"One!" I was told.

"One!" I snapped. "One in a ship of this size? You might as well stick a tom-tit on top of a mountain and expect him to warn the world."

Six buglers were placed at various points of the ship

THE LATE COMMODORE SIR JAMES CHARLES

"THE *AQUITANIA* DID NOT FAIL, BUT ON HER SPEED ALONE DEPENDED THE LIVES OF 6000 MEN"

with instructions to take up any danger call from a main bugler posted in a position near the bridge. I was taking no further chances. If we did bump into a U-boat, I was determined that these men would at least have a chance of escaping in the boats.

The instructions to the buglers had a comic sequel, which nevertheless solved a problem in my mind, and rather eased the worrying strain of the morning. We were steaming along that night as usual, with no lights showing, and hoping for the best. It was one of those quiet, muggy summer evenings when one can sort of feel the stillness. Far below I heard the buzz of many voices, with here and there the chorus of some happy song. Tommy had forgotten the cares of the day. Swiftly the ship was bearing them to a land that some had not even heard the name of a few months before. They were bent on the slaughter of Turks, but some did not know whether Johnny Turk was blue, green or black, nor did some know why it was necessary to wipe this strange being from off the face of the earth. Why worry about these things anyway? None of their business. Why even worry about submarines, the Captain and the crew of the big ship could be trusted to attend to that job. Six thousand Tommies climbed into their hammocks and went to sleep. But towards midnight their slumbers were most rudely disturbed. Without warning, the shrill sound of many bugles blowing the alarm in unison roused the whole ship to frenzied activity.

I immediately hurried to the main companion-way and there I met the General.

"What's up now?" he demanded.

"I was just going to ask you the same question, General!" I said politely.

"Didn't you give the order to sound the alarm?"

"No, sir, I did not. Didn't you?" I asked.

"I did not," he replied.

In the meantime, the men were pouring from the bowels of the ship, each hugging his "war-baby," and more or less silent. The General and I commenced an investigation. We had yet to discover the cause of the alarm, and to find out the person who had ordered the buglers to sound the call. The main bugler was the culprit. It seems that while playing a soft serenade on his bugle to while away the time he had inadvertently raised the key a little and, another bugler close by hearing this, and mistaking it for the alarm, had at once roused the ship. The delinquent bugler was immediately marched off to the cells. I felt very sorry about that, indeed my inclination was to compensate the lad. His serenade lulled my anxiety considerably. Thanks to that false alarm, every man of the 6000 were reported safely assembled at their respective boat stations within the remarkably short time of sixteen minutes as against the two hours which they had taken on the morning before.

The *Aquitania* carried them safely to their destination without further mishap. Many months later we carried a few back, but Yorkshire has not forgotten that many were left behind.

CHAPTER VIII

MERCHANTMEN AT WAR

Aboard R.M.S. "Berengaria."
At Sea.

IN this chapter I propose to deal briefly with the record of the Cunard Company during the Great War, a record perhaps equalled, but certainly not excelled, by any other of the great Mercantile Marine companies.

And first, let us examine the following amazing figures:

At the commencement of hostilities the company had in commission 26 vessels, apart from tugs, lighters and other subsidiaries, representing a total tonnage of considerably over 300,000 tons. As the war progressed, and to make up for depredations by the submarines, this tonnage was considerably increased, and it is estimated that the number of steamers handled by the company amounted to more than 400.

In all, 205,000 gross tonnage, amounting to more than 56 per cent, was sacrificed by the Company in the performance of services of the highest importance to the nation in the hour of its greatest jeopardy.

Some idea of the magnitude of the work performed by the Cunard organization may be gathered from the facts that in one year alone not less than 200 sailings were made in zones particularly exposed to hostile attack by enemy raiders and submarines, and that over 10,000 tons of cargo were often carried in one steamer.

In addition to cargo, the Company were responsible

for the transportation of 900,000 officers and men during the war period. When it is remembered that this aggregate is greater than the total population of either Liverpool, Manchester or Birmingham; that 900,000 men marching in column of route in sections of fours would take, without halting, nearly six days to pass a single point, it becomes possible to visualize the immensity of the task represented by these bald figures. When it is further remembered that the total British Expeditionary Force first thrown across the Channel in August, 1914, was only 80,000 men; that this was less than one-tenth of the number carried by the Cunard Company; and that the number so transported was equal to not less than one-eighth of the whole British Army at its greatest strength, the nation's debt to my company can be estimated.

Try and imagine the enormous task of provisioning these troops alone during the course of transport. Taking an average voyage as ten days, the food required to feed the number carried amounted to no less than 9,750,000 pounds of meat, 11,250,000 pounds of potatoes, 4,500,000 pounds of vegetables, 9,570,000 loaves of bread, 1,275,000 pounds of jam, 900,000 pounds of tea and coffee, and among countless other items 900,000 pounds of oatmeal, 600,000 pounds of butter, and 200,000 gallons of milk.

Vast as these figures are, they are dwarfed when we consider the enormous tonnage of cargo carried—a humdrum service, little appreciated, but upon which, fundamentally, our whole war structure rested.

Between August, 1914, and November, 1918, the records of my Company show that the Cunard vessels carried 7,314,000 tons of foodstuffs, munitions of war, and general cargo from America and Canada to the British Isles; over 340,000 tons from the British Isles to Italy and the Adriatic; over 500,000 tons from the British Isles to other Mediterranean ports; 320,000 tons from this country to France; and nearly 60,000 tons from

France to this country.   In addition to these colossal figures, cargo was carried westwards from this country, in the same period, amounting to over 1,000,000 tons. In all, 9,514,000 tons of cargo were carried by the Company during the Great War, the Cunard vessels steaming not less than 3,313,576 ocean miles, and consuming 1,785,000 tons of coal, to accomplish this feat. This distance is equivalent to the circumnavigation of the globe no less than a hundred and thirty-two times.

The toll of lives and brave ships sacrificed by the Company will never be fully told, but in the following pages I will deal briefly with a few of the vessels that fell victims, many of them after the pluckiest resistance, to the submarine menace.

At 5.30 p.m. on February 4th, about 40 miles north of Londonderry, Captain W. R. D. Irvine of the *Aurania* sighted the wake of a torpedo approaching his ship.   He saw it too late to avoid it, and it struck the vessel amidships, between the funnels.   The terrific impact of the explosion caused the *Aurania* to list heavily to port, but she righted herself again.   The boats were immediately lowered and the crew and passengers, with the exception of Captain Irvine himself and several of his officers, were all safely aboard them within ten minutes after the torpedo had struck.   No sooner had they got into the boats than the vessel was struck by a second torpedo, and just as the Captain and the remaining officers were clambering down the ropes into the last lifeboat, a third torpedo crashed into the *Aurania*.   Seven men were killed in the engine-room by the explosion of the torpedoes, and two others were lost by drowning.   The crew were in the boats for about one and half hours when they were then picked up by minesweepers.

In the meantime, as the *Aurania* was still afloat, Captain Irvine and some of the crew returned on board and made her fast with hawsers to a trawler that had arrived on the scene.   During the night, however, the *Aurania* broke adrift, and when day broke she had disappeared. A message was received from a naval patrol to the effect that she had drifted ashore at Tobermory, nearly fifty miles from where she had been torpedoed. Unfortunately, the stricken vessel had grounded at a very exposed position and, in the heavy weather that followed, she went to pieces. The loss of the *Aurania* was a particularly severe one to the company in that she was a new ship, having completed only seven voyages.

The *Dwinsk*, a steamer being operated by the Cunard Company for the Government, and in command of Captain H. Nelson, was torpedoed on June 18th of the same summer. She was struck about 9.20 a.m. some 650 miles east of New York, the torpedo hitting her in the region of No. 4 hold on the port side. At once seven lifeboats were lowered and all the crew were successfully embarked. Almost as soon as the crew had left the vessel the submarine appeared on the surface, and with a heavy-calibre gun fired nineteen shells into the *Dwinsk*, sinking her almost at once. Shortly afterwards a steamer hove in sight and fired five shots at the submarine, causing her to submerge. The unknown steamer then passed on her course, probably considering it was too dangerous to stop and pick up the men in the boats. After she had disappeared over the horizon, the submarine again appeared on the surface and, overtaking the lifeboats of the *Dwinsk*, she hailed the one in charge of the Chief Officer, and after interrogating him moved off in an easterly direction. During the night the little group of seven lifeboats became separated, but after undergoing the severest hardships, all except one ultimately reached port safely. Some of the boats landed as far apart as New York, Bermuda, Newport and Nova Scotia. The First Officer's boat, after sailing all through the first day and night, sighted a steamer on the second day, but, although distress signals were released, the anxious men received no reply. Toiling on, a barque, and then another steamer, were sighted on the evening of the third day, but again the little boat was unsuccessful in attracting attention. Luckily, the weather up to then had remained favourable, and continued to be good through the next day, on which another ship was seen, but she failed to perceive the lifeboat's stricken crew. Early on the following morning an empty lifeboat was sighted, and found to be one of their own boats from which, it was surmised, the crew, more lucky than they, had been rescued. On this day, to increase their sufferings, the wind rose and, by evening, a furious gale was raging. Towards dusk a great wave washed over the frail little boat, carrying one of the crew overboard, and filling the boat with water. On the day after, a Sunday, the wind dropped again, and remained variable until the evening of the following Wednesday, when it increased again to such an extent that by midnight a fierce gale was blowing once more. It may well be imagined that by this time, the ninth day adrift on the Atlantic in an open boat, exposed to wind and sea, the plight of the men was pitiable in the extreme. On Thursday morning the wind abated, but it was not until half-past nine on Friday that a steamer, the U.S.S. *Arondo*, sighted the famished crew and took them aboard, clothed them and provided them with medical attention, of which they were so sorely in need.

They had been drifting about in every condition of weather for no less than ten days, and the highest ration allowed them during the period of this terrible ordeal did not exceed one biscuit and half a glass of water per day per man. As a matter of fact this ration was reduced on the sixth day to half a biscuit, and a quarter of a glass of water per man. To the invincible courage, optimism and seamanship of the First Officer, who himself steered the boat for the whole of the ten days, the crew unanimously announced afterwards that they considered the saving of their lives was due. Of the other six boats, one was adrift for eight days, three for three days, and one for two days. One boat was lost, having foundered in the storm, and all twenty-two men of her crew were drowned.

The First Officer, Mr. Pritchard, as well as the Bo'sun's mate, who was in charge of another boat, were specially commended in the *London Gazette* for their great services. Lieutenant R. P. Whitemarsh of the United States Navy, who was one of the convoy officers to the *Dwinsk*, also played a gallant part in this epic story of the sea. Lieutenant Whitemarsh with another American and nineteen British subjects left the torpedoed vessel in No. 6 lifeboat, and this boat experienced a terrific storm, some four days afterwards. During the hurricane Whitemarsh volunteered to take the tiller and remained at watch without a break throughout the night. Great seas were sweeping the little boat, and one man was washed overboard. It seemed likely that the helmsman would suffer a like fate, so the gallant American officer ordered the other occupants to lie down in the bottom of the boat. This they did, two of them taking turns to hold on to the legs of Mr. Whitemarsh to prevent him, while at the tiller, from being washed away.

For this Lieutenant Whitemarsh received from His Majesty the King the Silver Medal for Gallantry in Saving Life at Sea.

It was three years earlier, and in a far distant sea, that the *Caria* was sunk, while proceeding in ballast from Alexandria to Naples in command of Captain J. A. Wolfe. She was not torpedoed. The submarine signalled to the *Caria* to stop and abandon ship, and as she was unarmed Captain Wolfe with his crew had no alternative than to obey. As soon as the lifeboats were clear the U-boat fired ten shots at her, several of which struck her about the bows and the bridge, and it wasn't long before she sank.

After twelve hours the crew of the *Caria* were picked up by the S.S. *Frankenfels*, ironically enough a German prize of war in the employ of the India Office, and landed at Malta. There were happily no casualties among the *Caria's* crew.

In this respect the *Carpathia*, which was sunk on July

17th, 1918, was not so fortunate. Proceeding in convoy and, at the time of the attack, about 120 miles west of the Fastnet, the escort had left some 3½ hours previously. She was easily the largest vessel of the convoy, and although travelling right in the middle of three lines of ships, the German picked her out with uncanny accuracy. Two torpedoes crashed into her within thirty seconds, one on the port side between No. 4 hold and the stoke-hold, and a second, half a minute later, in the engine-room. Satisfying himself that the ship was doomed, her commander, Captain W. Prothero, ordered everyone to the boats. Barely were they safely embarked, when a third torpedo struck the vessel. Three trimmers and two firemen were killed by the explosion of the first torpedo, but the remaining 218 members of the crew, together with 57 passengers, were picked up by H.M.S. *Snowdrop*, and safely brought to Liverpool. A letter was afterwards received from the Admiralty in which the Lord Commissioners stated that in their opinion the discipline and organization on board the *Carpathia* had been of a very high order, and that Captain Prothero was to be publicly commended in the *London Gazette* for recognition of his conduct in the crisis.

On May 5th, 1917, at 7.30 p.m., while *en route* to Avonmouth from New York, the *Feltria* was torpedoed without warning about eight miles south-east of Minehead off the Irish coast. A very heavy sea was running at the time. No. 1 lifeboat was capsized during launching, and No. 4 boat had been blown to pieces by the explosion of the torpedo. Boats Nos. 2, 3, 5 and 6 were successful in clearing the vessel's side. Most of the crew were in boats 3 and 5, the Captain and Chief Steward were alone in No. 2 boat, which was also badly damaged by the explosion. No. 6 boat contained the Chief Officer, Second Officer, Purser, plus three sailors, and the submarine coming to the surface ordered this boat alongside of her. Questioning the Chief Officer as to the nature of her cargo, the submarine made off but stopped to pick up Mr. Scott, one of the *Feltria's* engineers, and returned with him to the lifeboat.

From the U-boat's deck Mr. Scott was assisted back into the water, whilst Mr. Burt, the *Feltria's* quartermaster, very gallantly jumped into the sea and helped him to the lifeboat's side where he was pulled aboard in a very exhausted condition, while huge waves were washing over the little boat itself. Of the boat containing the Commander, Captain Price, and the Chief Steward, nothing more was seen, their lives being lost; by midnight three other members of the crew in No. 6 boat had died from exposure and exhaustion, one of the victims being Mr. Scott mentioned above. The remaining five in this boat were picked up early on Sunday morning by the S.S. *Ridley* and landed at Barrow. Twenty other survivors were picked up and landed at Queenstown, but out of a crew of 69 no less than 44 lost their lives, 17 dying from terrible exposure in the lifeboats.

Another vessel belonging to the Cunard Company, the *Flavia*, was more fortunate than the *Feltria* in that the whole of her crew was saved, when, early on the morning of August 24th, 1918, she was sunk off the Irish coast, while on a voyage from Montreal to Bristol. Her commander, Captain E. T. C. Fear, was below, resting, at the time of the attack, but the officer in charge had kept the situation well in hand, and H.M.S. *Convolvulus*, arriving on the scene, picked up the survivors from the boats and landed every man safely in Ardrossan.

On Sunday, March 11th, 1917, the *Folia*, commanded by Captain F. Inch, was sunk off the Irish coast, while on a voyage from New York to Bristol. It was a quarterpast seven in the morning that the Third Officer observed the periscope of a submarine some 500 feet from the ship and nearly abeam. Immediately afterwards he saw the feathery wake of a torpedo approaching, and a second later the *Folia* was hit amidships, the explosion smashing two of her lifeboats. Seven of the crew, including the Second Engineer, were also killed by the explosion, and the *Folia* herself began rapidly to settle. Four boats were at once lowered, and the rest of the officers and crew were safely embarked. While the lifeboats were still in the neighbourhood the submarine came to the surface, motored rapidly round the ship and fired four shots into her. She next backed away and fired a second torpedo into the sinking vessel. The U-boat then cleared off, but Captain Inch got his boats together and instructed the officers in charge to steer on a Nor'west compass bearing. Three of them made fast by painters so as not to get adrift from each other, and in this manner the frail boats stood on their course. About 11 a.m. the Captain, under the fog that had crept up, sighted breakers ahead. Creeping along the line of breakers they at last sighted smooth water at the base of towering cliffs. Pulling for these they saw the outline of a house high above, with people standing in front of it. Shouting in unison the crew succeeded in attracting attention and learned that the place was Ardmore, Youghal, Co. Cork, and from there they proceeded to Dungarvan, where they arrived in time to hear the church bells that evening.

In all the cases I have dealt with in this chapter of shipwreck every one of the vessels mentioned was unarmed and no resistance was possible.

But in the case of another vessel, the *Lycia*, under the command of Captain T. A. Chesters, a most plucky action was fought against heavy odds. It was at 8.30 a.m. on February 11th, 1917, and about twenty miles nor'west of South Bishop's Light, that the submarine was sighted, and by the time Captain Chesters had picked her up on the starboard beam his vessel had already been hit by a shot from the U-boat. The *Lycia's* course was at once altered so as to bring the submarine astern, and Captain Chesters himself opened fire, at about 3000 yards range. His gun, which was of Russian make and very light in calibre, was one of the first type supplied by the Admiralty to merchant vessels, at a time when there was a great shortage of ordnance owing to the needs of the Army and **Navy.** This gun misfired several times during the fight, and soon the Third Officer, Third Engineer and Steersman were badly wounded by the accurate shooting of the submarine. In the unequal duel the *Lycia's* funnel, starboard boats, forward cabins, chart-room, officers' and engineers' quarters were soon wrecked and in flames. At last, being unable to steer the ship under the continuous force and accuracy of the enemy's shells, Captain Chesters was forced reluctantly to abandon his vessel. Issuing orders to cease fire and stop the engines, as soon as the ship had sufficiently lost way, the crew were safely embarked in the port boat, with the exception of the Captain, Chief Officer, Third Engineer, the Gunner, and one of the boys, who succeeded in scrambling into the starboard boat which was dragging alongside.

When the lifeboats cleared the ship the submarine ceased firing, submerged and reappeared alongside Captain Chesters' boat. The submarine commander then ordered Captain Chesters to board the U-boat, which he did ; and he was at once asked why he had fired his gun without flying his ensign. Captain Chesters explained that this had not been possible as before he could fire his gun he had to remove the flagstaff aft. The German accepted this explanation and Captain Chesters, who had been treated with every courtesy, was allowed to return to the lifeboat. The submarine then ordered the lifeboat alongside again, and placing three German sailors in the boat, together with eight bombs, they rowed back to the *Lycia*, and there the Germans hung the bombs on each side of the rigging besides in the engine-room. The ship's papers, the breech block of her gun, her telescope and three live shells were lowered into the boat, after which the bomb safety-pins were removed, and the bombs placed below the water line. The U-boat sailors were then rowed back to the submarine, and before they were safely aboard the bombs began to explode. Shortly afterwards the *Lycia* sank, stern first, and the submarine went in chase of another vessel that had appeared on the horizon. The *Lycia's* lifeboats were picked up that same evening by two mine-sweepers, and the S.S. *Ireland Moor*, the crew being treated with the utmost hospitality and safely landed at Holyhead. Their conduct had been worthy, to use Captain Chesters' own words in praise of his men, " of all the best traditions of British seamen."

With the *Phrygia*, another Cunard vessel, there is happily a different story to tell. She was only a small vessel of 3350 tons, with a speed of not more than nine knots, but she put up a very gallant and successful fight against an enemy submarine. At 2 p.m., on March 24th, 1916, when homeward bound off the south-west coast of Ireland, two shots were fired at her by a U-boat, probably with the intention of bringing her to a stop. Captain F. Manley, her skipper, however, did not stop. Instead, he immediately ordered the helm hard aport and the crew to " general stations." There was a big sea running at the time, and this was fortunate, since the submarine, divining Captain Manley's intentions, continued to fire at the *Phrygia*. None of the shells, however, struck the little steamer. Captain Manley succeeded in manœuvring his ship to bring the U-boat astern, when he opened fire, and there began a running fight which lasted for forty-five minutes. During the whole of this time both the submarine and the *Phrygia* blazed away at each other incessantly under the most adverse conditions without either registering a hit. But at last one of the *Phrygia's* shells found its mark ; a great rush of black smoke poured up from the submarine ; her stern suddenly leapt high out of the water, and she disappeared to the loud cheers of the *Phrygia's* crew.

In connection with this fight the following resolution was passed by the Directors of the Cunard Company at a meeting of the Board in April, 1916.

" That the Company place on record their high appreciation of the gallant and successful efforts

made by the Captain, Officers and crew of the
Phrygia to save their vessel, and of the efficient
preparations made before-hand by Captain Manley
to deal with such an emergency, which contributed
towards the result, and finally extend their heartiest
congratulations to all ranks upon the splendid
gunnery and seamanship which put the enemy
submarine out of action."

Captain Manley and his crew also received recognition
from the Admiralty for their plucky achievement.

On March 27th, 1917, at eight o'clock in the evening,
the *Thracia*, commanded by Captain R. Nicholas, was
sunk at sight and without warning while on a voyage
with ore from Bilbao to Ardrossan. There was only
one survivor. Disappearing within one short minute
after being torpedoed, those on board had absolutely no
chance of saving their lives, and it was only by a miracle
that Cadet Douglas Duff, a young boy barely sixteen
years of age, was left to tell the tale. He succeeded in
saving his life by clinging for sixteen hours to the keel
of a capsized boat. While young Duff was in this parlous
predicament he was seen and jeered at by the crew of the
German submarine. Indeed, one of them raised a rifle
and aimed at him.

"Shoot and be damned to you," the plucky youngster
yelled, perhaps characteristically of the service to which
he belonged. He was ultimately rescued by a French
destroyer and at length landed at Le Palais, Belle Ile.
The body of the Chief Officer of the *Thracia* was also
recovered by the destroyer, and it is touching to reflect
that, as a mark of their respect and honour to the per-
sonnel of the British Mercantile Marine, a public funeral
was accorded to him by the inhabitants of this little
French seaport town.

Before her loss the *Thracia* had performed, like all the
vessels mentioned in this chapter, most arduous and
important duties, and one of her voyages, since it throws

a sidelight upon the multifarious activities of the Cunard Company during the war, deserves special mention.

On December 27th, 1914, under the command of Captain Michael Doyle, she sailed from Liverpool for Archangel with stores for the Russian Government. All the way to the North Cape she steamed in the teeth of a terrific gale, and under stormy skies; off that point, at this season of the year, entering a region where there is only one hour's so-called daylight of the twenty-four. Entering the White Sea, on the night of January 7th she ran into an ice-field, and on the next day this reached ahead of her as far as the eye could see. In the hope of breaking through to clear water Captain Doyle kept his vessel going until, the ice becoming thicker and closer packed with every yard, it at last became impossible for the *Thracia's* engines to drive the ship ahead. By prolonged and arduous exertions the *Thracia* was able to extract herself from this dangerous position and was finally brought back to the open water harbour of Alexandrovsk. From this port, on January 24th, 1915, accompanied by an ice-breaker, she again made a gallant attempt to win through to Archangel. Heavy ice-fields were once more encountered as soon as the White Sea was entered, causing the utmost difficulty in steering, and reducing progress to a crawl, until at last huge floes of ice again stopped her progress. The ice-breaker was also in difficulties, and therefore unable to render any assistance. For a considerable period the *Thracia* remained wedged in the drifting ice, and meanwhile a heavy nor'east gale had packed the entrance of the White Sea. The action of this wind, however, presently opened the ice in the immediate neighbourhood of the vessel, and a certain amount of further progress towards the south became possible. Here, however, the ice was found to be once again heavily packed, while the gale was choking the entrance with ever more and more drifting floes.

By this time the *Thracia's* propeller had become badly

damaged with the ice, and the ice-breaker was finding it difficult to secure her own safety. It was now clear that to remain in the drifting ice would eventually prove fatal, and so Captain Doyle made an effort to drive his vessel close to the land ice, where some degree of shelter might be found from the gales which were constantly driving enormous pieces of ice up and down with the ebb and flow of the tides through the narrow neck of the White Sea.

After many days and nights of the heaviest and most unremitting toil the *Thracia* was finally brought close to land, and a network of cables and ropes were thrown out from the ship to secure her position there. For seven long weeks, until March 18th, she was held here, during the whole of which time she was being submitted to the severest pressure owing to the alternating ebb and flow of the tides driving the packed ice against her side, under her bottom, and piling it up around her counter to a height of as much as 20 feet.

Her hull was seriously damaged, and for three weeks her pumps had to be kept going constantly, in order to keep her afloat, while the greatest skill and ingenuity had to be exercised in order to protect her rudder from the ice pressure under her counter.

So matters went on until the night of March 18th, when, owing to the heavy off-shore gales, the *Thracia* broke adrift, her anchors, cables and ropes being lost and her windlass broken. Fortunately, a few days later, the ice began to open here and there, so with the courageous assistance of another vessel, and under her own steam, she at long last succeeded in reaching a position inside the bar of Archangel river on April 9th, when her cargo was landed in good condition on the stationary river ice and conveyed by sleighs to Archangel.

But her troubles were not yet over. Within less than three weeks the river ice began to break, and the outgoing stream, carrying the broken ice to sea, drove the *Thracia* on to the bar. Her propeller blades were now reduced to the merest stumps, but in spite of this, she succeeded, at high water, in working herself free again by her own exertions. Obtaining ground tackle from another ship, which had arrived from Archangel at the first break-up of the river ice, the *Thracia* was enabled to come to anchorage in the gulf, and here she remained for about a week until the Dwina river was finally cleared of ice. She then proceeded slowly up the river to Archangel where she arrived on May 9th.

So great had been the damage sustained on this memorable trip, that it was necessary to place her in dry dock for the necessary repairs to enable her to return to England. When she at last arrived home, somewhere about the middle of August, 1915, her voyage had lasted seven and a half months.

After this diversion, let us return to the record of a few other Cunarders during the Great War.

On March 30th, 1917, the *Valacia*, under the command of Captain J. F. Simpson, left London for New York. At 5.30 the next evening, when in the English Channel off the Eddystone Lighthouse, she was struck on the port side by a torpedo. Very quickly her No. 6 hold, engine-room, and stoke-hold were full of water. Several British destroyers arrived on the scene and an attempt was made by one of these to take the disabled vessel in tow. She proved too heavy, however, so tugs were accordingly sent from the shore, and Captain Simpson was advised that the Admiralty Officials intended to try and beach her. The *Valacia's* Commander, in view of the fact that the bulkheads were holding, strongly advised that this course should not be pursued, but that an attempt should be made to tow her into Plymouth harbour. His advice was followed, and as it proved, with complete success. The task required herculean efforts, but the *Valacia* was taken safely into the harbour, where she was subsequently docked for repairs. The hole in the ship's side was no less than 25 feet long by 20 feet deep, but within a short time she was again able to take her place in the Company's fleet, and do much useful service for her country. The greatest credit is due to Captain Simpson for his splendid judgment and seamanship in bringing the vessel safely into port.

The *Valeria*, under the command of Captain W. Stewart, when homeward bound from New York on June 20th, 1917, came in contact with a submarine under the most surprising circumstances. About 3 o'clock in the afternoon both Captain Stewart, who was on the port side of the bridge, and the Second Officer who was on the starboard side, felt the ship quiver as if she had struck some obstacle. The Captain immediately crossed over to the starboard side, and was amazed to see an enemy submarine just under the waves, almost touching his ship. The working of her motors were distinctly audible.

For a moment the *Valeria's* gun crew were completely taken aback at this unexpected appearance of a U-boat at such close quarters. Captain Stewart, however, gave prompt orders to fire, and the gunners depressing the gun as far as possible fired a shell at literally point blank range.

Immediately a volume of vapour shot up from the U-boat, together with fountain-like spouts of water. A second shot was fired into her, but missed, but a third shot struck fair and square on her conning tower, and she sank like a stone. It is believed that the *Valeria*, when she first came in contact with the submarine, probably broke her periscope. Captain Stewart's first impulse was to stop in order to pick up any survivors from the U-boat, but in view of the fact that German submarines were at that time usually hunting in couples he thought it wiser to continue his voyage, and brought his ship safely back to Liverpool.

For this successful action, both Captain Stewart and the crew received special awards from the Admiralty, the Cunard Company, and other Associations, the destruction of the submarine being later verified by Admiralty trawlers. She was U-99.

It was perhaps not an unexpected fact, but one, nevertheless, of which the whole nation may well be proud, that the rescued officers and crews of these torpedoed vessels, never for a moment hesitated and indeed were anxious, as soon as possible, to render further service in other vessels.

An example of this occurred when the *Vandalia* was torpedoed on June 9th, 1918, her commander, Captain J. A. Wolfe, having already had a previous vessel, the *Caria*, torpedoed beneath him in the Mediterranean. The *Vandalia* was in a convoy accompanied by six American destroyers, yet she was picked out by a submarine and, although fortunately no lives were lost, she sank within two hours.

The gallant Captain Wolfe underwent this ordeal no less than three times during his war experiences, for a third vessel which he commanded, the *Volodia*, was sunk by submarines. As was usual, there had been no warning, and the *Volodia* was struck amidships, several of her engine-room crew, mostly Chinamen, being killed by the explosion. In addition, before she sank, the *Volodia* was also shelled by the attacking submarine. Captain Wolfe, with the survivors of the crew, succeeded in getting away aboard three boats, in charge respectively of Captain Wolfe himself, the Chief Officer, and the Second Officer, but these boats were chased by the submarine. On catching up with the Second Officer's boat, the German enquired for the Captain. He was told by the Second Officer that Captain Wolfe had gone down with his ship. The Second Officer was then ordered aboard the submarine, but after being closely questioned he was allowed to return to the lifeboat. The submarine clearing out, Captain Wolfe issued sailing directions, and the three boats kept together until nightfall, by which time the wind had increased to the violence of a gale. During the night the three boats became separated, so it was only the magnificent seamanship of Captain Wolfe and the two other officers, together with the splendid endurance and courage of the crews, that succeeded in bringing any of them to safety. For three days the frail boats were adrift in the open Atlantic, existing on one biscuit and one dipper of water per day. The Captain and Chief Engineer were actually on one occasion washed out of their little boat, but others of the crew succeeded in hauling them back again. The sea-anchors and rudder were carried away in the Captain's boat, but Captain Wolfe improvized a sea-anchor out of some canvas, sewing it with his penknife and some rope-yarn, and putting in it the last three remaining seven-pound tins of meat, the only articles of weight left in the boat. This weird, but effective contrivance he lashed to the broken rudder, and by this means the little boat was enabled to weather the breaking seas. How well to the course the vessel was kept can be gathered from the fact that when she was picked up by a destroyer, she was within 30 miles of the Lizard, having sailed 300 miles without sighting a ship. The other two boats, which had become separated, had similar adventures, but both were at last found, their exhausted and almost helpless crews being brought safely to land.

The *Veria*, Captain D. P. Thomson, was sunk on December 7th, 1915, in the Mediterranean, having left Patras in ballast for Alexandria on the 3rd of the month. At noon, on the fatal day, when about 50 miles from Alexandria, she sighted two lifeboats containing the crew of a Greek steamer, the *Goulandris*, which had been sunk by a submarine, and stopped to pick them up. Almost as once a U-boat appeared and opened fire. Captain Thomson, having no alternative, ordered his crew to man the lifeboats. During this operation the submarine continued firing, her shells destroying the chart house and the bridge, just as the boats were leaving the vessel's side. The submarine approached and demanded the ship's papers, but Captain Thomson had destroyed all those of a confidential nature, and all that the German commander obtained was the ship's register. The *Veria* sank shortly afterwards, and her boats which were not molested arrived at Alexandria next morning without the loss of one man.

The next vessel to claim our attention is the *Vinovia*, and, high as was the standard set by and expected of my gallant comrades of the Cunard, there were few instances, during the war of greater coolness and bravery than that of the *Vinovia's* skipper, Captain Stephen Gronow, when she was torpedoed in the English Channel on December 19th, 1917. She was then on her way to New York with a Chinese crew, and it was at half-past three in the afternoon that the torpedo struck her on the starboard side. As the *Vinovia* did not at first appear to be sinking, Captain Gronow ordered his engines full speed ahead, and made a gallant endeavour to reach the land. At 4 p.m., half an hour later, a small tug came on the scene and made fast to the disabled vessel, after some of her Chinese crew had left the ship in one of the lifeboats. A patrol boat then arrived and came alongside, when the remainder of the crew jumped aboard her. For the next three hours Captain Gronow, the only man left in the sinking vessel, steered her by means of the hand gear. Three hours later, at seven in the evening, a drifter approached when the Chief Engineer returned on board to assist his Captain in making a rope fast between the two vessels, and then returned to the patrol boat.

It was now quite dark, but still alone on board Captain Gronow stuck to his forlorn hope, continued to steer her and attend to the ropes. By half-past seven, as he noticed that she appeared to be making no headway, he groped his way forward by means of the rails, and found the fo'c'sle deck submerged four feet beneath the water. He also discovered that the tug had slipped the wire, and had disappeared. Clawing his way back aft to the steering gear, he was struck by a falling piece of wreckage from aloft and knocked unconscious. He lay thus for some time, but on recovering he made his way to the bridge and donned a life-belt. There he remained until, at eight o'clock, five miles from land and in pitch darkness, the *Vinovia* literally sank, beneath his feet, and he was hurled into the sea. He succeeded, however, in supporting himself on some wreckage, to which as it happened the ship's bell was attached, and it was this little fact that in the end proved his salvation. Attracted by the ringing of the bell, a small patrol boat the next morning decided to investigate the wreckage, and there the brave Officer was found lying unconscious. Unfortunately, his gallant efforts proved unavailing, as the *Vinovia* with her valuable cargo was totally lost. Still, Captain Gronow had provided yet another illustrious example for his successors at sea, and happily survived to receive from the Cunard Directors a handsome, inscribed silver vase, together with a certificate, and a silver medal and monetary gift from Lloyds.

CHAPTER IX

A GALLANT FOE

Aboard R.M.S. "Berengaria."
At Sea.

THE *Carmania*, another famous Cunarder, under the command of Captain Barr, sailed down the Mersey on August 15th, 1914, bound for the Halifax trade route, to carry out patrol duties. Arriving there, she received orders to proceed to Bermuda, and later she joined up with Admiral Cradock's squadron, which was then searching for the German raiders *Dresden* and *Karlsruhe* along the coast of Venezuela. She was with Cradock's ill-fated squadron for about a week, and was then ordered to make for the island of Trinidad in the South Atlantic. On September 11th information was received that the German collier *Patagonia* was leaving Pernambuco that night, and the *Carmania* was instructed to intercept the German vessel in conjunction with the cruiser *Cornwall*.

However, the *Patagonia* did not leave Pernambuco until three days later, and succeeded in evading the British vessels. In the meantime, Captain Barr had been instructed to continue on his course to Trinidad. This small and lonely island, barely 3 miles long by 1½ miles broad, about 500 miles from the South American coast, lies well out of the route of ordinary steamers, and presented an ideal coaling station for enemy craft seeking safe and unobserved harbourage during this operation. The land rises to a height of some 2000 feet, and on the south-west side of the island there is good anchorage.

On Monday, September 14th, 1914, about 9 a.m.,
the *Carmania* picked up the island, and two hours later,
as she drew nearer, it was observed that a large vessel
was at anchor on the far side of the land. It was known
that no British warships were in the neighbourhood, and
the island being uninhabited it seemed unlikely that any
British merchant vessel would be there. Therefore, it
was at once concluded that the strange vessel must be
an enemy. The day was exceptionally bright and clear,
and as the *Carmania* drew still closer, the mast and two
funnels of the unknown ship gradually took shape.
There were many conjectures aboard the *Carmania* as
to her identity. It was known that the *Karlsruhe* had
four funnels, the *Dresden* three funnels, the *Kronprinz
Wilhelm* four funnels, and an armed merchant cruiser,
the *Konig Wilhelm*, had one funnel. These were the
only enemy vessels that might possibly be in the vicinity.
But it could not be any of these, because even had the
number of funnels been altered, the outlines of the
above-mentioned vessels were known to the experienced
observers aboard the British ship.

It was soon evident that the *Carmania* had been
sighted, for smoke began belching from the funnels of
the strange vessel. She was getting up steam ready to
escape. The *Carmania* kept steadily on her course,
heading for the middle of the island, thereby making it
impossible to judge on which side she would pass.
The situation was thrilling in the extreme. The strange
vessel was the only one yet sighted, but behind the far
side of the island, hidden under the lee of the land, the
two German raiders, the *Karlsruhe* or *Dresden*, might be
lurking. Who would say that the visible vessel was not
a decoy luring the *Carmania* to her fate? Presently, a
small cargo vessel was observed backing away from
behind the enemy ship. Steaming away to the south-east
her evident object was to discover whether or no the
Carmania was alone, or in company with other vessels
hidden by the land. No sooner had the cargo ship

appeared than another small vessel was seen. Detaching herself from the large, unidentified vessel, she proved to be a cargo vessel of small tonnage also, and very soon made off in a nor'westerly direction.

At last it was learnt that only one big vessel was left, and this proved to be an armed cruiser like the *Carmania*. It was thought at first that she must be the *Berlin*, a German vessel of 18 knots. Later it was discovered that she was the *Cap Trafalgar*, the finest vessel of the Hamburg South American Line, 18,500 tons and capable of 18 knots. She had left Buenos Aires on August 17th and Monte Video on August 23rd. Captain Barr failed to identify her at first, because she was originally known to possess three funnels, but one, being a dummy used for ventilation, had been removed, reducing the number to two.

"General Quarters" was sounded in the *Carmania* at noon, and from the mastheads and the flagstaff aft fluttered the ensigns of the Royal Navy. Presently, the white flag with the black cross of the German Navy was run up by the *Cap Trafalgar*. As regards number and tonnage, at least, the fight promised to be equal.

To comply with the usual formalities, as it was not quite certain that the enemy was armed, a shot was fired across her bow. All doubt immediately vanished, for the distant bark of the enemy's guns was immediate, and two shells came screaming over the *Carmania's* bridge, just clearing that structure, pitching into the sea some fifty yards on her starboard side.

The fight was now on in earnest, and the firing on both sides was deadly accurate. Both vessels were registering hits at a rapid rate, and in the first few minutes one of the *Carmania's* gun-layers was killed, and the whole of the gun's crew lay wounded. Continuing to fire as coolly as if they were at practice, the British gun-layers were making things uncomfortably hot for the German. At first, only three of the *Carmania's* guns could be brought into action, but by a slight manœuvre to port other guns were brought to bear, and soon salvo after salvo was being poured into the *Cap Trafalgar*. All this time the vessels were gradually drawing closer to each other, and when about 3500 yards apart, above the din of the big guns, the staccato rat-tat-tat of machine guns could be heard coming from the enemy ship. Before this a shell had disabled the *Carmania's* control, and from the bridge it was no longer possible to give gun ranges by telephone. This must have been evident to the *Cap Trafalgar*, for her gunners were concentrating all their efforts in driving home the advantage, and shell after shell crashed into the neighbourhood of the bridge. It was, therefore, soon realized that to draw closer and allow the machine guns of the German to get within range, the gun crews on the unprotected decks of the *Carmania* would be mown down. To increase the range, therefore, the *Carmania* bore away to port. This manœuvre enabled the Cunarder to bring five guns to bear on the enemy, who was now astern. The *Cap Trafalgar* also ported, and our gunners were heartened when it was observed that she was now on fire and listing badly to starboard. The British gunfire had been steadily directed at the water-line of the enemy, and this policy was beginning to pay. But the honours were by no means one-sided, for enemy shells were constantly finding their mark. At one time the distance between the two vessels was less than 1½ miles, almost point-blank range, and it is amazing that the casualties aboard the *Carmania* were so few. So fast were the British gunners firing that the paint was blistering off the guns. The ship was also on fire in several places, and as the main water pipes had been shot away it was necessary to attack the fire with buckets of water, passed from hand to hand through the smoke and heat.

Soon the flames were licking the *Carmania's* bridge, and the Captain ordered the control to be changed to the aft steering position.

Still the fight continued. With the wireless gear

shot away, the ventilator cowls in ribbons, the port main
rigging hanging in festoons, and a great hole in the port
side aft, battered as was the *Carmania*, the *Cap Trafalgar*
was in a far worse plight. Shrouded almost completely
in smoke from the fire sweeping her decks, the list to
starboard gradually becoming more acute, her firing had
lost its deadly accuracy, and with each passing moment
was becoming more wild. Without warning her guns
ceased firing, she was seen to be heading back for
the island, and already preparing to man the lifeboats.

The battle was over, but there was still serious work
for the crew of the *Carmania*. The fire aboard was
raging furiously, and bucket gangs were employed in
a desperate effort to prevent the flames from spreading.
It was a fierce task, and one that demanded every energy
on the part of all on board, but, as they toiled and sweated,
they were cheered by the sight of their heeling enemy.
Already the crowded lifeboats from the *Cap Trafalgar*
had cleared from the side of the sinking vessel, and
were pulling towards one of the small German colliers
who could be seen standing by on the distant horizon.

Gradually the list on the big enemy ship increased,
until at last she lay completely on her side, her funnels
flat on the water. For a moment she lay thus, and then
with her bow submerged, she suddenly stood on end,
and sank swiftly beneath the waves. As she disappeared,
with her ensign still defiantly flying astern, a cheer went
up from the *Carmania's* crew, and it was a tribute, not
only for their own victory, but in praise of a very gallant
enemy.

Thanks to the unremitting exertions on the part of
the *Carmania's* crew, the fire was soon overcome, but
no sooner was this accomplished than a new danger was
reported. From the northern horizon the smoke of a
vessel was observed. Crippled and badly battered, with
nearly a quarter of her gun-crews killed or wounded,
for the *Carmania* to risk another action with the new-
comer would have been the sheerest madness. Wisely,

therefore, she increased her speed to the south-west, steering by sun and wind, until such time as she could assemble all that was left of her shattered navigating gear.

During the night the *Carmania* got in touch with the Cruiser *Bristol*, under whose care, and afterwards that of the *Cornwall*, she came to anchor near the Abrolhos Rocks at eight o'clock on the morning following the fight. Here, with the aid of the *Cornwall's* engineers, the worst of her holes were patched up, and with what navigating gear she could borrow, and in company with the *Macedonia*, the *Carmania* set out for Gibraltar at 6 p.m. on September 17th. Well did she deserve the hearty cheers of the *Cornwall*, with the two accompanying colliers, and those of the old battleship *Canopus* whom she passed early on the morning of the 19th.

She arrived at Pernambuco on the same afternoon, reaching Gibraltar nine days later. Her refitting took several months, but she remained as an armed cruiser until May, 1916, when she was again restored to the Cunard Company's Service.

Besides other honours conferred upon participants in this gallant fight, His Majesty the King decorated Captain Barr with the well-deserved Companionship of the Bath, in recognition of his splendid services during what proved a unique action of the war at sea, for it is on record that the *Carmania* was the only British armed auxiliary cruiser to sink a German surface war vessel in single armed combat.

After the war, on September 15th, 1919, there was an interesting sequel on board the *Carmania*. A piece of plate which belonged to Lord Nelson and was with him at Trafalgar was presented to the ship in commemoration of the fight. Twenty-four of these pieces of plate had come into the possession of the Navy League, who asked the Admiralty to allocate them to various ships. The *Carmania* was the only merchant vessel to receive the honour. In notifying the company of the

presentation, the General Secretary of the Navy League
stated :

> " The Navy League realizes that while every
> unit of the fleet has rendered service in accordance
> with the best traditions of the Royal Navy, H.M.S.
> *Carmania* has been able to render herself conspicuous
> amongst her gallant comrades, and in accepting this
> souvenir, the Navy League trusts that you will
> recognize it as an expression of gratitude to the
> glorious fleet of which that ship was so distinguished
> a representative."

That veteran Admiral, the Hon. E. R. Fremantle,
who was present, stated that there never was a single
ship action which reflected greater credit both on
the R.N. and on the Mercantile Marine, and more
especially on the R.N.R. It had very aptly been compared with the fight of the *Shannon* and *Chesapeake*.

Captain Barr, who retired from the Company's service
in 1917, said that the Captain of the enemy ship, the
Cap Trafalgar, put up a very gallant fight. "I do not
know his name," he said, "but he is the only German
I would care to meet."

CHAPTER X

A BRUSH WITH A SUBMARINE

Aboard R.M.S. "Berengaria."
At Sea.

IN New York, on April 10th, 1917, while in command of the *Ascania*, I received orders to load 1500 tons of T.N.T. explosive as a special cargo for Devonport. There were many spies in New York at the time, and therefore every possible precaution was taken to keep the nature of this grim cargo a secret. However, later events might tend to prove that the Germans managed to get wind of it.

John Duncan, my Chief Engineer, and myself were the only two Cunard officers aboard, although many of the lower ratings were members of the company. I have never sailed with any engineer who displayed so keen an interest in the navigation of a ship as did John Duncan. Every morning, as regular as the clock struck nine, John came stamping up on the bridge eager to know the exact position of the ship on the chart.

" Well, Skipper, where are we now ? " Duncan would enquire confidentially, nodding towards the chart-room. Solemnly we would both repair to the chart-room and gravely I would point a forefinger on our exact location.

"Fine!" John would whisper exultingly. "Fine, Skipper. Grand work! Grand work!"

I had the greatest admiration for Duncan, and implicit faith in his ability, and although the actual navigation of a ship is outside an engineer's department it was really a relief to have someone to take an interest in the work.

I felt that I was sharing a certain amount of responsibility with a friend, for friend he was indeed.

During the war the route which all vessels were required to follow was conveyed to the various commanders under sealed and secret orders by the Admiralty. The most careful precautions were taken to prevent any possible leakage of these routes from falling into enemy hands. We were required to destroy these precious documents by burning, immediately they were read, and to sign a certificate that this had been done.

On this particular voyage my secret orders instructed me to make for a definite point which lay about 100 miles sou'west of Plymouth, where, I was informed, I would be met by an escort of destroyers.

Our crossing was uneventful to begin with, but owing to that delightful cargo 'tween decks, you may be sure that every man aboard was very much on the alert for enemy submarines. Nerves were keyed to high-tension point. There were, also, several false alarms which tended to make life anything but dull. Then, on the last day of the voyage, only a few hours from our rendezvous, the wireless began to buzz.

"Enemy submarines active 100 miles sou'west of Plymouth."

This was cheerful news; a nice tonic before breakfast. These U-boats were probably waiting for me. At least, they were at the exact spot for which I was making. Duncan stamped on to the bridge at the usual time and I handed him the message. I left him reading it and walked to the chart-room. John followed, still gazing at the fateful pink form. Then he rubbed his chin reflectively.

"Where are we now, Skipper?" John asked.

Silently I placed a forefinger on the chart.

John gazed on the spot absently. Then:

"And where are the U-boats supposed to be, Skipper?"

My forefinger moved ever so slightly.

"Just there, John.   Slap on our course."

John again rubbed his chin reflectively, his eyes now glued to the chart.

"Hum!   What are you going to do, Skipper?" he demanded.

"What can I do, John?" I asked simply.   "I have definite instructions to proceed to that spot.   These orders have not been cancelled, so. . . ."   I shrugged my shoulders.

"You'll have to go!" said Duncan.

"Exactly!   I'll have to go, John," I answered quietly.

Duncan and I worked out distances on the chart, and we calculated we should be on the spot at noon.

"If our escort is there first I expect the submarines will beat it, John," I told him, our calculations concluded. John again rubbed his chin.

"Aye!   But what if the submarine gets there first . . . and there's no escort, Skipper?" he murmured enquiringly.

I smiled grimly at that, very conscious of the deadly explosive beneath our feet.   "In that case there's likely to be a nasty . . . a very nasty mess, John."

"Aye!   There will that!" John agreed, giving his chin an extra hard rub.   Solemnly we shook hands and Duncan departed to the depths of his engine-room.   I then beckoned my Chief Officer.

"Close all bulk-head doors, and clear all boats ready for lowering," I instructed.

It was unnecessary to tell the men to keep their eyes skinned for U-boats.   For a week past they had been treading the decks like cats, very much on the alert. During this period, the second week of April, 1917, we lost more tonnage than in any other period during the war. I am not certain of the total, but I know the figures were colossal.

Was my ship fated to swell those grisly figures?

As we steamed nearer and nearer the fatal spot a great

silence descended upon the ship. Every available hand was on deck, and the fo'c'sle-head was crowded with eager, silent men. From the bridge, with nerves tense and anxious eyes, my glasses swept the seas ahead. There was no sign of our escort. We had the Great Waters to ourselves.

"We ought to see their smoke soon, now, sir," my Chief Officer remarked quietly.

I did not answer, I knew that "soon" might be too late. Slowly the hands of the bridge clock crept round to noon. I could see now far beyond our rendezvous. Still no sign of our destroyers.

I was dead on time. In a few minutes we would sweep beyond the appointed spot. I dare not slow down.

Twelve o'clock struck.

"Submarine! Submarine! Starboard Bow!"

With the echo of the bell a mighty roar rose from the crew. Swiftly emerging above the waters, about two miles on our starboard beam, the sunlight glinting on her conning tower, we beheld the long, grey, menacing form of a gigantic enemy submarine. Even as the waters swirled from her decks, figures could be seen frantically stripping the cover from a great gun which covered nearly half her length. They were taking no chances of our speed defying their torpedoes, gun-shells would travel faster and farther. We had one 6-inch gun aboard and I decided to fight her. There was no alternative. But one enemy shot in the terrible cargo would mean the end of the world for us.

When I first saw that long, grey, cigar-shaped thing rising from the water I confess that, maybe for the tick of a watch, I stood petrified. But only for a second. Our 6-inch gun was aft and it was necessary to bring the submarine astern.

"Hard-a-port!" I roared, and we swung round just in time. We heard the distant "cough" of the enemy gun, almost simultaneously our own gun barked in chorus.

His shell went screaming wide, but a great spout of flying spray from our first shot sprang up almost under the nose of the U-boat. Our fellows cheered lustily. But their cheering was premature. As our gun again belched forth the bark of the German's was only a second behind. His shell came screaming over the bridge and landed uncomfortably close. Our second shot was wide. Bang went our gun again. "Cough" came Jerry's from the distance. Although our one weapon was an old type piece we were beating the German for time. Please God that we beat him for accuracy as well. The fight was now on with a vengeance. We were giving as good as we were getting. But one clean hit from the German into that 1500 tons of an explosive more deadly than dynamite would wipe us clean off the face of the seas.

This was my first scrap at sea. Curiously enough I felt quite calm. I suppose because my mind was very fully occupied, for, of course, I was constantly manœuvring my ship so as to present the least possible target. Still the bulk of our vessel presented a bigger object to them than their much smaller craft did to our gunners and I expected to be hit at any moment. Another shell came screaming over, missing us by yards. With every miss our fellows sent a chorus of jeers and catcalls ringing across the waters which must have reached the Germans' ears.

Bang! Bang! . . . Cough! So it went on. Our gunners were now firing two shots to the German's one. The submarine was manœuvring as quickly as we were, but at one time the spouts of spray from our shells seemed to completely envelope her. At last one of our shells seemed to land smack on top of her, her nose leapt out of the water, and down she went to the loud, exultant cheering of our crew.

My gun-layer swore he sank the U-boat, but actually she was not sunk. Certainly the German submerged much quicker than he came to the surface in the first place.

When I glanced at the bridge clock, at the end of the scrap, I was amazed to find that the battle had lasted for barely five minutes. It seemed like hours to me.

Allow me to pay a compliment to my gunners. Had it not been for the deadly accuracy and uncanny speed of the naval ratings manning our gun, an obsolete type, I am quite certain that the ship and every soul aboard would have been blown to Hades. I never made any claim that we had sunk the German. None the less my Jack Tars certainly made it so hot for him that he reckoned it was much cooler in the depths than above the water. We didn't wait to make certain. We cleared like the deuce for Plymouth. About an hour after the fight we ran into a sea strewn with wreckage. Ship's boats blown to smithereens, cargoes of every description, sea-chests, bedding, life-buoys, rafts—all floating in one great tangled mass, and the sea was thick with oil. When I beheld this flotsam any feelings of regret which I may have had for the fate of my late antagonist left my mind. That wreck-strewn sea was unmistakable evidence of his devil's handiwork. By the amount of the wreckage it was evident that more than one vessel had been destroyed. Where were the survivors? Was this the reason why he had challenged me with his gun? Had he expended all his torpedoes before he met me? I decided that was the sole reason which had forced him above the waters in open fight. I slowly circled the sea of wreckage, searching the waters for sign of life. There was none. I learnt later that three ships had been blown up in that very spot, and all aboard had perished.

Safely in harbour that night John Duncan, my Chief Engineer, came marching solemnly into my cabin, as was his wont at the end of every one of those perilous war voyages. He always stood for a moment in the doorway, rubbing his chin reflectively, and eyeing me in silence. Then solemnly he would advance with outstretched hand, and exclaim:

"*We* have done it again, Skipper!"

"Aye, John. *We* have done it again."

On that voyage at least he was certainly worthy of any honours which were going. Had a German shell landed in our cargo we, above decks, had half a chance of escape. For Duncan and his men, working far below in the bowels of the vessel supplying the speed and helm-control, there would have been no escape.

CHAPTER XI

MORE WAR ADVENTURES

Aboard R.M.S. "Berengaria."
At Sea.

AS an example of what war meant to the lower ratings of the Merchant Service, in this chapter I will describe the adventures of two of the present staff of my vessel, the *Berengaria*.

James Gibson, my Storekeeper, joined the *Ausonia* early in 1917, and in May of the same year, passing the old Head of Kinsale, under the escort of two cruisers, a submarine attacked the vessel without warning.

Gibson says: "I remember it was a beautiful evening about five o'clock, the sun shining brilliantly, the sea calm and placid, and I was having a quiet smoke on the boat-deck when suddenly I saw the long, feathery trail of a torpedo making dead for the ship. I yelled a warning, but almost before I shouted my voice was drowned by the roar of the exploding tube as it struck our stern, carrying away the rudder and two propellers.

"We at once took to the boats, but stood by; and later, when we saw that she was not sinking very rapidly and there was no sign of the submarine, we all returned to the ship again. The *Ausonia* was a vessel of 15,000 tons register, and towards dusk that night a cruiser bore down and attempted to tow us, but had to cast off as she was incapable of handling a vessel of our size. We drifted about until 2 a.m., gradually sinking, when a tug, the *Woodcock*, came to the rescue just in the nick of time, and towed us into Queenstown.

"After laying there eighteen days the *Ausonia* was taken

in tow by three tugs, and with two American destroyers circling us to ward off submarines we were towed to Bristol, where a new tail and stern were put on her. This took about six months, during which time I made several trips in the *Carpathia*, which was also torpedoed, and then I again rejoined the *Ausonia*.

"The *Ausonia* was some 620 miles west of the Irish coast at 5 p.m., on May 30th, 1918, when again a torpedo struck her, causing a terrific explosion. As our Commander, Captain R. Capper, afterwards said, he saw rafts, ventilators, ladders, and all kinds of wreckage, coming down as if from the sky, fall round the after-part of the ship. Captain Capper who, at the moment, was at the entrance of his cabin when the ship was hit, at once went to the bridge, put the telegraph to 'Stop'—'Full Speed Astern'; but received no reply from the engine-room. All hands were at once ordered to their boat stations, and the wireless operator tapped out the ship's position on his auxiliary gear. Seven boats were got away, and within a quarter of an hour after the ship was struck we had safely left her. About a quarter of a mile astern Captain Capper mustered us together and called the roll. It was then discovered that eight stewards were missing, having been at tea in a room immediately above the part of the ship struck by the torpedo.

"Half an hour after we were torpedoed we sighted a periscope on our port bow, and an enemy submarine came to the surface and fired about 40 shells at the ship, at point-blank range, some of these dropping within fifty yards of the boats. After the *Ausonia* had gone down the submarine approached the boats, and Captain Capper, who was at the oars in one boat, was ordered to go alongside. On the submarine's deck several of her crew were lounging, laughing and jeering at us. After enquiring the nature of the *Ausonia's* cargo the submarine commander ordered us to steer in a north-easterly direction. She hovered about the open boats until nightfall, but at dawn she had disappeared.

"Captain Capper gave orders that we were to keep together and endeavoured to get into the track of convoys, the weather being fine at the time. Until midnight we were successful in remaining in each other's company, but the wind having risen in the night, two boats, one of them in charge of the First Officer, and the other in charge of the Boatswain were, on the following morning, not to be seen.

"There were 22 of us in my boat, including the Captain, a stewardess, Mrs. Edgar, and a youth with both legs broken.

"We were all very scantily dressed as it was warm weather when we were attacked, and everyone had taken to the boats just as they were clad. The Stewardess was a brave little soul, asking no favours and trying to appear as cheerful as the rest.

"At dawn on the first morning adrift two of our boats were missing. Captain Capper gave orders for the remaining boats to be fastened together in a long line, by the painters. In this strange formation, we continued throughout the following day and night, when the ropes began to part. They were also retarding progress and were therefore cast off, the boats, however, still continuing to remain pretty well together. On the third day adrift, a Sunday, the weather became bad, heavy rain falling and soaking us all to the skin. On Monday and Tuesday, conditions improved a little, but on Wednesday a storm broke, and by midday a heavy sea was running, with a gale blowing from the north-west. The boats were now running before this, with great seas breaking over them and saturating everybody on board.

"We made progress at the rate of about 60 miles a day. The nights were terrible, no one slept and it was perfect hell, it being so dark sometimes that you could not see the person sitting next to you. We sent up several red flares each night, but as nothing resulted, Captain Capper decided to conserve our supplies for the direst emergency. We had sails up and as there was no need to row, there was nothing to do but sit and think, and hope, and suck buttons or anything that would bring saliva to our swollen tongues, our parched and broken lips.   Captain Capper allowed everyone, including himself of course, half a biscuit a day and a fifth of a dipper of water, a wise and strict rationing which was to save us from complete starvation.   On the afternoon of June 5th a NW gale sprang up, separating the remaining boats, each going their own way.   We never saw each other again.

"We were nearly all in when on the tenth day adrift we sighted land, but it was another fifteen hours before we were picked up by H.M.S. *Zinnia*, at 5.15 a.m., when 12½ miles south of the Bull Lighthouse.

"We had only 25 biscuits left together with half a bucketful of water—but one day's meagre supply when the terrible ordeal ended, and we were all in such a pitiable condition that we had to be pulled up the ladders of the *Zinnia*."   The boat herself was in a strained and leaky condition, and although Captain Capper had been without sleep for ten days, he was still in full possession of his faculties and able to give the probable position of his other boats.

So much for Gibson's story.   May I supplement that story by an extract from Sir Archibald Hurd's book, *A Merchant Fleet at War*, in which he graphically describes the ordeal of the survivors of the *Ausonia* during their ten terrible days adrift in open boats.

"The conduct of the Cunarder's crew was of the highest order, that of the stewardess, Mrs. Edgar, of Orrell Park, Aintree, the only woman on board the vessel, being particularly courageous."

He continues: "Special mention must also be made of the butcher's boy, Robinson.   At the moment of the explosion, together with the pantry boy, Lister, he was in one of the cooling chambers, and the explosion made it impossible for the two boys to get out.   Robinson had

several wounds on his hips and thighs, and his left arm
was lacerated. Both boys, in addition, had both legs
broken above the ankle. Robinson, however, managed
to crawl out on his hands and knees and secure a
board and place it across the gaping hole in the deck,
thus enabling Lister also to reach a place of comparative
safety. The two boys then crawled on hands and knees
up two sets of ladders to the boat-deck, and were placed
in the boats. The doctor attended to the boy Robinson's
injuries, as far as was possible, but it was not for 30 hours
that Captain Capper was able to transfer him to the boat
in which Lister was lying, so that he also might receive
medical aid. In spite of their experience and injuries,
both boys remained calm and cheerful, and indeed in
high spirits, but it is sad to record that Robinson subsequently succumbed in hospital as the result of his
injuries.''

More, however, to Captain Capper than to any one
man was the salvation of the rescued men due, and it was
in recognition of his dogged determination and splendid
seamanship that His Majesty the King afterwards
bestowed upon him the Distinguished Service Cross.

My Chief Steward, Mr. Pimbly, was Second Steward
aboard the *Orduna* in the very early days of the war.

He tells me:

"Commanded by Captain Taylor, we sailed out of
Liverpool one Saturday evening, carrying passengers
bound for New York. At about 6 o'clock the following
morning I was on deck speaking to one of the quartermasters, when we observed the wake of a torpedo coming
towards us. One must be quick to see a torpedo coming ;
the torpedo is always about 20 yards in front of the wake,
and only the wake is discernible to the eye. It was coming
towards the stern of the ship, and only missed us by
twenty or thirty feet. The Quartermaster immediately
notified the bridge. I ran to warn the Chief Steward.
He instructed me to wake up the passengers and crew,

and acquaint them that we had been fired at by a submarine. The passengers came streaming out of their
state-rooms, the women and children in their night-
dresses, approximately five hundred of them. It was a
pitiable sight to see them rushing out, clad in this way,
with their faces as white as ghosts. We had instructions
that they were not to be allowed on deck, and I quickly
posted men at stations to see this order carried out.
Meanwhile, Captain Taylor had started zigzagging.
Failing to hit us with his deadly tubes, the submarine
came to the surface, and commenced firing at us. We
were unarmed—at this stage of the war no passenger
liners were armed, and were consequently unable to do
anything except try and get away when attacked. I was
on deck and could actually see the Germans mount their
gun. It was obvious that the order that no one was
allowed on deck was to avoid injuries from shell-fire. In all
he fired about sixteen shots at us, some falling short, some
going over us, but all very near the mark. It was the first
time that any of us had been under shell-fire, and it was
distinctly unpleasant. During the attack the women were
ordered into the smoke-room to dress. Then we
gradually zigzagged our way out of range, and everyone
breathed sighs of relief.

"That was my first taste of submarine warfare, an
experience from which I emerged unscathed.

"My next experience was fated to end more
disastrously.

"This was aboard the *Carpathia*—well remembered as
the ship that went to the rescue of the *Titanic*. In
July, 1918, under an escort of destroyers, the *Carpathia*
was one of a convoy of sixteen ships sailing from Liverpool
to New York. Some three hundred miles west of
Ireland the destroyers left us and a few hours later we
were struck dead amidships by two torpedoes, one after
the other. How this happened will never be known, as
the submarine picked us out right from the middle of the
convoy, and none of the other ships were struck. We

had on board from 200 to 300 passengers, mostly women
and children, English and American.   We at once
lowered the boats, and got the women and children—in
fact, all the passengers—out safely, and nearly all the
crew.   The majority of the unfortunate men in the stoke-
hold were blown to pieces.   Two of the engineers, who
were badly scalded, managed to crawl out of the engine-
room, and after all the passengers had been safely disembarked two of the assistant cooks and myself managed
to lower a boat containing only the two wounded engineers
and the doctor.   I never thought it possible that these two
youngsters—for that's all they were—and myself could
have lowered a huge ship's boat without any assistance,
but we did it somehow.

"The engineers were scalded beyond recognition.
One of them was unconscious.   The doctor absolutely
soaked them in oil, but the agony these poor fellows
suffered, particularly when the salt water soaked through
their bandage, is beyond description.

"The last persons to leave the ship were the Captain
and the Quartermasters.   They had remained on the
bridge to the end, sending up daylight stars.   Captain
Prothero scrambled off the stern of the *Carpathia* when
she was well up in the air.   From the boats we could
just see the remainder of the convoy disappearing over
the horizon: they dared not stop even to pick us up.
The Captain ordered the boats into formation, and then
it was seen that some were overcrowded, and it was a
tricky business transferring the women and children to
equal the loads.   We took a number of women and
children into the boat I was in, as we only had the
doctor and two wounded engineers together with myself
and the two young cooks.   I was at the helm steering
and the two cooks rowing, the engineers were still at
the bottom of the boat, with the doctor constantly
anointing their wounds with oil.   Just as we were all
ready to pull away we observed the periscope of the
submarine about a mile off our port beam.   She came to

within about a quarter of a mile of us and fired another torpedo slap into the *Carpathia*. There followed a tremendous explosion, the great vessel rose on end, and the last thing we saw of the gallant *Carpathia* was the Red Ensign, fluttering proudly at her stern as she plunged beneath the waves.

"The women and children were terrified as the submarine approached the boats and we, the crew, were afraid that they would take off our Captain, as was the usual wont. But about this time we heard the sound of distant gun-fire, and on the horizon we saw the smoke of an approaching vessel. Hearing the shots the submarine immediately submerged and was not visible when the sloop *Snowdrop* appeared on the scene. With black smoke belching from her funnels, the *Snowdrop* dashed towards us at full speed and swept round in great wide circles dropping her deadly depth charges. About an hour afterwards she came alongside, and gave us orders to keep rowing away, and she would eventually pick us up. Then off she dashed again in her relentless search for our attacker. We were in the boats about three hours when she suddenly reappeared and instructed our Captain to send his boats alongside one at a time.

"Everyone was taken safely aboard the sloop though not without some little difficulty as there was a moderate sea running. The *Carpathia's* lifeboats were finally abandoned, and I remember they looked very forlorn as they gradually drifted away. We then proceeded at full speed for Queenstown, but the *Snowdrop* received orders by wireless to take us direct to Liverpool. With our rescue, however, our troubles were not yet over. Owing to lack of accommodation, and the small space of the sloop, the majority of the women and children had to lie down on the decks all night. As many as possible received shelter in the Captain's and Officers' quarters, but the space aboard was so small and there were so many of us, that we of the crew had to remain standing all night.

"Towards midnight a violent gale arose and great seas washed the decks of the sloop, and one can imagine the plight of the poor women and children exposed to these terrible conditions. However, we arrived at Liverpool the following day without the loss of a single life, and I am glad to say that even both the scalded engineers eventually recovered."

Shortly after the war Mr. Pimbly was for a time Chief Steward of a Russian liner named the *Kursk*, a vessel which was chiefly engaged in rescuing the White Russians from being massacred by the Reds. His adventures on that happy ship are worthy of record in these memoirs, if only for the fact that they will give the landsman some slight idea of the many difficulties with which the Steward's department of a large vessel is sometimes faced.

Pimbly says :

" I will never forget the name *Kursk* as long as I live. The fun started with the very first voyage. We embarked about 1400 White rebels at Murmansk and we couldn't get rid of them. Nobody would have them. These people had rebelled in Finland against their own country, and had joined the Russians. But now the Russians had driven them out and we rescued them from slaughter just in the nick of time. We made for Reval in Estonia, but before we reached there we received orders to land them at Helsingfors. The authorities at Helsingfors had other ideas. As soon as they learned the nature of our human cargo they gave us one hour to clear out. The actual words used were :

" 'Get out, or we will sink you!'

"Then we tried Reval, but got out of there as well . . . under the hour. My supplies of food were running short so we made for that part of Estonia, in the Baltic, which was then under British protection. Here the Admiralty instructed us to lie up with the Baltic Fleet and wait for orders.

"Wait! For how long, with 1400 hungry rebels aboard?

"There was only one place where food could be bought and that was in the live market. Moreover, the Russian traders would not accept English money, and as the rouble was about a million to the pound, I required two suit-cases to carry the money for my stores, and half of my staff to lead the cows and pigs (all live) and hens aboard which we purchased. This went on daily for about two weeks. Then destroyers came along and the rebels were taken back to Helsingfors where they were quickly tried by court-martial. The majority were shot.

"Back we went to Murmansk, where we embarked another crowd of Russian refugees, men, women and children. These had been driven out of their homes by the Reds and were in a deplorable condition, half-starved and in rags. Our work at this time was really a work of rescue, inspired in the name of mercy, trying to save these unfortunate people from destruction. Once aboard, the problem was what to do with them, where to take them and how to feed them. It was almost impossible to get sufficient supplies of food. The Reds had not penetrated to the Crimea, so it was decided to take them to Novorossiisk in the Black Sea, where they would at least be free from persecution.

"Novorossiisk is a bleak, desolate place, with countless miles of barren steppes stretching for miles around. It was winter, and bitterly cold, and there they were landed. We gave each a loaf of bread and a piece of meat and set sail for Constantinople. I have never forgotten the sight of these poor wretches as they watched our departure. Except for the whimpering of children they were mostly silent, like dumb animals, not knowing what was to become of them, or where they were to go.

"Constantinople was crammed with Russian Royalists. I went into a restaurant one night and every waitress in the place, about fifty of them, was a Russian Princess.

In the streets, ladies were offering fur coats, sables, rings, necklaces and jewellery of every description to get money to buy food which was almost unprocurable. Daily the Reds were driving the aristocrats through the Crimea, and everything that could float—rafts, barges, boats— were used to bring them through the Bosphorus. I saw a derelict timber barge go floating by one day, packed with women and children bedecked with furs and jewels. Later I went aboard. They had had no food for days and were sleeping, packed like sardines, on the bare decks. Without lavatory accommodation, and not even a drop of water to perform the most meagre ablutions, their jewels and furs enhanced a state of filth indescribable.

"All night long my bakers were making bread, yet that was all we could spare them—dry bread and water. But had it not been for the assistance of the British and American Governments, the majority of the Russian Royalists must have perished from exposure and starvation. Personally, the Russian Revolution was no concern of mine. What did concern me was the inhuman and ghastly hardships which women and little children had to bear as a result of that affair. The full horror of their sufferings will never be told.

"The *Kursk* was instrumental in rescuing General Wrangel and several members of the Russian Royal family. General Wrangel had commanded the Royalist Army and he was smuggled aboard secretly in civilian attire. He and his whole party lived and slept in the smoke-room, never once leaving the place, not even to come down to the dining-room. I had a little chat with him daily. The old man was very grateful for everything that was done for him, but one could see that his heart was broken over the fate of his country.

"In addition to the White Russians I had a lot of troops aboard, and before we sailed, as I was anxious to procure a supply of poultry, I went ashore and interviewed the Naval Transport Officer. Owing to the shortage of food, these things had to be arranged through this officer.

" 'Can't be done,' he told me. Then he thought for a moment and said : 'Tell you what, call at Chanak as you pass through the Bosphorus. I have a poultry farm there, and have raised about three hundred turkeys. You can have a hundred of these.'

"I thanked him profusely.

" 'You'll have to catch and kill them yourselves,' he added, as I was leaving him. I barely caught that last remark, but I was to remember it very distinctly later on.

"Chanak is a bare, barren wilderness, and when we arrived we found these long-legged turkeys running about wild. I sent three stewards ashore to rope in the stipulated hundred. Later I increased the number of stewards to twenty—thirty—forty, until the whole ship, Russians, soldiers and nurses included, were dashing madly after these swift, lanky-legged birds. They were on a wide, open range, and led us a merry dance. I'll swear we chased some of them half-way to Gallipoli. We roped in a hundred eventually. Those proved to be the halt, the lame and the gouty. That night the exhausted soldiers and stewards were too tired to eat turkeys, which at any rate were so tough that even the hungry White Russians couldn't eat them.

"Several months later the *Kursk* sailed out of Liverpool with 1500 Australian civilians aboard, and the most eventful voyage of my career commenced. These fellows had been employed as munition workers in England during the war and were being repatriated to Australia. For our consort we had an Australian troopship sailing with us, laden with 'Digger' Tommies. Before we sailed the two rival crowds had a pitched battle on the dockside. The reason was apparent. Whilst the Australian Tommy had been fighting in the trenches for a few shillings a day, his civilian brother had been living in comfort in England, earning £10 a week. That was one reason.

The other reason was that the civilians were going back as second-class passengers, while Tommy was being taken back slung in a hammock, aboard a troopship. An hour before sailing the Shore Superintendent came aboard to see me.

" 'You've got the toughest crowd that has ever sailed the seas, Chief, so look out for squalls!' he warned me.

"Before we had even left the Mersey a delegation of four of this tough crowd, headed by a big, black-bearded leader, came to my cabin and demanded audience.

" 'Say, Chief,' said he of the black beard. 'We've formed a food committee and we'll tell you what we want for eats. Just sling out a few menu cards, and we'll make them out ourselves.'

"I told them I was delighted to hear of the arrangement.

" 'Good!' said the leader. 'To begin with we want fried potatoes at least once a day.'

"I explained that this was impossible, owing to their large numbers, but that I would try and meet all their demands as regards other dishes.

"The first squall commenced in the dining-room one morning, shortly after we sailed. Someone insulted one of my waiters, hurling a particularly loathsome epithet at the lad. Several other waiters heard it and, quite justly, demanded an apology. My stewards were mostly ex-service men, lately released from active service, and had not yet learned to suffer insults gladly. The Australians refused to apologise, so my stewards in a body went on strike.

"I called a meeting of all my troublesome passengers, and I politely told them that unless they learnt to behave decently to my stewards they would have to bring their own food from the kitchen. The food committee, led by Blackbeard, promptly apologised and for a time everything was tranquil. Then both vessels reached Port Said together, and there was another scrap between the Tommies and the Munition Workers. A few of my stewards carried a few scars next morning but I never enquired the cause. Several British Tommies stationed at Port Said were also mixed up in the battle and news of this must have preceded us.

"The Suez Canal was, at this particular time, protected by British troops owing to the Turks breaking out down the Nile Coast. We were stoned from one end of the Canal to the other, and the most frightful language was bandied between ship and shore. Every porthole on the ship was smashed to smithereens.

"During this time I had frequent visits from Blackbeard and his gang demanding fried potatoes.

" 'We want fried potatoes!'

" 'Impossible!' I told him finally. 'My kitchen isn't big enough to fry potatoes daily for fifteen hundred of you.'

"Eventually the *Kursk* steamed into Colombo and the troopship arrived at the same time. The Goldface Hotel, near the docks, has quite a big yard, and there two of the rival factions met that night. I saw the scrap from a bedroom window. The yard resembled a shambles within seconds. The majority of our passengers arrived back well battered. Some were left behind for repairs. A number were lodged in gaol.

"After leaving Colombo we eventually reached the Equator, and as the temperature was well over a hundred I decided to give them cold luncheon. Down came Blackbeard and his food committee, protesting loudly at the cold fare.

" 'You want hot fare in this weather?' I asked.

"They did! So next day, when it was so hot that even to breathe was an effort, I gave them:

"*Pea soup . . . Hot Roast Pork . . . and Hot Plum Pudding*.

"They all enjoyed it immensely. Many asked for more.

"Again we had comparative peace for a time (with the exception of about twelve fights daily). Then one day I was informed that the whole crowd had gathered on deck and were holding an indignation meeting. From an upper deck I beheld the big bearded Australian urging the crowd to mutiny.

" 'We want fried potatoes,' he was chanting. 'We want fried potatoes at least once a day, men. And if we don't get them we'll tear this ship to pieces, and boil that X.Y.Z. Chief Steward in oil.'

"The situation was serious, and I was on the point of sending word to the 'Old Man' when another incident solved the problem. Several of our firemen, off watch and having a quiet smoke on deck prior to turning-in, overheard Blackbeard inciting the crowd to mutiny. Now the firemen we had in those days—the old coal-heaving Liverpool men—were just about ten times as tough as anything on earth, and it appears the listening men had run down and warned their mates of the state of affairs above deck.

" 'We want fried potatoes!' Beardy was still yelling when up from the stokehold, like black devils emerging from the nethermost pit, streamed a crowd of stokers. This gang had first proceeded to the potato lockers and, with bags and buckets loaded with the entire store of the ship's supply, they swooped down on the indignation meeting.

" 'You want fried spuds, do you . . . you X.Y.Z.s. Bang! Wallop!—We'll give you fried potatoes.'

"They pelted the mutineers round and round the ship, and at the end of the battle there wasn't a potato left on the vessel . . . either fried or boiled. After this affair we had no further trouble from Blackbeard and his gang.

"Finally we arrived at Albany and commenced to disembark a number of them. From Albany we proceeded to Melbourne, where we landed a few hundreds more, and then sailed for Sydney, where we disembarked the last of our unruly passengers. We remained at anchor in Sydney for nearly a month awaiting instructions from the Admiralty. Then we embarked the German internees, who had been imprisoned in Australia since the beginning of the war. These consisted mostly of well-to-do tea planters and their families, many of their wives being English. We also took on board the captured crew of the *Emden*, eventually sailing with a total of 800 internees. After being at sea two days we ran into a real cyclone ; the ship had to be battened down, influenza broke out on board, and at one time we had 300 cases down at once.

"There were several doctors among the internees, who did all in their power to fight the dread epidemic. Many of the crew were sick as well, yet somehow, although I was busy ministering to them all, I was among the few aboard that escaped infection. As far as I can remember we buried about 100 at sea—men, women and children. I attended funeral after funeral, and on one black day the number ran well into double figures. All the services were conducted in real Naval fashion, with our officers and crew present, supported by the crew of the *Emden*.

"When we arrived at Durban a special staff of doctors and nurses were engaged to enable those aboard, who had worked day and night for weeks, to get a well-earned rest. We remained in Durban for four days, and every corner of the ship was disinfected. While this was in progress the internees were marshalled in a field ashore with cans of coffee and sandwiches.

"Eventually we sailed from Durban with a clean bill of health, and three weeks later we arrived in Holland.

"That was the end of the *Kursk* as far as I was concerned, but, as I said in the beginning of this chapter, I will never forget the name as long as I may live."

CHAPTER XII

SHIPS THAT PASS

Aboard R.M.S. "Berengaria."
At Sea.

AT sea I believe it is counted an honour to sit at the Captain's table. Many of the world's celebrities, and some lesser lights also, have sat at mine, and some of the friends I have made on both sides of the Atlantic are very dear to me.

Not many months ago we carried Mr. Ramsay MacDonald and his daughter, Miss Ishbel MacDonald. I was amazed by the late Prime Minister's energy and vitality. My Gymnasium Instructor told me that he was in the gym sharp at seven o'clock every morning and he was always first into the breakfast room. A great mixer, entering into all the sports and games, he endeared himself to everyone on board by his simple charm and naturalness.

Before sailing the Fox Film Company gave me a reel which showed the main political activities of the Prime Minister over a number of years, requesting me to present this to him during the voyage. I did so at a little ceremony in the Palm Court and he at once released it for the benefit of our passengers, and it was shown to all classes in our cinema aboard.

One night, at the end of dinner in the saloon, I beckoned the cigar steward, who was standing near with his portable trolley, but Mr. MacDonald at once waved him away. Jumping to his feet with " excuse me a minute," he hurried from the room and a moment later returned with two special cigars. A small thing, maybe, but I felt honoured to think that the Prime Minister of England should interrupt his dinner and hurry to his room just to give a humble sailorman the pleasure of smoking an exceptionally good cigar. I appreciated that very human gesture even more than I enjoyed the weed.

Monsieur Hubert Marty, the big, genial French Chef of the *Berengaria*, will not soon forget that once we carried Mr. MacDonald. At Southampton, a few hours before we sailed, a group of reporters saw Marty return to the ship in a great state of excitement. These scribes were awaiting the arrival of the Prime Minister, and one Southampton reporter, recognizing our Chef and sensing a story, asked Marty why all the bother.

"I beena all over ze Sout'ampton for ze haggis," said Marty, frantically waving a paper parcel. "I wire Londres, and, Mon Dieu! I onla get ze two haggis for ze whole trip."

That night the London and Southampton papers came out with a headline:

"Shortage of Haggis on the *Berengaria*. Prime Minister likely to be deprived of his National Dish."

There followed a dramatic description of the desperate efforts made by Marty to find an adequate supply of haggis to supply the demands of Mr. MacDonald, and his disgust at only being able to obtain two in the whole of England.

On our return from New York there were about a dozen mail-bags all addressed to our Chef.

"Ah, Mon Dieu! Mon Dieu!" cried the distracted Marty. "Everybody ina Scotlan' send me the haggis— haggis in ze tins—in ze paper bags—in ze cloths—in ze box—and for moanths and moanths—evera time ze Ber'gara comma back to England, I get ze packeet and packeet ofa haggis ... plenty haggis."

"What did you do with them, Marty?" I asked him.

"I giva them to ma friends, monsieur," Marty

SIR EDGAR BRITTEN WITH MISS EVELYN LAYE

TWO BELLES OF MANILA

OFF FOR A RIDE IN MADEIRA
See Chapter XIII.

shrugged his shoulder. " And now I have no friends, Capitan."

On another trip I met George Arliss, that great actor of stage and screen. He was fresh from a Hollywood success and looked dog-tired and, I thought, very down-hearted. In one of our many pleasant talks we discussed the high salaries paid to the brighter stars of the cinema world.

"The few that draw the high salaries earn them, Commodore," he said to me, with that winning, whimsical smile of his, and I have never met any man with a sweeter smile. The first few days at sea I observed him from a distance, generally sitting silent and still in a deck chair, and, as I have said, looking very despondent. It was cold and misty when we entered English waters and I was somewhat amazed to see him quite cheerful.

"You're looking pounds better now," I observed on the last day of the voyage.

"I feel better, Captain," he said, with that wonderful smile. Then he waved towards the English coast. "Thank God for the damp of old England," he added fervently.

It sounded like a prayer to me.

Then John Barrymore came up into my cabin one morning. All the ladies on the ship had been most anxious to catch a glimpse of the handsome star, but he generally hid himself in his private suite all day. I have met most of his family (Holt), and a very charming crowd they are. John told me he was educated in London, which rather surprised me. He spoke very highly of British films, and of our artists.

"They will lead the world one day, Commodore," he told me, emphatically.

Incidentally, and I have met hundreds of them, these film stars always appear tired and fagged when they arrive fresh from Hollywood. Maybe they earn those colossal salaries, and maybe that's why some are just a wee bit eccentric. There is one who has a curious way of amusing himself when he has had a few drinks.   His hobby consists in kicking boots and shoes, which have been left out to clean, round the corridors, and knocking on doors to wake people up.   Then there was another bright star who went a bit silly one voyage.   We placed a watch on him for his own safety, but as he seemed to recover this was withdrawn.   Presently a report came, about 2 a.m. one morning, that the bright youth was serenading the officers on watch from the highest yard-arm on the ship.   He had climbed up the outer rigging, up past the crow's nest, and there he was perched on a yard-arm higher than any sailing ship's mast.   He came down safely, but I am quite sure none of my crew would have cared to have followed his example.

In the long gallery of the *Berengaria* we have a delight-ful picture entitled: "Eve and the Serpent."   One morn-ing this picture was missing and on a search being made it was discovered in the cabin, propped up at the bottom of his bed, of another one of our eccentrics.   This picture must assuredly possess "It," for a copy of the same picture has been stolen twice, and found in like circum-stances, aboard the *Aquitania*.

I have the happiest recollection of charming Evelyn Laye, who is always keen to help the cause of seamen's and other charities.   She always makes a point of sitting at my Purser's table, and I remember how she thrilled my passengers one evening in the crowded dining saloon.

She had offered to sing at the usual concert staged during the voyage, at which a collection is generally taken for the Seamen's Orphanage.   Owing to the lack of talent on board Mr. Owen found it impossible to stage a show.   He was very down-hearted about this, and con-fessed his sorrow to Miss Laye.   Unknown to anyone else she got in touch with the leader of the orchestra, and in the middle of dinner, on the last night of the voyage, we were all startled into delighted silence as, without warning, she stood up from her table and com-menced to sing a selection from *Bitter Sweet*.   As she sang, slowly she moved from table to table with a salver in one outstretched hand.

> "I'll see you again
> When skies are blue again."

Certainly she created a few blue skies for the Seamen's Charity for, as a result of her effort, that salver was soon piled high with notes and silver coins. Miss Laye keeps herself exceedingly fit, playing deck tennis strenuously, attended by Miss Yorke, our masseuse, regularly every morning and evening throughout the voyage.

In December, 1928, the King lay dangerously ill, and Prince George, who was serving in the Navy at the time, was brought by a destroyer from the West Indies and boarded the *Berengaria* at New York. At this time there was much distress amongst the Welsh coal-miners in South Wales, and the Prince of Wales had opened a relief fund in their aid. Despite his own natural anxiety and worry Prince George had still a thought for the suffering miners, and during the voyage, entirely off his own bat, he staged a stunt which considerably swelled the funds for the miners' relief. But as my Purser, Mr. Owen, can give you a little more about this than I can I will call on him to tell this yarn.

Mr. Owen told me: "Before leaving New York, with Prince George aboard, I was informed that his birthday, December 20th, 1928, would fall on the last night of the voyage. I therefore got in touch with the Chief Steward and the confectioner, and a beautiful cake, complete with candles and decorations, was prepared for the occasion. We also decorated the dining saloon, and, with a spotlight shining on the white icing and glittering silver decorations of the cake, tastefully arrayed on the Prince's table, the effect was somewhat striking.

"The great saloon was crowded with passengers when the Prince arrived, and as he was not aware of the little surprise awaiting him, all eyes were focused on him as he approached his table, wondering what he would do.

"There was not the slightest hesitation; the thought must have come into his mind spontaneously, for immediately Prince George saw the cake he at once sent his equerry over to my table with a suggestion that the cake might be sold to aid the Lord Mayor's Mansion House Fund for the Welsh miners.

"After dinner I had the cake placed on exhibition in the main lounge, procured the services of a professional auctioneer whom I knew was aboard and announced that, at the Prince's request, the cake would be sold to the highest bidder.

"When the auction started His Highness was present, seated beside the stand containing the cake, and after a little speech stressing the terrible hardships the Welsh miners were experiencing as a result of the trade slump, the ceremony opened.

"The bidding was fast and furious to commence, opening with a £1 bid, and finally being knocked down to a Birmingham gentleman for £200. The latter at once presented the cake to Prince George, and suggested that it should be put up again.

"Lord Weir was the next buyer, again for £200, and he also very generously handed it back to be re-auctioned.

"The Prince then suggested that it might be sold in slices, and I at once hurried off for a confectioner's knife.

"His Highness personally cut the slices, and the first was sold for £5. There were many Americans aboard, and soon they were bidding from twenty-five to a hundred dollars for a slice of Prince George's birthday cake.

"As I passed from table to table handing out the cake and collecting the dollars, one lady grasped my arm.

" 'Make my husband buy a slice, Purser. I want one, please,' she asked me imploringly. The husband didn't seem particularly keen about the suggestion, but he tossed me a note and at the same time handed me his dinner menu.

" 'Here, Purser,' he growled, 'you tell the Prince I've bought a slice of his cake and ask him to autograph this menu card for me.'

" 'Certainly, sir!' I murmured with suave politeness. 'That will cost you another twenty-five dollars.'

"His wife laughed delightedly.

"I approached the Prince, explained matters and asked if he would mind signing the card.

" 'Delighted!' he said with a smile, quickly appending his signature. 'Rake in as many more as you can, Purser—but double the price,' he added with a wag of his finger.

"When no more slices could be got from the cake, the Prince personally commenced to sell the crumbs. The last crumb was sold for £5 and the total realized the handsome sum of £2062 13s. 4d.—a record collection."

Everybody aboard knew that his Royal Father was gravely ill, hourly messages were being flashed over the wireless acquainting Prince George with the King's condition, yet, in the midst of it all he had a smile and a thought for the cares of others.

Truly, indeed, a regal gesture.

"On another occasion," Mr. Owen continues, "I was anxious to persuade Lord Birkenhead to officiate as Chairman at our usual concert for Seamen's Charities. I knew that if the passengers were informed that the great lawyer was to speak during the entertainment that the lounge would be filled to capacity and a rich harvest ensue for a most deserving cause.

" 'Do try and get someone else, Owen,' his Lordship pleaded. 'I am sure there must be someone aboard who can speak far better than I can,' he added modestly.

"But I was determined to get him, so I reminded him that I was a Liverpool man, and also of a certain hot-pot supper at which I had attended and over which he had presided. This hot-pot supper was held in connection with a Rugger team called Parkfield Old

Boys, captained by that famous amateur, Tom Pollock. We were only a second-league team, but as we had beaten every team in our class in Lancashire, we applied to the league for first-team fixtures. All the teams in the league consented except Liverpool, but mainly through the influence of Lord Birkenhead, Liverpool eventually relented. Naturally when Parkfield Old Boys met Liverpool in their new status as a first-league team we went at them hammer and tongs and beat them. That epic victory was celebrated in the good old Lancashire manner with a hot-pot supper, over which F. E. Smith presided.

"When I gently reminded Lord Birkenhead about this glorious memory, he at once agreed to act as my Chairman at the concert.

"At another concert a rather distressing *faux pas* was made by a very nervous speaker who was acting as Chairman. The lounge was filled with ladies, but it so happened that there was only one voluntary lady artist on the programme. After making a few flurried remarks at the opening of the entertainment, the nervous gentleman waved his hands, as if including the whole of the lounge, and remarked :

" 'I will now call on the only lady present.'

"The men roared, but we know what ladies are, bless them—some of them walked out, and the unhappy Chairman became the most unpopular man on the ship.

"One of the most embarrassing duties I have to tackle on occasion is the finding of dance partners for lonely ladies on Carnival night. There was one lady, an extremely plain spinster who particularly wanted to dance with one man. She craved my co-operation, and as I happened to know the gentleman intimately, I approached him full of confidence.

" 'Will you do something for me?' I asked him.

" 'Certainly, Owen,' he remarked quickly. 'I'll do anything for you, old man.'

"Discreetly I drew his attention to the distant, expectant lady.

" 'Please go over and ask her for a dance,' I implored.

" He gave one quick glance, then raised his eyes to heaven.

" 'Owen!' he said fervently, gripping my hand, 'I'll do most things, old man. But not that . . . not that!'

"Edgar Wallace crossed many times in the *Berengaria*, and I knew him intimately. Kind hearted, sympathetic and ever generous, he always consented with alacrity to officiate at any function organized in the name of charity. He was remarkable for his enormous consumption of cigarettes, which he smoked in an endless chain with his long cigarette holder. He had a special writing-desk aboard, which we used to call the 'Edgar Wallace desk.' No matter how busy he was he would always send for me daily to have a yarn. One of my most cherished possessions is an author's copy of one of his books, *Bones of the River*.

"I can picture him still walking up the gangway of the *Berengaria* on his last fateful voyage to Hollywood. A short time later his remains were brought on board the same vessel in a casket, on his last journey of all. I had to go down with the Staff Captain to fit up an 'Arden Chapel' in one of the rooms, and there, midst a profusion of flowers he lay in state as we crossed the Atlantic. The passing of Edgar Wallace will always be one of my saddest memories.

"A few years back the charity concerts generally lasted for two and a half hours, and one collection only was taken at the end of the first part of the programme.

"Sir Harry Lauder appeared in the first half of one of these concerts and was, of course, enthusiastically encored. During the second half he appeared in the lounge, merely as a member of the audience. But as soon as he was recognized he received another tremendous ovation and was persuaded to give another turn.

" 'Are there ony Scotsmen present?' Sir Harry demanded, as he mounted the stage for a second time.

" 'Aye! Aye! Aye, mon!' cried about a score of voices.

"Sir Harry turned to the Chairman.

" 'That's fine,' he said drolly. 'Mair wur-rk, Maister Chair-r-man, mair pay . . . send the hat roond again.'

"There was much happy laughter at this dry sally, and another considerable sum was raked in for the Seamen's Charities.

"On another occasion, in the dining saloon, Fanny Ward was my guest at table. Sir Harry was also present, but sitting at a table some distance away, overlooking the balcony. Without warning, the orchestra commenced to play a selection of Harry Lauder's popular airs. A young lady in his party immediately started to sing the chorus, 'I love a Lassie,' which reduced everyone to silence. With the next song, 'Roamin' in the Gloaming,' which if I remember rightly was one of his first successes, the great Scottish comedian jumped to his feet and commenced to sing this in a very low tone, motioning the leader of the orchestra to reduce the accompaniment to pianissimo. As he sang there was not a sound in the dining-room. Everyone was held spellbound. Even the waiters, in the act of carrying trays between the kitchens and the dining-room, stood motionless until the last notes of the chorus died away. There followed a moment of tense silence, and then Sir Harry, motioning again to the orchestra, the whole of the passengers in the dining-room rose to their feet spontaneously and joined in the chorus once more led by Lauder himself.

"On a certain occasion some years ago we made a record crossing to America, arriving at the Ambrose Lightship with everybody thrilled at the prospect of getting home quickly; then happened one of those strange things which are so puzzling. While we were waiting for the pilot to come on board, a dense fog settled down and we could not move; and there we remained for thirty-six hours. Naturally, the passengers were a little restive, and some amusement had to be found for them. It so happened that we had two wonderful pianists on board, both of whom had appeared at the Charity concert the previous night—the German pianist Guiseking, and Elly Ney. The two great artistes had a little private meeting and themselves put up a notice that they would give a special entertainment in the Palm Court that evening. They had no preliminary practice, but just sat down at the same piano, and what they did with it is quite beyond me to tell you, but they kept the crowd in a roar of laughter for over an hour.

"I can remember once when we were approaching Port Moresby in the Pacific Isles, just before getting to New Zealand; the weather being tropical at the time, it was decided, owing to a number of gentlemen coming in to lunch and dinner not suitably attired, to post the following notice :

> 'Will all gentlemen kindly conform to the proprieties of conventional dress in the dining-saloon ? '

"Some wag in the night pinned the following underneath :

> 'Those conforming to the proprieties of conventional dress of the people at our next port of call had better not go ashore at Port Moresby.'

"The people of Port Moresby go about in complete nudity."

So much for Mr. Owen's yarns, but now I think I ought to conclude this chapter with a few more of my own.

Not long ago I carried Sir Frederick Williamson, C.B., C.B.E., Director General of Postal Services, and Sir Edward Campbell, M.P., Parliamentary Secretary to the Postmaster-General. They walked up the gangway at New York rather weary and tired, for they had just completed an adventurous trek right round the world. This journey may well go down to posterity, for as a result of their efforts it is hoped to connect the British Empire by regular and frequent air-mail and passenger service.

Sir Frederick Williamson described the story of this epic journey to me in person, and as he walked off the ship at Southampton unseen or unheard by a crowd of camera men and press reporters, who were too intent on making contact with cinema and sporting stars to bother about the adventures of mere pioneers of Empire; and as these two great but very modest men are unlikely to repeat the story a second time, I think it is worthy of a permanent record in this log:

"On January 29th last (1935), Commodore," Sir Frederick began, " we left London for Brindisi, travelling by train and steamer. At Brindisi we embarked on an Imperial Airways flying-boat and flew across the Mediterranean Sea to Alexandria, Egypt. Here we transferred to a land plane and crossed Palestine to Bagdad.

"On we flew again, after a brief halt, following the banks of the Euphrates and crossing to the south-west of the Persian Gulf, until we reached a little desert outpost called Sharjah. This latter place comprises one solitary building, a little block-house specially built for the convenience of Imperial Airways and standing lonely and desolate in the midst of vast, rolling miles of sand dunes.

"From Sharjah we flew along the south coast of Persia and Beluchistan to Karachi, India.

"Here we transferred to another plane owned by the Indian National Airways and proceeded to Delhi.

"At Delhi our first discussion took place, and the real object of our journey commenced. We met all the Indian Government Officials concerned with the scheme, which I will explain in due course, and at this stage I may only say that the discussions were very satisfactory indeed.

"Lord Willingdon, the Viceroy of India, with whom we remained as guests for ten days, was extraordinarily helpful to us, and His Excellency was exceptionally interested in our proposals.

"Off again, the different planes in which we travelled growing gradually smaller in size as we proceeded further east, to Calcutta, Rangoon, Bangkok, Singapore, to Koepang in the Dutch East Indies. Leaving Koepang, the last jumping-off airport of the Dutch Settlement, we travelled over the shark-infested Timor Sea in a land plane, as no seaplane was available, arriving safely in Darwin, the first airport in Australia. From Darwin there commenced a long and lonely journey of over 2000 miles across the desolate plains and bush of unexplored Australia to Brisbane and Sydney.

"At Sydney we were met by the Ministers and Officials of the Commonwealth, including the Postmaster-General of New Zealand, who had come over specially for the Conference. I need not say more than that the Australian and New Zealand Governments have accepted the scheme in principle.

"No air-mail service as yet connects New Zealand with Australia, as over 1200 miles of open sea divide the two countries, so, for the first time since leaving Brindisi, we were obliged to forsake the fast air transport for the ordinary steamship.

"In New Zealand we not only discussed the scheme in question, but other important business which will eventually lead to the advantage of the postal service of the Empire.

"At Wellington we embarked on the Union Steamship Company of New Zealand's vessel, the *Maunganui*, and crossed the Southern Pacific to Tahiti. We had rather a thrilling experience in this region, as near Tahiti the vessel ran into one of the worst cyclones experienced in these seas for many years past. The storm hit us without

warning about 2 a.m. one morning, and for six hours the
vessel was hove to, buffeted by the hurricane, and swept
by terrific seas. One great sea completely dismantled
the wireless masts and aerial, and for a time we were cut
off from the outer world.

"From Tahiti to San Francisco and Vancouver. On
again across the broad rolling prairies of Canada to
Ottawa. Here we met the Dominion Officials, and again
the discussions were highly satisfactory. From Ottawa
to New York, and so aboard the *Berengaria* for home,
rather tired after our long journey, but happy with the
thought that our efforts will bear fruit, and result in a
closer union of Empire.

"Now for the scheme, Commodore:

"We have been absent for three months, having
covered close on 30,000 miles, and I think that Sir
Edward Campbell and myself are the first who have
completely encircled the world by this particular combination of air and steamship routes.

"The object of the expedition was to discuss a very
large Empire Air-Mail and passenger scheme which was
outlined in the House of Commons last year.

"The principle of the scheme is the dispatch of all
letter mail to every part of the Empire without special
charge or marking, and at the same time arriving at a
great increase in frequency and speed. In other words,
it will be possible to post a letter to any part of the
Empire exactly at the same price as one posts an
inland letter for delivery in the home country, to ensure
that this will automatically be despatched by air service.

"The proposal will also ensure a bi-weekly service to
Australia, New Zealand and South Africa, and as frequent
as five times weekly to India.

"Further, when the necessary improvements in aero-
dromes and installation of directional wireless and other
essential apparatus for safe night flying have been installed
along this great route, we shall be able to fly from London
to Sydney in seven days, as compared with the thirty-one

days which it takes at present. India, also, will be reached in three days.

"Moreover, if we can link New Zealand to Australia, as is probable, we shall have a twice-weekly service which will connect London to Wellington by an all-air route, which will be covered by an eight-day flight.

"We hope, with the co-operation of India, the Dominions and Colonies concerned, to bring the scheme into operation some time in 1937."

Sir Frederick smiled grimly as he concluded his yarn with the following reminiscence of the flight across the shark-infested Timor Sea.

"At one of our meetings in Australia, Commodore, I remarked upon the fact that Sir Edward and myself were the first passengers to be carried from Singapore to Darwin across the Timor Sea, as this service so far has been confined to air-mail only."

"Yes, we were the first," remarked Sir Edward drily. "And had the sharks got us we would have been the last."

Tay Pay O'Connor, that grand old Irish Politician, travelled in the *Berengaria* on several occasions. He was a lovable, ever-cheerful character, and the friend of everyone privileged to meet him. I forget what mission he was on, but at any rate he was *en route* to Washington on a visit of some political importance during his last voyage with us.

One day the Purser invited several important personages, including Tay Pay, to his room for a coffee and a cigar and during the conversation someone said:

"Did not Mr. Balfour go out to the States in a cruiser?"

Tay Pay immediately broke in with:

"An' why the blazes did they not send me out in one? Begorra, I'm going out on an equally important mission."

"Another injustice to Ireland," someone else retorted, amidst general laughter.

"Shure, 'tis not an injustice this toime, it's an insult to America," said the irresistible Tay Pay.

Another fascinating personality was Vincent Blasco Ibanez, the famous Spanish author, who was banished from Spain on account of his personal views. The writer of the *Four Horsemen of the Apocalypse*, in addition to his occupation, was a great curio collector, particularly old pottery, and his collection was worth a king's ransom. Mr. Owen tells me he was extremely excitable, and liable to "go off the deep end" at the slightest provocation. One night, raging with temper, he bore down on the Purser and demanded that the orchestra should at once cease playing, as it was disturbing his slumbers. THIS WAS AT TEN P.M., when it had only just commenced its dance business. Had his request been carried out there would probably have been a mutiny aboard, especially among the younger passengers.

"The only solution I could find to the problem was to change his cabin," said the long-suffering Purser. Then Mr. Owen added wistfully: "Every night, as the clock struck ten, the same thing happened, and I had to find him a different cabin. It became a habit right throughout the voyage."

Royal Princes are not quite as temperamental as authors. Next to Prince George's suite a party of young people had a gramophone, which they loved to play in their cabin. His Royal Highness generally retired to his room early and Hughes, my chief Master-at-Arms, was posted discreetly nearby to watch for his approach and to see that he was not disturbed. The Prince came down rather earlier one night, and Hughes, observing him coming from a distance, at once went into the cabin occupied by the young people and very politely suggested that the noise of the gramophone might disturb the Prince. When His Highness arrived outside his suite he saw Hughes standing by. As a Naval man he, of course, knew the duties of a master-at-arms, who are, what one might call, sea-police.

"Why are you posted here, Hughes?" asked the Prince.

"To see that you are not disturbed, sir," answered Hughes.

"That's very nice, Hughes," the Prince remarked, politely. "But please go away. I don't require anyone to look after me."

Hughes saluted and was walking away when Prince George called him back. Waving a hand towards the adjoining cabin he asked:

"Did you request these young people to stop playing their gramophone on my account, Hughes?"

"Yes, sir!'

"Then please inform them that it is my wish that they continue to play the machine. They will not disturb me in the least."

Tetrazzini! Who of my generation, privileged to have heard her golden voice, will ever forget her? Always generous, with a heart as big as her small, diminutive frame, she did not require to be pressed to sing for charity: she always volunteered. The last time she crossed in the *Berengaria* the great lounge was packed with influential people; many were travelling just to hear her sing on the ship. Standing on a dais in the centre of the lounge, dressed all in silver white, she sang to us, and long after the echo of her glorious voice had died we sat on in silence, too deeply moved even to applaud. There was an aisle, leading from the dais right down the centre of the lounge to the exit, and as the old lady passed down this, beaming on everyone, the passengers literally "rose" to her. In all she sang three songs, but immediately she left the lounge she sent for Owen.

"Is it not that there is another two classes on this ship, Mr. Owen—the Tourist and the Third Class? Yes?" she asked.

"Why, yes!" said Owen. "But have you not done enough, Madame? We do not care to trespass on good nature!"

"Good nature!" she exclaimed. "Is it not for the seamen who have not the ships, and for the little children who have not the food—and would not the good people of the other classes like to hear me sing, yes?"

So the beloved prima donna moved from class to class, enthralling them all with her wonderful voice, and reaping a rich harvest in the name of charity.

Some time later we in the *Berengaria* read of her death, and for a space the "Happy Ship" was sad.

In April of this year I carried back Mr. J. H. Whitney to New York, and a little yarn which he and I had together may be of interest to readers interested in horse racing.

Mr. Whitney's horse, Thomond II, finished third in the Grand National at Aintree this year, and all America was rather disappointed at this result, as over in the States they expected the horse to win.

"The Grand National distance was perhaps a bit too far for him," Mr. Whitney told me, "but he will win other races in England, and will certainly have another crack at the Aintree classic next year," he added.

It will be remembered that Golden Miller, a hot favourite, fell at a thorn fence early in the race. There were conflicting reports concerning the failure of the horse to clear the obstacle, some stating that a flash let off by Press photographers caused the favourite to refuse the jump. Others claimed that Golden Miller first refused, and then shot straight up into the air unseating Jockey Gerry Wilson.

The mishap was reputed to have saved many book-makers from complete bankruptcy, because of Golden Miller's heavy support.

"I never heard one word of suspicion amongst racing men," Mr. Whitney told me. "I had a chat with Miss Paget after the race and she was well satisfied with the performance of her racer. We were all convinced that Golden Miller's failure was due to his gruelling race a week previous to the Grand National when he set up a course record in winning the Gold Cup race at Cheltenham."

On another recent voyage I carried a trio famous in racing circles. I allude to Mr. A. C. Bostwick, another well-known American, our own Steve Donoghue, and Mr. Bostwick's well-known racehorse, Mate. The famous horse was a sheer delight to the eye, a thorough-bred and a gentleman. I never missed a morning without having a yarn with him. Steve told me that Mate pulled harder than any horse he had ever ridden.

"After I had exercised him a few times," said Steve, "I got hold of his groom: 'What makes this horse pull so darned hard?' I asked him.

" 'Oh,' said the groom, 'you're probably pulling him on both reins. Hold him tight on one rein only, and you'll find he'll go all right.'

"Well, in the first race in which I rode him, Commodore, I didn't follow the groom's advice. I simply let go the reins and gave Mate his head."

Steve paused and chuckled delightedly.

"As soon as I let go the reins he cocked his head up and I got a look at one eye. I have never in my life seen a horse look more surprised. He was still pulling like the dickens, with nothing to pull at. The result was he ran like Hades and won the race in a canter."

As all racing men will probably recall, Steve won the Grand Prix, in Paris, in 1934. He and Mr. Bostwick came up for a yarn in my cabin one morning, and Steve's description of how he won the French Derby rather thrilled me, although I am not a racing man.

"I hadn't a mount in the Grand Prix and was not expecting one," Steve told me. "But thinking I'd like a busman's holiday I flew over to Paris a few hours before the race and the first man I met on the course was Lord Derby.

" 'Hello, Steve,' greeted His Lordship. 'What brings you over here? Are you riding in the Grand Prix?'

" 'No, sir,' I answered. 'Just a busman's holiday. I haven't a mount,' I added.

"I strolled into the pavilion to have a drink, Commodore," Steve continued. "And about half an hour before the race was due to start I was offered a mount. I wasn't too keen about accepting this at first because I was without kit of any kind, but I was finally persuaded to ride in the race.

"It was rather a jumbled-up race and at half the distance my mount and I were all alone in the field, well behind the bunch. I crept up and up, my horse going beautifully, but at two-thirds of the distance there didn't seem a hope of getting through the black, bunched-up mass of horses in front."

The little jockey paused, and I saw his strong hands clench tensely as he lived that race over again.

"Then all at once, Commodore, the horse's eye just caught an opening between the ranks of that thundering mass in front, and like a flash he was through, and we led the field to the winning post."

The great little man smiled as he concluded his yarn.

"Rather nice of you to give the horse all the credit, Steve," I told him.

Again the world's greatest jockey smiled.

"I would never have won a single race without a horse, would I, Commodore?" he asked me quietly.

No, Steve, no more than I could ever have sailed the seas without a ship.

CHAPTER XIII

CORAL REEFS AND ENCHANTING ISLES

Aboard R.M.S. "Berengaria."
At Sea.

IN this chapter of my memoirs I will endeavour to instil the atmosphere of a world's cruise. On January 1st, 1929, in command of the *Franconia*, I sailed away from the cold, grey climate of wintry New York to the sun-kissed lands of the warm South. That wonderful voyage will linger long in my memory. Sailing the Atlantic "Ferry" as I have done for the greater part of my life, covering well over a million miles of the same old waters; as the *Franconia* nosed her way down the broad waters of the Hudson I felt as happy as any of the eager, laughing holiday throng who crowded our decks. My chart-room was literally piled to the roof with charts, for we were to visit many strange places never touched before. There was no hurry, no Blue Riband of the Atlantic to hold or reclaim; just long, lazy days of enchantment, drifting among strange islands in far-lying seas, skirting the coral reefs of Polynesia, cruising through narrow straits in spice-scented air, sailing ever to the East, chasing sunshine and happiness.

Funchal, Madeira, was our first port of call, and the clamorous diving boys, the cobalt blue waters, the lazy ox-waggons lolling leisurely over the cobbled streets of old Funchal held an enchantment never to be forgotten.

It was in 1479 that Christopher Columbus made his home in these islands before sailing westward in search

of the New World. Life in Madeira has progressed
very little since then. The soft equable climate is not
conducive to change or hurry. One never rushes in
Madeira and you soon fall under the spell of leisure and
contentment that pervades the narrow streets and quaint
little shops. One of the great thrills of a visit to Funchal
is the celebrated excursion up the Monte to Terreiro da
Lucta. A cog-wheel railway takes one up through gorges
whose sides are covered with masses of purple bougain-
villeas, honeysuckle and flaming azaleas. As you
ascend, the glorious panorama of Funchal spreads out
below—the cobalt blue of the surrounding sea, the little
town of Funchal, its tiny harbour with many ships lying
at anchor and the jagged outlines of the surrounding
mountains. The descent is made in basket sleds that
coast down over the smooth cobbled roadway, guided by
two fleet-footed natives. It is great fun and a most
unique experience.

Leaving Madeira astern, our next port was Gibraltar.
Here we lay for a day in the shadow of the grim fortress
which guards the gateway of the Mediterranean. Many
of our passengers went ashore and witnessed a bull-fight
at Linea, and came back loudly denouncing the cruelty
and ghastliness of this popular Spanish entertainment.

To any of my readers who may chance to visit the great
rock, while you will enjoy wandering about the quaint
streets of Gibraltar, I would point out it is the history of
the place that makes the greatest appeal. It has witnessed
centuries of strife. In 711 the rock was taken and fortified
by the Moorish chieftain Tarif, and ever since has been
considered the key to the Mediterranean. It was not until
1704, during the war of the Spanish Succession, that it
was captured by the combined forces of the British and
Dutch and the British flag was finally hoisted above the
fortifications. The present population presents a great
variety of types: British soldiers, Spaniards, natives of
Italian descent, Maltese and Moors.

At Algiers, our next port of call, the whole of the

British Mediterranean Fleet was riding at anchor in the Bay, and it gave even our American tourists quite a thrill when they beheld the lean, grey vessels of the Senior Service drawn up in two proud lines.

"They look like watch-dogs, Captain," one passenger remarked to me. "Great, silent, watch-dogs, docile as lambs, but ready to pounce if danger threatens old England. That's the impression they give me."

Lean grey watch-dogs!

On the boat-deck, from where the passenger and I were gazing on the Fleet, a few yards along, one of my junior officers was surrounded by a group of ladies. He was pointing one outstretched hand towards the south coast of Europe.

"Over there, ladies, lies France!" His hand moved ever so slightly in the same direction. "And about there lies Italy!" He turned completely round facing Algiers, and again his hand moved. "Behind there is the great Sahara Desert!" The hand moved again, but an elderly lady interrupted him.

"Say, young man," she asked, with arms akimbo, "and where is Kintucky?"

From Algiers, lazily we sailed the Mediterranean. We looked in at Monte Carlo, where fortunes have been won and lost, but its glory has passed; then on to Naples—Posilipo—Pompeii.

There is a wonderful fascination about Pompeii and its history. Imagine a modern city of to-day, with its teeming life and customs not only suddenly stopped, but preserved so perfectly that centuries later its life could be opened up and lived over again. As one walks over its cobbled streets, its stones worn into grooves by the actual wheels of Roman chariots—imagination is not necessary to bring back the past. It lives all around, and is in every breath one draws. Intelligent guides are there to give the specific facts—but their task is not difficult. Pompeii is not mythical, its facts are living, they are there for all to touch, walk upon and see.

But there are people who have eyes and cannot see, as the following yarn may vouch.

Dr. O'Brien had rather a disgruntled old gentleman sitting at his table. He had his wife with him, a dear little lady, rather subdued by her husband's forceful personality.

The Doctor says: "Both had visited the ruins of Pompeii, and that night the old fellow seemed in a heck of a temper. I asked him what was the matter.

" 'Matter!' he barked. 'Lying dog of a guide, not only robbed me, but insisted that his measly ruins were thousands of years old!'

" 'Well, aren't they?' I murmured. 'I always thought they were.'

" 'Bunk!' he snapped. 'Pompeii was busted less than thirty years ago. I distinctly remember reading about it in the papers.' He turned to his wife and fixed her with a glare. 'What I say is true, isn't it?' he demanded.

" 'Yes, dear,' the little lady whispered gently. 'I remember reading it with you!' "

Leaving Italy astern we sailed for Phaleron Bay, the aristocratic watering place of Greece, and after a brief visit to Athens we made for Haifa in the Holy Land. At Haifa a number of our passengers had arranged to fly to Jerusalem, and from there to Cairo, where we were to pick them up again. One American gentleman brought back a rich yarn from the Jerusalem trip. Whilst there the party had paid a visit to the famous Mosque of Omar. The guide was rather long-winded, explaining how the great Mosque had changed hands through the centuries from Christian to Moslem and back again a thousand times.

"Ah! if you vill only spare zee time, ladies and shentlemens, I tell you much more of ze wunderful Mosque of Omar."

One old lady waved an umbrella under his nose.

"I think you've taken enough time, young man!" she snapped. "And get this," she added, "you cannot tell me anything about Omar Kayyam. I know him from A to Zed."

What with poets and mosques the old lady had got a little mixed up.

From Haifa we made for Port Said, and then on through the Suez Canal—a ditch in the middle of the desert, holding little of interest, yet one of the world's most important waterways.

At our various ports of call we picked up groups of passengers who were coming only part of the way with us, and at Port Said we had a spot of bother with a party of Egyptians. At the top of the posters advertising the world's cruise there appeared prints of the *Aquitania* and the *Berengaria*, and this fact led to a slight misconception, and rather a comical episode. These two vessels appeared on all the Cunard posters, those advertising the ordinary passenger routes and otherwise, and were merely there to show the world their two proudest ships. Anyone who could read the text of the posters advertising the cruise would learn at once that neither the *Aquitania* nor the *Berengaria* was concerned in the trip. But this particular party of Egyptians couldn't read English very well. The outstanding object on the poster to them was the four gigantic funnels of the *Aquitania*, and when they came down to the docks and beheld the lone funnel of the *Franconia* they set up a helofawail.

"Ah—no good—no good!" they howled, waving four fingers at the solitary funnel. "We wanta four smokes. No good! No good!"

The good Purser put matters right, but how he explained the absence of the missing funnels I never troubled to enquire.

On from the Suez to the Red Sea, crossing the line which divides East from West, and so to Bombay. Here we lay at anchor for nine days to allow our passengers a brief visit to the interior of India.

Bombay with its wide harbour is the most modern and prosperous of Indian cities. It is laid out around the lovely Malabar Hill from the top of which one gets a glorious view of the city and harbour. The splendour of the great Parsee mansions on Malabar Hill and the Towers of Silence, the occupants of which, at death, are finally placed to be devoured by the vultures, are sights which linger in the memory.

Bombay's streets are a riot of colour, seething with pink turbans, green scarves, scarlet stockings and purple robes. Few cities show greater variety of racial type. In addition to Magrattas, the predominating element of the population, there are Arabs, Afghans, Sikhs from Northern India, Rajputs, Bengales, Tibetans and, of course, the Parsees.

From Bombay we sailed for Ceylon.

According to the natives the island of Ceylon is "situated only forty miles from heaven"—a fortunate thing for Adam, who is supposed to have landed on its highest peak when he was thrown out of Paradise. Be that as it may, its yellow sands are fringed by rows of palm trees, its hills rise above fertile valleys and culminate in superb mountains whose peaks are hidden among the clouds, its flowers and shrubs flame with colour, its commonest birds wear plumage bright as humming birds, its fields are rich in luxuriant vegetation, and whether or not it is the Garden of Eden, it is rightly called "The Garden of the World." The Singhalese wear brightly coloured sarongs and tortoiseshell combs —the children wear nothing at all. In the terraced hills the planters live among miles of tea and rubber, and rice. . . .

In Ceylon the Buddhist religion holds sway. According to their creed all life is sacred, and nothing that lives must be destroyed. They believe that every tiny insect is working its way through salvation to enter Nirvanah. But the trade in tortoiseshell must go on. They adhere to their religion, their method of separating the shell from the body of the turtle is appallingly cruel. They tie the poor animal over a roasting fire until the heat causes the shell to come away from the body. Immediately the shell is free they quickly release the turtle, when it at once dives back into the water, to die a slow, lingering death with half its poor body torn away. But the fact remains, they do not kill it, so their religion is adhered to.

From Ceylon on to Penang.

The approach to Penang, Prince of Wales Island, is really enchanting. Through long bays of quiet waters, dotted with low-lying, palm-decked islands, we nosed our way, and from the high decks of the *Franconia* we could see great forests of rubber trees stretching for miles inland, with here and there the white, gleaming mansion of some wealthy Chinese.

I made a personal visit to the Temple of Snakes in Penang, and its name is no mere matter of speech. There are thousands of snakes in that delightful house of worship—real, live, slithery reptiles—entwined about the various idols, crawling round stands and braziers, squirming and dangling from the blackened rafters overhead, whilst white-robed priests kneel in pious supplication around.

There is a magic in Penang—the faint odours of spice and of pepper, the far sound of muffled gongs —a strange enchantment born of foreignness—of strangeness. . . . The maze of people. The paper lanterns outside the shops. The rickshaws on the streets, and the curious, clumsy native row-boats in the harbour. The thick forests of rubber trees, the great mansions of the wealthy Chinese. The curiously alert yet veiled eyes of the Malays, driving their tiny bullocks through the dust—eyes at home in the jungle, where the elephants march. . . . In Penang you have the sense that this pretty town with its sprinkling of Europeans, its modern hotel, its awareness of the west, is only a seeming, an appearance, and that beyond in the jungles the realities and the hidden mysteries lie—waiting.

From Penang we made for Siam, and Bangkok the

capital made even an old Sailorman rub his eyes at its variety and contrasts. From tiny sampans dancing on a silver river, and frail mat-huts nestling in a golden valley, to the magnificent palaces of Princes with their splendour of marble and mosaics—poverty and riches, cheek by jowl, reality and make-believe. As I gazed on the marvellous throne halls of the Princes in that ancient-modern city of Old Siam, the genius of man held me in speechless amazement.

Some of these magnificent buildings, I learnt later, are devoted to quite prosaic purposes, and this reminds me of the best yarn of the trip.

We had a party of elderly spinsters aboard who were determined to visit every temple and Mosque in the East. The majority of my passengers were American, but we had several Englishmen in the ship and one of these, whom we will call George, being also partial to Mosques, had attached himself to the spinsters as their leader and shore-guide.

George was a rotund, rather bald, middle-aged gentleman, somewhat self-opinionated, and just a little pompous. He was extremely correct and very attentive to the ladies however, although he treated his own sex with a suave aloofness which was to lead to his undoing.

Bill and Harry were two young American scamps, always up to some mischief or another, and as George had had the temerity to admonish them openly on several occasions they hatched a plot which was fated to cost George his popularity with his feminine flock.

It was the night we reached Bangkok, and our two young Americans knew the city intimately. They also knew of a certain mysterious mosque which stood on a great hill several miles from the town.

The pompous George had a habit of sojourning to the smoke-room a few minutes before dinner every night, and it was during this time, and in George's hearing, that they discussed the mysterious mosque.

They ignored George, did not even see him, or so they pretended, but George was all ears.

"Far more interesting than the Temple of Snakes, I assure you, Harry," said Bill.

"But I've been to Bangkok a dozen times, Bill," Harry declared, "and I've never heard of the place."

"Nor will you, Harry, not if you visit Bangkok a thousand times. For some mysterious reason the natives are afraid of the place, never discuss it. If you attempt to obtain a guide, or a conveyance, all you get is a shrug of the shoulder, and an emphatic declaration that no such mosque exists."

"And does it exist?" asked Harry with mock eagerness.

"Most certainly it does!" declared Bill. "It is built on a hill about four miles north of the town—you can't miss it—a great marble building with hundreds of steps leading up to it—one of the most beautiful mosques in the East."

That night, on the boat deck, with the moonbeams dancing on the oily waters, George gathered his flock around him and described the wonders of the mysterious mosque on the hill.

"I counsel you to secrecy, ladies. Very few white men know of this holy place, and we must keep the knowledge to ourselves."

"But how d'you come to know of it, George?" one inquisitive lady demanded.

George pressed a forefinger warningly over his lips.

"Don't press me, my dear. I assure you the information is reliable—most reliable."

Early next morning, as soon as the gang-plank was lowered, the party of spinsters, headed by the redoubtable George, set off on the road that lay northwards from the city.

It was a blazing hot day, with a road covered in sand that would keep getting into the ladies' shoes, and in consequence progress was painfully slow. After walking for several hours they came to a bend in the road, and suddenly espied a great marble building perched on a hill, but still several miles away.

"There, dear ladies," declared George, waving a complacent hand towards the building. "There is the famous mosque of——!"

"You said it was only four miles out, George," a limping lady snapped peevishly. "It seems more like twelve miles to me."

"Never mind, as long as we get in when we do get there, dear," a chorus consoled her.

"Get in!" scoffed George disdainfully. "Of course we'll get in, ladies. Follow me!"

They all followed, and after several more hours, they came to a great flight of steps leading up to the portals of the mosque.

Half-way up they all sat down on the steps for a brief respite, and to remove some of the sand which covered them from head to foot.

Their toilet completed, they still sat on. It was hot work toiling up those steps after their long trek, and there were still hundreds of them to climb.

It was whilst they were still sitting, now mostly silent and very close together, that one lady breathlessly whispered:

"D-do you think there is any danger, George? I—I feel just a little bit scared."

The great place looked eerily silent, and there was that strange stillness in the sunlit atmosphere which can be felt at noontide in most tropical countries. Moreover, with the exception of themselves, there was no living thing to be seen in all the quiet countryside around.

"Scared!" said George airily. "Nonsense, ladies. I assure you that you are as safe as if you were aboard ship."

He stood up, and the whole party prepared to follow him. But George remained motionless for a minute, deeply pondering.

"Ah, yes!" he declared at last. "I knew I had forgotten

something. It will be necessary for us to remove our shoes just to—ah—conform with the religious rites of the—er—mosque."

There was some faint murmur of protest at this suggestion, but George earnestly assured them that it was the proper thing to do, so they all, including George, removed their shoes.

In this manner they negotiated the remaining flight of steps until they reached the top landing. They stood for another moment to admire the grandeur of the building, and then, very piously and reverently, they tiptoed in stockinged feet towards the great carved portals.

George knocked once, a discreet, apologetic, gentle tap. There was no reply. He knocked again, a little louder, but still there was no reply.

"Don't you think w-w-we might come back another day, G-George?" one lady whispered tremulously. "P-perhaps the p-p-poor things are all asleep."

"They never sleep!" declared George, banging the knocker a third time, imperiously, impatiently.

Before the echo of that knock had died, the great doors swung suddenly open and the astonished party were confronted by a tall white man arrayed in a long khaki smock.

Hiding his surprise, George quickly explained that the party were on a brief visit to Bangkok and craved permission to view the place.

"Why, sure!" said the tall man in a rich American accent. "Step right in."

They all trooped in with many delighted squeaks of thanks whilst the tall man carefully re-shut and bolted the door. Then quickly viewing the party he drawled:

"I'll say you all look darned hot and thirsty, and I propose we tap a barrel of beer pronto, before we give the old joint the once over."

"Beer!" gasped an elderly and very prim and proper spinster. "Beer, my man! In a mosque?"

The American fixed her with a glassy stare.

"Mosque?" he repeated. "Say, sister, I don't get this. What d'you figure this joint is?"

"Why!" said the lady indignantly. "Isn't this the holy mosque of——?"

The American interrupted her, wagging a grubby finger under her nose.

"Holy nuthin'!" he growled contemptuously. "This is the John D. Gower's Slake-a-Thirst Brewery Company, Incorporated, and let me tell you this, sister, we brew the best beer . . ."

But only George remained behind to test the virtues of John D. Gower's excellent brew.

The ladies had hurriedly fled in search of their shoes.

I believe George was just a little tight, and a much nicer fellow, when he lurched up the gangway that night, and he wasn't a bit interested in mosques and temples at any other period during the remainder of the voyage.

From Bangkok we sailed for the fabulous island of Java, and cast anchor at the first port—Semarang, opposite the huge island of Borneo, on Java's north coast.

Java is the epitome of the tropical island. Marvellously fertile—the cultivated fields amazingly rich—growing, and growing in sun-forced violence—the massed tangled growths of the jungle—ferns, vines, bamboos, mango tree and banana and palm, wild orchid and a hundred other parasites—encroaching whenever the cultivator's vigilance for a moment relaxes on the tamed fields. The island teeming with people—Malays, Hindus, Arabs, Paquans—is one of the most densely populated areas in the world. Java bears traces everywhere of the centuries of commerce she has known with the outside world—the European colonizers—the Portuguese in 1509, the Dutch, the English. Java is Javanese still—but the island wears European clothes. The clear, pale-green of the native rice-fields is bordered not only by the dim green of the jungle, still peopled by the monkey-folk, the leopards, the brilliant birds of the tropics—but also by the wide-reaching plantations of the Europeans. Modern cities like Batavia—as Dutch as Amsterdam— erect their immaculate houses along canals as Dutch as wooden shoes—and the natives do their wash in them. Motor cars on the highways—rhinoceros along the streams, Dutch missions and Mohammedan temples, fox-trots in the Hôtel des Indes, wayong and wayong wong (the fascinating Javanese plays and shadow plays), the bustle of trade in the ports by day, and at night the incredible windless quiet that lies over the forests like folded wings—that is Java.

Semarang lies among low hills, with sudden high-lands rising just behind the town and the Soembing mountains in the distance. Tandjong Priok, world famous port of Batavia, lies farther west, with Batavia six miles inland. In Batavia, the Arab quarter, the Chinese quarter, the native bazaars—where, among curious Eastern wares, you will see batik in its native lair—are all fascinating to the strangers. The extraordinary tropical gardens of Buitenzorg that lie across rivers and around small lakes, and include an unequalled collection of orchids, are known all over the world.

Singapore is another of the names that sing and shout to anyone with the sea or the salt of the seas in his blood.

Singapore—the "cross-roads of the world"—where, sooner or later, every ship in the East, every race, every colour, is seen—every speech east of Suez is heard.

Singapore is an island—a small island off the southern-most tip of the Malay peninsula—and it dominates the seaways between India and China, Japan and Australasia.

Its early history rests on the traditions that "leaving Palembang in Sumatra some Malays settled in Singapore about A.D. 1360 under Sang Nila Ultima." But it is known that in 1703 the Rajah of Johore offered Singapore as a gift to a Captain Hamilton (for what unimaginable services no one knows), who, prodigious man! declined it, though he remarked that it was "a proper place to settle a colony in, lying in the centre of trade, and accommodated with good rivers and safe harbours, so conveniently situated that all winds serve shipping both to come in and go out of the port."

To-day it is (in spite of Captain Hamilton) a colony of the British Crown, but a Chinese city really, and one of the most valuable ports of the seven seas.

Our next port was Bali, in the Dutch East Indies.

Up to a few years ago Bali had practically never been visited by denizens of the outside world. It is completely charming and unspoiled, and as one lives its sunny delightful life one may pause and wonder just how much the advent of the automobiles, telephones, subways and airplanes, have advanced the civilization of the world! Everywhere one is amazed and held spellbound by the beauty of the lush, tropical forest, the purple-topped hills and mountains, and of the people themselves. The Balinese are the most beautiful and perfectly formed of all the Malay peoples and the women in their colourful costumes, predominate everywhere. This is not strange, when it is learned that they constitute seventy per cent of the population! As you cross the island you notice that wherever there is a picturesque cleft in the hills, or a magnificent group of trees, a temple is built dedicated to the gods and to the spirits of the hills and forests. The temples are marvels of intricate carving and design, and one cannot help but admire the constant throngs of festively-dressed worshippers so innocently and devoutly proffering up their offerings of rice and flowers.

I wax lyrical over Bali, for of all the places I visited I loved this fair isle best of all.

This small island, that has hardly altered one aspect of its culture in a thousand years, living divorced from everything that we mean by "progress" yet has a culture, a native art, a cult of beauty, and a deep faith in many gods. To over-sophisticated, over-strained senses, Bali brings the peace of sunlight after shadow, cool water after thirst. And there is magic in these islands—magic taken

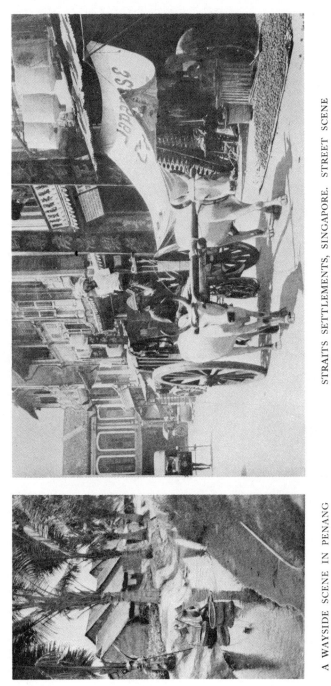

STRAITS SETTLEMENTS, SINGAPORE. STREET SCENE

A WAYSIDE SCENE IN PENANG

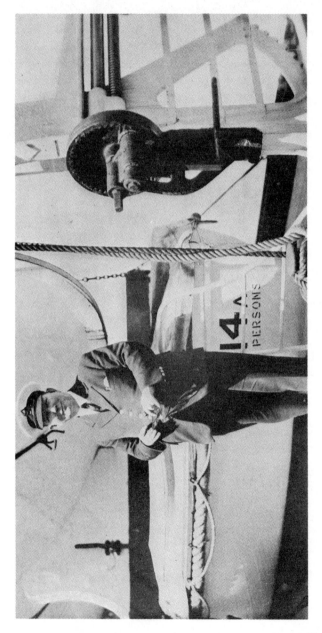

MR. RODGERSON ("RODGY")

(See Chapter XIV.)

for granted and made daily, with due ceremonial, and every formality of beauty and respect. Each small patch of rice land has its own tiny lantern swinging from a high pole, an airy temple to the rice god who has that field in charge. Near each small thatched house of plaited bamboo each member of the family therein dwelling has his own tiny temple and makes, every day, his small offerings of cups of rice, of bamboo tassels, of carvings or silver work or shell to the god whose jurisdiction covers that particular day. And, almost daily, into the great and strikingly beautiful temples, unlike anything seen anywhere, or dreamed—except that they are reminiscent of Hindu temples (legitimately, for a modified Hinduism mingled with the more primitive beliefs in magic is the religion of the Balinese), the natives throng in festive dress, bearing offerings to the gods of the sun, of the rice, of the rain, and the winds—to cajole and propitiate. For these enchanting people, living on this far-enchanted island, live very closely with their gods, and feel them concerned either as protectors or as menace, with every smallest matter of the day or night. One realizes in Bali how mysterious life has always been to the primitive—how full of evil coming without herald or good reason, of good coming whimsically and by chance. No wonder that it seemed necessary to coax the presumable sources of inexplicable events into kindness, into friendliness, to stave off evil. Actually, in Bali, the whole life of the people centres around their religion. Their festivals are religious fêtes, their most important ceremonials concern the cremation of the dead—their houses are small and plain, but their offerings to the temples and to the priests are the best and loveliest things they can lay hands on. And, the ceremonial propitiations of the gods, great and small, observed—the daily toil of simple households done, they seem to spend their days in tranquil play and laughter.

Bali is still so unspoiled, so remote from the clamour and clatter of our living, so endearing, with its charm of a very young, very innocent, yet serious child, so utterly lovely to look at, that people who have been once to Bali, like the fallen angels, have always a nostalgia to return to heaven. Certainly here, more than anywhere else in the world, one has the sense that the world is still young, that the dew of creation is still on the leaves, and that here the world, like the Balinese, wears flowers in its hair.

It was at Bali that I had occasion to log one of my crew for drunkenness. This seems a small thing to record in my memoirs, but I remember I sat in my cabin musing for an hour after I had punished him.

"Ships and men!" I thought. How drastic the change in both since those far-off days of my first vessel, the *Jessie Osborne*. Both are now so prim and proper—almost prudish. In the old days it was quite the usual thing to see a whole ship's crew hauled aboard in cargo slings, every mother's son roaring drunk.

> "Fifteen men on a dead man's chest,
>   Yo! Ho! Ho! and a bottle of rum."

Aye! And we put to sea with the men in that condition, and we officers were required to do all the work until Jack Shellback sobered. Yet here was I on a world's cruise with a crew of seven hundred men, and although we had been at sea for months, and had called at some hectic places where wine and women's smiles might lure even the pious George to get tight on occasion, yet, out of all that crew I had only found it necessary to log one man for drunkenness.

"How'd you get adrift, my lad?" I asked him, when he was brought before me.

I was loathe to punish the lad, but discipline must be maintained, and regulations obeyed.

He hesitated, gulped once or twice, but remained silent. I sensed, however, that he was searching his mind for some plausible excuse so, to give him a chance, I asked him quietly:

"Haven't you anything to say for yourself?"

"Nan-nan-no, sir!" he stuttered. Then I saw an eye brighten cheerfully as it lit on a calendar hanging over my desk.

"P-p-please, sir!" he added quickly. "I—I—was celebrating Easter."

Celebrating Easter! In Bali!

"Was that her name?" I asked. "Was she nice!"

"I—I beg your pardon, sir?"

I didn't answer, but his piety cost him five shillings and an entry in the log book.

From Bali we sailed to Macassar.

Macassar is another lovely port far off the beaten track of regular tourist travel. It lies opposite the wild coast of Borneo, north of Java in the Celebes, which is shaped somewhat like a star-fish, with its four great peninsulas. As you softly glide into its attractive harbour, native outrigger canoes swiftly dart out for a thorough inspection of the great monster that has so smoothly slipped into their midst.

In Macassar you will not find trolley cars, or even automobiles in any quantity. While the life of the town is commercial, it smacks more of the commercial days of the great clipper days, and bales of rattan and copal: bags of copra and coffee fill the rude warehouses along the wharves.

While there are no great temples and monuments to see here, the very primitive simplicity of the life has its own special appeal and charm.

Zambonga, our next port of call, which is situated on the south-western coast of the great island of Mindanao, is the most important town of the Sulu Archipelago.

The town is still under the influence of the early Spanish settlers, and as one drives along the sweeping stretches of shore road everywhere are the great spindle-like forms of the coco-nut palms towering above the small native Philippine huts, built high off the ground on stilt-like poles.

We had a grand picnic at this island paradise, the whole ship went ashore, including crew and stewards. Our dining-room was a deeply-shaded palm grove, and it was quite an art dodging the falling coco-nuts as we sat under the shaded trees at luncheon. During the course of our meal we were serenaded by thousands of monkeys indignantly protesting at our invasion of their sacred domain.

From Zambonga to Manila in the Philippines. And here again one can still trace the influence of the old Spanish raiders. At Manila the best cigars in the world are made, and they are so cheap that even ship's officers can afford to buy them.

The city of Manila covers an area of about twenty square miles of low ground through which flows the Pasig River and several tidal creeks. To the west lies Manila Bay, and beyond this rise the Mariveles Mountains. Manila itself is a most interesting picture of American colonization, and you feel that it is done very well.

From Manila to Hong Kong, a fair harbour in old China.

There is something about the natural beauty of Hong Kong which immediately appeals, and I heartily endorse its reputation for being called the loveliest harbour in the Far East. First seen, the city resembles a giant layer-cake, rising in successive tiers from the esplanade along the water-front to the handsome villas and official residences perched high on the "peak," 1800 feet above.

Moreover, it is so perfectly Chinese.

Chinamen, and their little ladies, in full native dress, scurry through the busy little streets, huge fantastic banners wave in front of jumbled shops, rickshaw bells tinkle, and about all is a queer distinctive babel of sound found nowhere but in this land that can never be "Westernized."

With the exception of Peking, no other place in China compares with Hong Kong with the quantity, quality and amount of things offered by its shops. Amber, antiques, brass, men's clothes, cloisonne, camphor wood, wicker furniture, carved ivory, carnelian, amethysts, jade, rose quartz, crystals, lacquer, Mandarin coats, porcelains, silks, embroideries, wood-carvings, all in bewildering display at breath-taking low prices.

The Chinese merchant tells you with tears in his eyes (you almost weep with him) that if he sells at your price he'll lose money. Often the bargain ends by the merchant saying: "Take it, master, I lose money," followed by a quick: "Buy something else, please?"

From Hong Kong I visited Canton, and its four-hour train journey brings home how ridiculously minute has been the Europeanization of China. Only a few minutes out of Hong Kong all traces of "outside influence" disappear—past native villages, rice fields, and farmlands done entirely in the Chinese manner. Most of the villages have a tall tower-like building, and if block houses were still built to-day, you would feel you had guessed what they were. Curiosity triumphs and you question a passing Chinese conductor, who, in queer "pidgin" English confirms that your guess was quite correct!

It is not always peace and quiet in these tiny villages between Hong Kong and Canton, and when trouble comes the inhabitants quickly ensconce themselves in safety in these forts, and hope that when they once more emerge, a few of their pigs and chickens may still be spared by marauding bands of robbers. After all, our Puritan ancestors were but copying just an old Chinese custom!

Canton is the human ant-hill of South China, with a population variously estimated upwards to four millions, and the city is substantially to-day what it was a thousand years ago. Its narrow tunnel-like streets are beehives of activity: every man, woman and child works, and notwithstanding the daily wage of a few cents, are quite good-natured about it. Everything under the sun seems to be manufactured in some shape or form by the Cantonese. The river life also presents an amusing spectacle, and after you have looked over the hundreds of sampans, you are not surprised to hear that more than a million of the city's population live on the water. I was somewhat startled, however, when I was told that thousands of these amphibious human beings never set foot on shore from birth to death.

North of the Philippines lies the island of Formosa, and at Keelung, the principal town, the Japanese governors received the whole of my passengers into his palace, and presented everyone with a pound packet of tea.

Mr. Guy Gundaker, President of the International Rotarians, who was present, then made such an able speech in thanks, that the Governor promptly made it a two-pound packet. Mention of Mr. Guy Gundaker reminds me that I often meet people who are rather hazy as to the object of the Rotarian movement, therefore a few brief words of explanation may be of general interest, particularly as I personally believe that this Society will eventually do more to solve the peace of the world than any other influence I know.

The object of the Rotarian movement is to establish a society in each town throughout the world, no matter what nationality or creed, composed of men drawn from all professions and trades, and to meet at luncheon for one hour weekly for the purpose of discussing the best means of promoting business, and also to preserve good fellowship between members of competitive trades.

Commencing in Chicago, this society is daily increasing in thousands, and some of the best business men in England and America are already behind the movement. Not long ago the Society chartered no less than three Cunard ships, and went round the world establishing their clubs and lodges. The three vessels proceeded by different routes, and all met, by arrangement, in Japan, and, as a result of their efforts the Japanese Rotarians are now a power in the land.

During the past five years many prominent Rotarians have crossed in the *Berengaria*, and a special "Rotarian luncheon" has always been the means of bringing them together during the voyage across the Atlantic when a sufficient number have been on board. As many as twenty-seven have been present at one of these luncheons, the popularity of which has been proved by the fact that a special Rotarian register is kept in the ship, and is one of the first things asked for by those belonging to the organization.

Amongst the well-known Rotarians who have travelled in the *Berengaria* may be included Wilfred Andrews, Herbert H. Merritt, Guy Gundaker, Everett Hill, Canon Elliott, Frank L. Mulholland and Vivian Carter. These gentlemen are regular *Berengaria* travellers, and much of the fame of the *Berengaria* Rotarian luncheons may be put down to their being in evidence so frequently, and assisting in perfecting the arrangements connected therewith.

The outcome of these frequent crossings was that two of those mentioned above, i.e. Wilfred Andrews of Ramsgate, and Herbert H. Merritt of Cardiff, Wales, looking round for a suitable trophy for presentation to the *Berengaria* in connection with Rotarianism, had an inspiration, and in consequence this ship is now in possession of a *Rotarian wheel with silver gong attached*, to be placed before the chairman at these gatherings, so that he, as presiding officer, can call his brethren to order at any time during the meal.

The *Berengaria* greatly appreciates the honour conferred on her in being the recipient of this novelty, and we feel sure that Rotarians throughout the universe reading these lines will not only appreciate the spirit of kindly thoughtfulness which prompted these two fine fellows to get together and think of this very clever idea. It is more than probable that the example will be copied, and that Rotarians using the *Berengaria*, and seeing the trophy—which, by the way, will be jealously guarded by the ship's officials—will find that before long every ship giving "Rotarian luncheons" will be following suit, and adding a "musical call" to their establishment.

Not long ago I met a Roman Catholic priest who had a church in New York for over twelve years. He knew no one outside his parishioners. Then he joined the local Rotarian Society, and at his very first meeting, among others, he met a Presbyterian and a Baptist minister.

"I tried to convert these two misguided men to my faith, Commodore," he said, with a sly twinkle in his eye. "I failed, of course, but still, we were drawn together in a bond of Christian fellowship that might never have been possible had we not been brother Rotarians. That is Rotarianism, Commodore, and the finest religion I know," he added.

In America they all address each other by their Christian names, and at one meeting which I attended in New York it was rather funny being addressed as "Edgar." At this same meeting one member told of a distressing case—a little cripple girl of poor parents whom the member declared might be cured of her deformity by a costly operation.

"All right, hand in her name and address, we'll take care of her," rapped out the chairman, and the business was settled.

I have said that this movement may go a long way towards promoting world peace. Well, it is a known fact that the Rotarians of Lima, Peru and Santiago, Chili, banded together and approached their respective presidents, and were responsible for bringing that long and bitter struggle between the two countries over the Tacna–Rica line to a peaceful and permanent conclusion.

I have met all the great leaders of the Society, and am personally very keen about the movement, as I believe, and I again repeat, that in my humble opinion its growth will lead to a better understanding between the nations of the world.

With this digression we will get back to the ship,

as my passengers are impatient to continue the cruise.

From Formosa we sailed for Shanghai, and the first indication one receives on approaching Shanghai is that the churning waters about the ship become extremely dirty and muddy in colour. The town, although situated on the banks of the Whang-Poo, is also near the mouth of the great Yangtse River, whose amber flow discolours the water for many miles out to sea.

The waters of the Whang-Poo were not deep enough to allow the *Franconia* far up the river, so at Woosung it was necessary to embark my passengers on a tender for the rest of the journey inland. On the way we passed countless "junks," river steamers, merchant ships, and battleships of all nationalities. It is a queer sight to see the Union Jack, the Stars and Stripes, or the French tricolour, flying in these Chinese waters, so far away from their own home ports.

Shanghai is a marvellously modern city, at least, in the European sections, and tall office buildings, smart shops and attractive-looking clubs predominate along its famous Bund.

Leaving Shanghai, our next port of call was Chemulpo, Korea. The Koreans were entirely different from any people I had ever seen before, and I was extremely attracted to them.

Long ago when Korea was called the Hermit Kingdom, and the barbaric foreigner was denied access to the land, the better classes prided themselves on making as little physical effort as possible. To-day, while a reversal in fortunes has obliged the Koreans to forego the ease of their ancestors, they still outwardly maintain an all-pervading calm. It is hard to suppress a smile, when one first sees the male of the species. He will leisurely pass by with an expression of complete resignation that is particularly comical in his long white night-gown and funny little fly-trap hat.

The low-lying, mushroom-like houses are distinctively

typical of Korea; as also is the capital city's traffic, composed mostly of miniature ponies trotting along under loads that might break the proverbial camel's back, and wooden carts whose construction surely antedated that of Noah's ark!

The capital city, Seoul, lies thirty miles inland from Chemulpo, and the Japanese governor, hearing of our arrival, invited my passengers to luncheon. We were then eight hundred strong, and the only means of locomotion across the thirty miles of roadless land to Seoul was by rickshaw. I conveyed my respects to the governor, and informed him, that owing to lack of transport we must reluctantly refuse his kindly invitation. Within a few hours of the despatch of that message rickshaws, drawn by great muscular Koreans, began to roll up to the ship. The governor must have collared every rickshaw in all the villages around. In one long line, which stretched for nearly a mile, my eight hundred passengers rode down to Seoul, and in a great banqueting hall, complete with stage, and after a glorious luncheon, the Japanese waiters stripped off their togs and rendered a wonderful theatrical display. It was, indeed, a great event, and I think the Koreans got as much pleasure out of seeing us as did we from their unstinted hospitality.

From Korea we sailed from Chinwangtao, and from this port the majority of my passengers went inland to Peking. This ancient capital of China still enthralls with the mystic glamour and proud glory that only a comparatively few years ago was Imperial China. At first it seems terribly complicated with its "outer," or Chinese city, and the "inner," or Tartar city. Then, too, in the centre of the Tartar city, is the old Imperial city enclosed by a high wall, and in the centre of this stands the purple forbidden palace surrounded by lakes and gardens.

The trip to the Great Wall is accomplished by train. It entails a considerable journey up through very mountainous and rugged country. The train finally stops at a station not far from the Pa Ta Ling Gate, and the Wall is about half an hour's walk away. There are sedan chairs available for those who might not feel up to the walk, managed by two husky bearers, who bid furiously for patronage. Suddenly over a brow of a hill appears the first sweeping view of the wall—a great python of stone winding its stubborn way over cragged peaks and sunless valleys, its powerful air of permanency seemingly, and for ever, conquering the impossible. It is quite easy to climb the Wall and walk upon its broad surface. Perhaps one will prefer to pass through the gate to the Mongolian side and contemplate it with the eyes of the invader. So great is the spell of this great marvel, that even to-day it somehow feels much safer on the Chinese side.

Next came Japan, land of butterflies, kimonos and geishas, and our first port of call was Miyajima.

Miyajima is a fitting introduction to Japan.

While one may have heard that the Japanese are a small people, one cannot imagine just how tiny they are until one sees them by the score in their native land. They are more like children and, after the more repressed and sombre faces of the Malay people and the Chinese and Koreans, their spontaneous gaiety is very charming. They are extremely naïve—in fact, to an almost embarrassing extent, as they group themselves about you frankly taking you in, and, judging by their laughter, finding your height and clothes terrifically amusing. The first delighted impression of these gaily dressed little people, laughing and scuffling along with their absurd wooden clogs over the stone pavements of the streets, will linger for all time in the memory.

The island of Miyajima is sacred and bounds in temples and shrines, not only extending to the water's edge, but into it. The great red Torisis stand out high above the waters of the bay and, while religious in purpose, they add tremendously to the artistic effect of an enchanting scene.

Kobe, our next call, with its great modernized pier, is now thoroughly Westernized. Foreign influence is apparent everywhere, and as a result there is little of attraction. But a visit to Kyoto, a train journey inland, is well worth while.

Kyoto is the ancient capital of Japan, with its nine hundred temples, palaces, gardens, quaint little shops and bazaars. One cannot help being impressed by the surging life in this busy city so characteristic of the Japanese.

Yokohama, though filled to overflowing with shops, is more of a modern seaport, but we used it as a base to allow our passengers to travel inland for brief visits to Kamakura, Tokyo and Nikko.

Kamakura is not a city, but a lovely little seaside village situated on Sagami Bay. Here one finds two of the most interesting sights in Japan—the ancient temple of Hachiman, God of War, and the world-famous statue of Buddha that towers high above the trees. There is a long approach leading to this marvellous statue, though it is not until you have come under its shadow that its great size impresses.

Tokyo is a complete surprise. It is so glaringly modern and its great buildings, street cars and many automobiles are more of America than the Far East. Perhaps its youth accounts for its modernity, for in the eyes of the Japanese the city is just a baby whose birthdays hardly tote up to six centuries.

Ninety miles from Tokyo lies Nikko, the most beautiful place in all Japan.

There is an old Japanese proverb: "Never use the word magnificent until you have seen Nikko." Here among other countless lovely things I remember a great red lacquer bridge, spanning a swift mountain stream and which may be crossed only by members of the Imperial Household. Most lovely of all, however, are the temples that melt into the age-old landscape under the tremendously tall and stately cryptomeria trees. Over the doorway of the sacred stable there is the original carving of the three famous monkeys of Japan, "Hear no evil—see no evil—speak no evil."

In Nikko one can buy long, beautiful strings of cultured pearls for a mere song. These cultured pearls are, to the eye, the same as the true Oriental, and, therefore, amazingly beautiful. As a matter of fact the cultured pearls are real pearls, the difference being that the Oriental pearl is made naturally by the oyster to protect itself from some obstruction that has become a source of irritation. In the cultured pearl this source of irritation is inserted by the Japanese into the oyster, which, when replanted in especially marked beds, immediately proceeds to cover it with the secretion that makes the pearl. When comparing the two, the only way an expert can tell the Oriental from the cultured is by examining it in a rather expensive and large machine, and that enables enables him to detect the substance around which the cultured pearl has been formed.

Leaving Japan, the long cruise was nearing its end, but we had yet to call at Hawaii.

Hawaii, the never to be forgotten—Isle of Love and the passion flower. I remember that it was dusk as we nosed our way towards the enchanting island, and clear across the placid waters came the soft voices of the natives calling out their unforgetable greeting. . . .

"Aloha! Hawaii! Aloha!"

Here, at Hawaii, largest island of the Hawaiian group, one encounters the semi-tropical vegetation—passion flowers, hibiscus, bougainvillea—and the volcanic cones, the white beaches, the breathlessly blue seas, in intensified form, typical of the islands of the South Pacific. In Hawaii vegetation is extraordinarily lush, fragrant— the volcanic source of the mountains is obvious, and the whole island exciting in its strange wild beauty.

Next Honolulu—away from the native villages and ancient temples of Hawaii to the sophisticated modernity of the capital of the islands—a curious city—not Oriental, not Occidental. A mingled population—Hawaiians, Filipinos, Hindus, Chinese, and every possible combination of races—a natural setting of extraordinary beauty—

for Honolulu lies at the foot of evergreen mountains, its streets are fringed with hedges of brilliant flowers, and the blue Pacific rolls in and breaks in foam on the city's beaches.

As we approach the pier of Honolulu a lovely sound reaches the ears and one discovers that a group of natives are serenading the arrival of the ship with the soft sweet music of the islands.   As the gang-planks are lowered, groups of native girls board the ship, carrying hundreds of beautiful flower necklaces or leis.   They mingle freely with the passengers and everyone soon finds they are wearing three or four of the sweet-smelling leis—the whole ship is filled with their perfume.   It is truly a charming welcome and is so in keeping with the lovely spirit of friendliness and beauty that greets one everywhere in Hawaii.

In the soft twilight we are once more bedecked with leis, and the soft Hawaiian "Farewell to Thee" rings out across the ever-widening stretch of water as we sail away. Take warning, however, that if you ever wish to return to these lovely islands, your leis must be given back to the waters ere you pass Diamond Head!   It is a terribly hard thing to throw the lovely smelling flowers away— but with such an alternative—what else can one do?

From Hawaii to San Pedro, and my American passengers are thinking of home. We stay one night at San Pedro, long enough to explore the long bright roads, to visit Hollywood, to dine at one of the fashionable hotels.

Then on to the Panama—the Isthmus—the new set in the old—the canal with its marvellous air of achievement —of tenacity—a giant among canals—built to handle the largest ships afloat—the lock chambers' enormous size; 1000 feet long, 110 feet wide—romance here, too— the modern romance of engineering—but Balboa is old— and so is Panama—old as the Savannahs. We have time to go and explore—and savour the contrast—until we steam once more into the Atlantic, leaving the Pacific behind.

A few days later we steam up the mighty Hudson—a river with no flowering vines, no coral beaches, but lovely, too, in its tense abstract way—on past the tall Lady of Liberty, her shadow aslant the waters—on to the very edge of the towering sky-scrapers—New York. . . .

So ended the most wonderful picnic I have ever enjoyed, and as many of my readers may decide to embark on a similar adventure one day, I will conclude this chapter with a few hints, or words of advice, which, if followed, may help towards the better enjoyment and comfort of the voyage.

Round-the-world cruising has become almost a habit, and in the great 20,000-ton liners that make the cruises to-day it is also a luxury and a very interesting one, too. The great travel firms in England and America that organize and carry out these cruises, publish beautifully illustrated handbooks, or itineraries, months before the cruises begin. If you contemplate taking a cruise, get these handbooks and read them. The spirit of contemplation will quickly change to one of determination, and the next thing you know you will have booked your passage and be making preparations for the journey.

Some cruises go round the world east about, that is through the Mediterranean and Suez Canal, and return via the Panama Canal. Others go west about, starting out through Panama Canal and returning via Mediterranean, or in some cases round South Africa. The only difference is that going east about the clock is being put on half an hour or so each night as you steam eastward, and going west it is put back correspondingly. To make up for this, when crossing the 180th meridian east about, you will experience an eight-day week, and west about a six-day week. Thus it will be seen that what you gain on the swings you lose on the roundabouts, and vice versa. However, as it doesn't matter very much on a cruise when you go to bed or when you arise, the alteration of the clock should not make much difference, although I have heard several people complain of it interfering with their proper rest, especially at the beginning of the cruise.

The cruise ships are well-known vessels belonging to the various Transatlantic lines, and they are chartered lock, stock and funnel by the travel companies, and manned by the same captain, officers and crew as they carry on their ordinary runs. This is a great factor towards smooth and efficient running. The best ships provide an experienced physician, a tip-top orchestra, gymnastic, swimming and squash instructors, barbers, ladies' hairdressers and manicurists, a well-equipped laundry and valet service, a well-stocked library, indoor and outdoor swimming tanks, garden lounges, deck games, etc., etc. The charterers put a staff on board, in charge of a cruise director, and this usually includes lecturers, clergymen, surgeon-dentist, bankers, and host and hostess, photographers and travel experts, and a librarian with an ample stock of travel books, guides, etc., etc. A good supply of clothing, such as is ordinarily worn in temperate climates, should be taken, and also several Palm Beach suits. There is an impression that these can be best obtained abroad, in places like India or China, but my experience is that they are rarely satisfactory, and you will do well to get them at home. Bring flannels, sweaters and sneakers for deck games, also a gymnastic costume. A swimming costume suitable for the outdoor pool should be brought, as this pool is well in the public eye, as it were, and always a great source of attraction. A heavy coat or wrap is required for cool evenings, and a light raincoat or dust-coat is useful for motoring.

Many of the motor drives are very dusty trips, and on occasions passengers are advised by the "staff" to wear old clothes; so bring along that old suit, and you can get it cleaned up occasionally on board.

Do not bother about a sun-helmet; they are a nuisance to pack, and can be obtained better and cheaper in tropical countries.

For gentlemen, a dinner-jacket is the usual dress for evenings, and should be sufficient, unless you expect to attend any formal functions aboard. For hot weather, a couple of loose dinner-jackets made of white alpaca or duck, look and feel cool, and can be laundered on board as required.

For ladies I am advised by several very charming authorities that amongst other things they should have dresses of materials that do not crush or wrinkle, and which, upon opening the trunk and being shaken out, will look "perfect." I had no idea such material existed. The same authorities also advised Kayser silk for certain items, but I'm getting into deep water now and guess I'll drop the subject.

If you are in the habit of taking any particular kind of tonic or patent medicine, don't forget to bring a good supply, as it may not be obtainable aboard. Umbrellas, sunshades, tinted sun spectacles, fans, cameras (still and movie) binoculars, pedometers, altimeters, small clothes-line and pegs in neat package from department store, flasks (thermos and otherwise), drinking cups, are amongst the handy things seen on cruises.

If you bring anything in the way of valuable furs or jewellery (and it is not advisable to do so), you will do well before sailing to get a certificate from the customs authorities, which on your return to the United States can be produced to show that you did not purchase them abroad. Without this certificate you might have difficulty in establishing the fact. American citizens returning from abroad are allowed to bring in, duty free, one hundred dollars' worth of personal articles, that is, articles purchased for personal use during the voyage. Curios and presents for friends are, of course, not included in this. You should, before sailing, get from the customs authorities a list of dutiable goods so that you can discriminate in your purchasing abroad. It is inevitable that you will return from the cruise loaded with "junk." Yes, I think that is the word. It is bad enough to have to carry the "junk" home without having to pay duty on it.

By the way, bring a couple of fancy costumes. The masquerade ball is always a great event, and the first one usually takes place early in the cruise, as it gets folk together.

The question of tipping on board is one that exercises the minds of a good many travellers, but the cruise staff will readily inform you of what is usual, in fact, what they themselves give for personal service. It is generally paid weekly on a cruise, and if you make up your mind to it and pay it when the time comes round, you will cease to be annoyed by this irritating subject. There is nothing to be gained by putting it off week after week, generally against your better nature. Roughly 30s. or $8 dollars per week should cover all tipping.

In order that your cabin may not be cluttered up with great wardrobe trunks during a cruise, a large baggage-room is provided, in charge of a baggage master. Having unpacked what you immediately require, you can send your trunks down to the baggage-room, where they will be conveniently placed under your initial letter, and at stated times during the day (or any time if you wish it) the baggage master will be in attendance, so that you may pack or unpack as desired. For shore excursions extending over several days, good sized suit-cases are recommended. A cabin trunk to go under the lower bunk is a convenient stowage, and should not exceed 13 inches in height.

As regards cash during the cruise, the bank or exchange on board will negotiate all travellers' cheques, letters of credit, etc., but I would advise everyone to carry a stock of small bills of one, two and five dollars. These are good all over the world, and you can purchase many small articles with them without bothering about exchange. The purser will keep all money and valuables for you. For some unexplained reason, on a world cruise, small bills become as scarce as hens' teeth.

Dogs or animals of any sort are not allowed to be carried on a cruise, so don't make any rash promises to bring your friends home a monkey.

The social side of the cruise consists of dances, masquerades, bridge and whist drives, concerts, sports, lectures, etc., and frequently dinner dances are arranged at the large hotels in various ports. Committees are selected from the passengers to take in hand all these activities, and if you are fond of such things, you won't have a dull minute.

For those who prefer quietness and peace, what could be better than a comfortable deck chair, your books and diary, and the glorious restful scenery of tropic seas? A poet once hit the nail on the head in a very aggravating manner by writing: "How little they know of England, who only England know." I suppose the same applies to America, or any other country.

My own company, the Cunard White Star Ltd., Cunard Buildings, Liverpool 3, are the pioneers of big ship world cruises, and as experience counts for everything, if ever you want to see the world in comfort, write to the above address.

CHAPTER XIV

ODDS AND ENDS

Aboard R.M.S. "Berengaria."
At Sea.

AWAY back in Southampton Water, now three thousand miles astern, I commenced writing this log, and in a few hours time one half of the voyage will have ended.

"Ambrose Lightship ahead, sir!"

Croughan, my "Tiger," has called me early this morning. It is not yet dawn. From the port-holes of my cabin I observe three bright flashes, at eight second intervals, cutting the darkness. New York lies not far beyond, and even now the waters of the mighty Hudson are swirling past our bows. Mount to the bridge with me and take a look at this great river.

Dawn is just breaking now, but already the fairway of the Hudson is black with craft. Night and day it is always the same.

The Americans sing the praises of Broadway's million lights, wax lyrical about their coal-black "Mammies," chant liltingly about their cornfields, and their old Kentucky homes, but no poet, or jazz merchant has yet thought fit to immortalize the mighty Hudson, the life-stream of Manhattan. Allow an English Mariner to pay due homage.

Sailing up the Hudson in the old days of the Gedney Channel gave most masters of big ships heart disease, and the bottom of many a vessel has rested comfortably for hours, and sometimes days, on the shoals of Sandy Hook.

But with the opening of the Ambrose Channel the river is now one of the most comfortable known to navigation. The dredging of this channel was one of the most marvellous engineering feats of the age. It is about six miles in length, 2000 feet broad, and, cut out of the very centre of the river's bottom, it allows the world's largest vessels to sail right up to the front doors of New Yorkers. The *Lusitania* was the first ship to sail up the fairway in 1907. To my mind it was rather a fine gesture on the part of America to bestow this signal honour on a British ship, for the formal opening of the channel was delayed for two days to await the arrival of the great Cunarder.

To describe life on this vast inland waterway is quite beyond the power of my amateur pen. Widen old Father Thames by at least twenty miles, multiply the normal number of vessels passing up and down the river by about ten thousand, and Londoners may obtain some idea of the traffic on the Hudson. Blaring sirens, screeching whistles, huge double-decker ferryboats, crammed with humanity, tearing slant-ways across the river from New Jersey to Manhattan, and vice versa; tankers, barges, sailing ships, cattle boats, giant liners, fussy tugs; long, floating contraptions like gigantic rafts, transferring whole trains complete with engine, trucks and carriages from New York City to the mainland—these are just a few of the craft, and the scene of hustle, bustle and animation beggars description. To me, the tall Lady of Liberty, gift of France to a sister Republic, towering slap in the midst of this hurly-burly, always seems to be waving her torch in triumph, commanding the world's admiration.

"Lady of Liberty!" said an American to me once, during the days of prohibition, as he gazed sneeringly on one of the world's greatest works of sculpture. "Guess Uncle Sam has divorced her these days, Cap."

"Maybe he has, for a time," I retorted, "but Uncle Sam will marry her again some day," I added.

No one can sail up the Hudson and fail to admire the

daring and ingenuity of the American people. The first
glimpse of the mighty skyscrapers, towering sheer to
the heavens, is breath-taking, awe-inspiring, and no first
sight of any other port in the world can compare with the
thrill which the first glimpse of New York inspires.
Under the shadow of these swaying mountains of steel
and mortar, the tall masts of the *Berengaria* seem like
match-sticks in comparison. When one realizes that
eight million souls are crowded in mighty New York it is
hard to imagine that this rock of Manhattan was inhabited
solely by wild boars and the savage red man less than three
centuries ago.

I have the greatest admiration for the American people,
and it has always been a source of wonder to me why the
two great Anglo-speaking nations have not come closer
together, and to a better understanding. We in England,
spoon-fed on gangster films, are apt to consider the race
as the most lawless in the world, forgetting that America,
in her short history, has absorbed fifty million foreigners,
all types, creeds and classes, a large percentage ignorant
and illiterate, and the scum of middle Europe. These
are the type from which the gangster thugs have sprung.
In the old pre-war days I was engaged in the emigration
trade in the Mediterranean, transporting these people
from Middle Europe to New York, and I knew then that
America was importing trouble. The shipping agents
at the different Mediterranean ports were paid a certain
sum per head for every emigrant shipped to America.
I remember at one Italian port, a family came aboard,
father, mother and six children, and as the father was
suffering from glaucoma, a disease of the eyes, they were
refused permission to board. We learnt later that the
father was also a notorious Austrian bandit, lately escaped
from prison, and America has to thank our ship's doctor
from preventing at least one family of potential gangsters
from entering the country. The yarn is a good one,
but before I tell it, allow me to introduce the medico
concerned, now famous in the shipping world.

Doctor MacIntyre, the present Board of Trade Doctor for Southampton, and I were associated for a long number of years, moving together from ship to ship. Mac was scratch man at golf in New York, as he is now at Southampton, I believe, and there was always a pipe band and a big crowd of golf enthusiasts waiting to greet him when we docked at New York.

When the family mentioned above came aboard as third-class emigrants, Mac, as I have said, refused to pass them. This was a big loss to the agent so, knowing that Mac had several hundreds of people to examine, he thought he might wangle them aboard in another class. To carry out this purpose the agent took them ashore, rigged out the whole family in totally different attire and marshalled them aboard again as second-class passengers. Mac told me that he didn't recognise them the second time, but he again detected the father's disease, and refused to pass them. Nothing daunted, that persistent agent herded the family ashore again, dressed them in a third rig-out, once more entirely different from the first two rigs, and ushered them aboard as first-class passengers. But Mac's eagle eye found them out again and, to the loud lamentations of the agent, for a third time he refused to give them a clean bill of health. There was no higher class, or I believe that this family would have been brought aboard again for the fourth time.

With that yarn my mind goes back again to my early days with the Cunard.

Naturally, there are occasions, although remarkably rare, when someone dies at sea, and I remember one ocean burial which, for pomp and splendour, is outstanding in my memory. It happened aboard the *Carpathia*. The vessel had been chartered in New York by about 350 Roman Catholic priests who were making pilgrimage to meet the Pope in Rome. The reverend gentlemen occupied the whole of the accommodation in the first class. In the third class we were carrying some 1500 ordinary passengers, and it so happened that during the course of the voyage one of these died, a Catholic Italian. When this fact was made known to the Cardinal in charge of the priests, he instructed his entire concourse to attend the funeral in full regalia. I have never witnessed a more impressive ceremony either on land or at sea.

I remember another burial which was not quite so impressive. We were cruising the Mediterranean at the time in the *Laconia* during her maiden voyage. The Captain concerned, a strict disciplinarian, we affectionately called the Rajah. I was Chief Officer. At Algiers one of our male passengers, a Roman Catholic, died. The Rajah sent for me, and said he:

"Well, Britten, I think we might make a little show at the funeral. Send a few officers and a party of sailors to attend the ceremony."

Now it appears that the nearest graveyard was in the desert a few miles outside of Algiers, and we left the engagement of a priest and all shore arrangements to our local agent.

I detailed the Second Officer, a typical Scot of the West Highlands, to take command of the funeral party. As the *Laconia* was on her maiden voyage we were carrying our naval architect aboard, a Mr. Holmes, who was making his first voyage at sea. Mr. Holmes attended the funeral and later that night, in conversation with the Rajah, he innocently "let the cat out of the bag," and very nearly got the Second Officer hung, drawn and quartered for the part the latter played at the burial ceremony.

"You know, Captain," said Mr. Holmes admiringly, "this is my first trip at sea, and frankly I am amazed at the number of jobs which you ship's officers are called upon to tackle at a moment's notice, jobs which I might say an uninitiated landsman like myself would consider far outside your sphere."

The statement appeared to contain a leading question, so the Rajah demanded:

"How so, Mr. Holmes?"

"Well, as you probably know," continued Mr. Holmes, "I attended the funeral this morning, and after we had walked for miles across the desert in blazing sunshine, everyone was dismayed to discover that, owing to an oversight by the local agent, there was no priest in attendance at the graveside—that is, everyone was dismayed with the exception of your excellent Second Officer.

Mr. Holmes paused, and the Rajah sat up, very interested.

"Is that so, Mr. Holmes," he murmured ominously. "Pray tell me what happened?" he invited.

"There was no telephone or other means of communication back to Algiers," went on Mr. Holmes, "so your excellent officer whipped off his cap and promptly conducted the burial service—and I thought he did it very well indeed," concluded our architect enthusiastically.

I saw the dark eyes of the Rajah flash disapproval.

"Oh, you do, do you?" Then turning to me, he demanded to know if I was aware that no priest had attended. I answered in the negative, so he immediately instructed me to see the Second Officer and demand an explanation. The Rajah was very annoyed so I sent for the culprit with all despatch.

Said I, when the delinquent entered my room: "The old man distinctly disapproves of your leanings towards the Church. What made you bury that man this morning?"

The Second Officer was not repentant.

"What made me dae it, Chief?" he repeated indignantly. "We were staundin' in the sun wi' oor heids bared an' a' leeble to catch sunstroke at ony meenite, so ——" here Jock lowered his voice and wagged a decisive finger—"I buried yon mannie unner a' th' rites o' th' kirk o' Scotland, an' Catholic or Protestant he'll be nein the waur o' yon bit service."

The Rajah was rather keen on ceremonies and, whilst we are on this subject, here is another yarn which I recall. The corpse of some prominent American was due aboard the *Laconia* at 5 p.m. one day, twenty-four hours prior to sailing, and I was instructed that due ceremony was to be displayed as the remains were brought on board. Accordingly I detailed a full party of seamen and stewards, with the usual buglers to line the deck near the gangway. We waited there for three solid hours and when, at 8 o'clock, the flag-draped casket of the embalmed corpse was carried solemnly aboard, my men stood to attention, whilst the buglers played the "Last Post."

Later, the casket safely deposited in the mail-room, I reported to the Rajah that due ceremony had been carried out according to his instructions.

Arriving at New York the first person up the gangway was a huge American stevedore, and behind him trooped about a dozen of his tough guys.

"Say, Chief," drawled the stevedore, "heve yuh got the key of the mail room?"

I handed him the key.

"Come on, boys," blared the big fellow to his minions. "There's a 'stiff' aboard, let's lug him out first."

Later, the Rajah approached me.

"Well, Chief," said he, "has the corpse been safely disembarked?"

"Oh, yes, sir," I said. Then I added somewhat drily: "But not quite with the same amount of ceremony which he received when he was brought aboard."

The Rajah did not ask for details.

I remember a yarn about another Scotch officer, a Chief Engineer. We called him Sandy, and his face, on which I seldom saw a smile, was adorned by a small pointed "Captain Kettle" beard. Those whiskers play an important part in this yarn, therefore I want you to keep them in mind.

Sandy spent heaps of money on his clothing, but despite this fact, he always looked a bit mottled and untidy, chiefly because he spent most of his time in his beloved engine-room.

About the time I write, the Chief Engineers of the

Line dined in lonely majesty in their own cabins, but then instructions were issued by the Company that they must take a table in the saloon with the passengers. When I acquainted Sandy with the new instructions I saw his ears go back, and the red hair bristle.

"That means dressing for dinner every night, Sandy," I chuckled mischievously.

He waved an oily sweat rag in my face.

"I'll dae naethin' o' the kind," he snapped. "I've never worn a daggoned laundry on ma chest in ma life, an' am no startin' at ma age."

"Orders is orders, Sandy," I reminded him with a grin.

"Damn yer orders, and damn——!"

"Now! Now! Sandy!" I interrupted admonishingly. "I'll be looking forward to seeing you in your nice boiled shirt next voyage."

He was still growling like a hungry bear when I left him. But like all good sailormen, Sandy cursed yet obeyed orders. Next voyage he duly turned up for dinner during the first night resplendent in evening dress, albeit his whiskers were bristling with bad temper, and he looked darned uncomfortable. I got a close-up of him after the meal, and the imprint of five oily finger-marks on his virgin-white shirt-front told their own story. Although in a modern ship, with telephone leading from his cabin to the engine-room, which enabled him to communicate with the officers below, Sandy always considered it his personal duty to go down into the engine-room at the last moment just prior to dinner to see that everything was well with his beloved engines. Hence the finger-prints. It appears that that infernal stiff-starched shirt-front would insist on bulging out and tickling Sandy's whiskers as he descended the steep iron stairways leading down to the engine-room. One can imagine the irate Scotsman cursing and swearing beneath his breath as he hammed the offensive garment back beneath his waistcoat with five oil-begrimed digits.

One night during the voyage something detained Sandy

longer than usual, and he appeared late for dinner, all hot and bothered, and, as usual, with the shirt-front well oiled.   The rest of the table, which included a distinguished Hungarian nobleman, were already seated, and had reached the meat course.   Sandy set out to catch them up, commencing with soup.   It was then that dire disaster overtook our admirable Scotch engineer.   It appears that he was wearing one of those convenient, but now somewhat old-fashioned hook-on dress ties and as Sandy bent low over the *consommé* the offending tie, which had probably worked adrift owing to his recent exertions, slid from beneath his whiskers and flopped into the soup.   The table noticed the incident but, although inwardly convulsed, like well-bred people they pretended otherwise.

When Sandy's baleful eye beheld the tie floating in his soup he was seen to glance furtively around the table and, concluding the disaster had passed unobserved, he quickly salved the garment with two fingers of his left hand, and, whilst still spooning the soup into his mouth with his right hand, he gave the somewhat damp tie a quick wipe on his trousers and then attempted to hook it back into place beneath his pointed beard.   Had it not been for his whiskers he might have succeeded, but the darned thing refused to go back into place.   Then, to crown matters, the greasy tie slid from between his fingers and once more flopped into his soup.   This was too much for Sandy.   With a muttered curse he openly fished out the tie, carefully dusted it with his napkin, jammed it viciously into one vest pocket, patted his whiskers over his tieless collar, and went on with his soup.

I learnt later that the whole of his table companions had acute abdominal pains throughout the rest of the voyage, as a result of their desperate efforts to suppress the mirth which they dare not display before the irate Sandy.

Mr. Rodgerson, the present ship's writer of the

Berengaria, on account of his ability to write shorthand at speed, has within recent years been called upon to assist many prominent people, and tells some very interesting yarns concerning many noted celebrities who have travelled on the "Happy Ship."

Lord Dawson of Penn, Mr. Winston Churchill, the late Sir John Harrington, Sir Malcolm Campbell, Miss Ruby M. Ayres, the late Edgar Wallace, are just a few of the notabilities who have claimed his services from time to time.

Of Sir Malcolm Campbell, the great racing motorist, Rodgerson says:

"Sir Malcolm Campbell is very delightful to work for. On the first occasion when the 'Bluebird' broke all world records, I took down in shorthand his account of the record run, and afterwards clean drafted it for the Press. Then recently I assisted him with his broadcast of the latest record. Listening to him while dictating you could almost feel that you were in the car; and despite his fame he is so absolutely unassuming. I hope he crosses in the *Berengaria* next year again, and that I shall be able to assist him with the account of the 300 m.p.h. record which I feel sure is his final object and, I hope, achievement.

"Lord Dawson of Penn is another charming man with whom I have come in contact. When I last assisted him he was preparing a series of lectures for a tour in the United States. He was very interested in a short-hand machine, which he felt sure would ultimately be a success, and showed me details of its working. I am always looking out to see whether this will achieve popularity during my time. His Lordship is one of the quickest men in action I have ever met. I can recall seeing him on one occasion coming out of our swimming pool after a Turkish bath, in his dressing-gown, at 8 p.m. to the minute; he had to run up four flights of stairs (we call them decks) to go to his room, and eight minutes later I was amazed to see him coming down the companion-way, immaculately dressed, ready for dinner, with his daughter on his arm.

"Mr. Winston Churchill I shall never forget. His amazing vocabulary and memory for words rather bewildered me when first I met him. On his last voyage with us I assisted him by taking down in shorthand a series of articles for the Press. All the time when he was dictating he was pacing the room like a caged lion, opening a door, or a drawer of a cupboard, picking up and throwing down books and ornaments, throwing himself down on a settee, and jumping up again, but never still. The words simply pour from his mouth, there is no other expression, but he phrases each separate sentence completely before delivering it. Sometimes he will pause abruptly, and after less than a second's thought, he will snap: 'Turn back about six pages to where I was talking about so-and-so. You will see I used the word "horse," substitute the word "animal." '

"I merely give these words to bring out the point I have in mind—his amazing memory. All the time he was at work he drank inordinate quantities of soda water, and he had a bucket full of these bottles on ice in his cabin.

"It was fatiguing work keeping up with him, but a fascinating labour, and I think I enjoyed working for Mr. Churchill as much as for anyone during my long career as a ship's writer."

Winston Churchill keeps himself very fit aboard, regularly calling upon the services of Mason, my Turkish-bath attendant. Like Rodgerson, Mason has also come in contact with many well-known people. He claims that he assisted Gene Tunney to win the world's heavy-weight boxing championship, but I have a better yarn than this to tell about him. One day an elderly gentleman, world famous, and whom we will introduce directly, sought the services of the good Mason. Incidentally, Mason is a Cockney, and although I do not accuse him of impoliteness, he is somewhat blasé in respect of persons. He

likes to get on with the job, which he does thoroughly
and strenuously. Well, this old gentleman sought him
out one morning, and said he:

"Mason, I want to place myself entirely in your hands
during the voyage. I have just completed a strenuous
lecture tour in America, and feel somewhat run down."

"Right, sir," said Mason, unaware of the identity of
his victim. "Jump into the hot bath."

From the hot bath to the cold shower Mason, who is
rather voluble, carefully explaining that the hot bath
opened the pores of the skin, and the cold shower closed
them again, and so on. Then on to the slab, and as Mason
massaged he delivered a lecture in anatomy, volubly
explaining, as he rubbed each separate muscle of his
patient, their function and their purpose. Presently a
bell-boy poked his head into the sacred domain. It is
warm work massaging in the hot atmosphere of a Turkish-
bath, and Mason, who is inclined to be irascible, does
not like to be disturbed.

"Lord Dawson of Penn! Lord Dawson of Penn!
Wireless message for Lord Dawson of Penn," shouted
the bell-boy, looking at both Mason and his patient
enquiringly.

"Get to hell out of this," shouted Mason fiercely.
"We've got no damned lords down 'ere."

The boy shifted—quickly.

"Excuse me," said a quiet voice from the slab. "D'you
know, Mason, I've an idea that that message is meant for
me?"

Mason tells this story against himself.

He had delivered his lecture on anatomy to the King's
Physician, Lord Dawson of Penn.

Mason generally finishes work just prior to dinner
every evening, but one night, or rather, during the early
hours of one morning, he received a message that another
world-famous gentleman required his services urgently.
It was carnival night, and our friend had entered into
the spirit of carnival, and as we were due to arrive in New

York in a few hours time, he reckoned that Mason would be able to rub some of the flies away.

In the Turkish baths aboard the *Berengaria* there is a spacious hot-air lounge where the patients dry off, and recover after Mason has finished with them. For the purpose of the yarn, I might also mention that there is always a night chef on duty. Mason's patient became a little peckish as a result of the massaging, and requested Mason to repair to the kitchen and obtain him something to eat. The good Mason departed to oblige, and in due course arrived back with a dish of fish and chips, tastefully arrayed on a silver platter, with plates and fish-knives and forks complete.

"Get me a—hic—newspaper and—hic—some vinegar, Mason," commanded the great one, viewing the fish and chips.

Mason went to his cabin, procured an old copy of the *News of the World*, called at the kitchen on his way back, and returned to the baths. Very carefully, the great one —and he really is one of the bright stars of our aristocracy —emptied the dish of fish and chips on to the open newspaper, dusted the contents with salt, and well soaked the lot with vinegar.

"This is the only—hic—damned way—to eat—hic— fish and—hic—chips, Mason, in the good old—hic— English way."

Mason was not in the least perturbed, as a matter of fact, he shared the repast with the noble gentleman.

Mention of Mason and Rodgerson reminds me that my present crew as a whole deserve a place in this log. Indeed, I think they have well earned special mention. Here are just a few things outstanding to their credit, which may agreeably surprise the average landsman.

Off their own bat, and at a cost of £600, the crew of the *Berengaria* have endowed a cot at the Children's Hospital in Southampton, and every year, out of their own pockets, they hand the hospital £100 towards its upkeep. In addition, they make an annual grant of £60 to the Royal South Hants Hospital. These grants are made by the lower ratings—sailors, firemen, stewards and kitchen hands, and it is this spirit, which permeates my crew, that has earned the title "The Happy Ship" for the *Berengaria*. My fellows have also an athletic club, an insurance club, and a savings bank. Each member of the crew pays into a common fund the sum of one shilling per voyage, and half of this is credited to the social and athletic side, and half to the insurance club. When members of the crew are not re-engaged, the Ship's Doctor certifying them medically unfit, the club pays them 30s. for each voyage they are stood off, and then a special grant of £5 at the end of three voyages if they are still unfit and unable to resume duty. There is also a death benefit of £25 paid to the dependants of any of the crew, should he die ashore or afloat, whilst still a member of the club. Every year the Big Lady must have her annual holiday for repairs and clean-up, and it is during the lay-up that they pay out their dividends.

As I have said, these things have been entirely created by the men themselves, and I think they are worthy of mention in this log if only on the off chance that many other ships may read, and be pleased to copy.

The athletic prowess of the crew, in all departments of sport, is extraordinarily high, and two huge show-cases aboard are required to display the many wonderful trophies which are competed for annually.

These include:

The Cunard Steam Ship Company's Rowing Cup. Presented by the Company and competed for annually by crews chosen from the Sailors, the Firemen and the Catering Department, the winners receiving either medals or prizes.

The Crosse and Blackwell 100 yards Challenge Cup. When Mr. Goff, Managing Director of Messrs. Crosse and Blackwell, first crossed in the ship, he was so interested in the activities of the Athletic Club that he wirelessed to London for this cup to be ready and delivered in Southampton when the ship arrived. It was there at the dock when we berthed, and he personally presented it to the club. The trophy is an exact replica of the Football Association Challenge Cup.

The Mrs. Charles Augustine Robinson Athletic Shield. Mr. and Mrs. Charles Augustine Robinson are very old friends of the *Berengaria*, and Mrs. Robinson suggested that this trophy be presented to the finest all-round athlete in the ship, at our annual sports' meeting, which is generally held in New York.

Mrs. Augustine Robinson will be remembered as the American Flag Lady, President of the American War Mothers' Union, and the Founder of the Lighted Torch in Paris, which she used to cross over annually to rekindle.

The Laughland Swimming Trophy. Mr. Laughland, of Messrs. Laughland and Son, Southampton, was a breast swimmer enthusiast, and gave this cup for annual competitions amongst the juniors, or boys under nineteen, to be competed for annually. Mr. Laughland was a prominent member of the Southampton Town Council, and obtained free concessions for the members of the crew to use the swimming baths in Southampton, and did everything possible to encourage our fellows to become expert swimmers and to qualify for life-saving certificates.

The Y.M.C.A. Football Trophy. This cup was presented to the *Berengaria* by the Y.M.C.A. in New York to mark the occasion when our crew wrested the Atlantic Championship from the *Olympic*, who had held it for five consecutive years.

The Carlton Cricket Cup. This trophy was presented by Mr. W. E. Toomer at the Hippodrome, Southampton, on a *Berengaria* gala night. Mr. Toomer, who is well known in the golfing world, was for many years a partner of Phil Mead, the famous Hampshire cricketer, and he greatly appreciated the fact that the *Berengaria's* different departments turn out eight teams to compete for this trophy annually.

The Grover Higgins Tennis Trophy. (With which is a trust fund deposited to provide a gold ball annually for the winner.) This trophy is competed for annually on the top deck in New York, a special court being marked out, and the competition is always carried through on a Sunday when in port.

The Parkhouse Cup. Presented by Messrs. W. E. Parkhouse and Son for annual competition for the 440 yards championship. This firm have always shown the greatest interest in the Social and Athletic Club, and it was a spontaneous gift which has been greatly appreciated by our fellows. A valuable prize always goes with the winning of the trophy.

The Dixie Cup. Presented by F. Webber, Esq., for the annual contest between the "Ins" and the "Outs"; that is, teams from the Deck Stewards against the Public Room Stewards (or inside workers), and the method of the contest is changed at every sports meeting; perhaps one year it is a walking match, the next a running match or a cycling contest, and this always proves one of the events at every sports meeting.

The "Berengaria" Smile Cup. This is the only trophy in our show-cases which is not won by athletic prowess. It was presented to the *Berengaria* to perpetuate the appreciation by Mr. and Mrs. Beander McCormick Goodhart, who are regular passengers in the ship, of the *Berengaria* Smile, and the general air of cheerfulness which pervades "The Happy Ship."

The Inter-Departmental Football Challenge Cup. This was bought by the Club itself for competition throughout the ship, and there are seldom less than eight competing teams. The competing teams fight like demons to win this coveted trophy, and the rivalry is always intense. This year, owing to the fact that the ship has been so little in port during the season, in order to sustain the interest, the contest was conducted, for the first time, on six-a-side lines.

In addition to our inter-crew competitions, we sometimes challenge the crews of other ships, should they be in port at the same time as ourselves, of course, and there is the story of one great cricket match which ended somewhat tragically for the *Berengaria*.

The battle took place in the Van Courtland Park in New York, the *Berengaria* supplied the gear, and towards the end of the game, when our side was batting, the property man packed up all the surplus gear and sent this back to the ship, leaving our fellows with only one ball. There was quite a crowd present, and with five minutes left for play, and with ten runs wanted to give the *Berengaria* victory, excitement was intense. Then there came a mighty hit from one of our fellows which sent the ball crashing into the distant roadway for a six. The crew cheered hilariously, but presently their applause gave place to groans. A passing tram ran over the ball, cutting it in half, leaving the game unfinished with four runs to win. When, on a subsequent voyage, the *Berengaria* replayed that match, the other ship beat them by an innings and umpteen runs.

Every year the *Berengaria's* crew gives a Christmas treat to a thousand poor children in Southampton. Mr. Le Grand Gould, a well-known American gentleman, came to hear of this some years ago and, as a result, for years afterwards he annually supplied sufficient quantities of odd pieces of silk to dress a thousand dolls. The social club aboard purchase the dolls and my stewardesses work at odd moments, over long months, dressing them for the kiddies.

To provide for the children's treat a draw is promoted aboard, and much fun is aroused by the way the hand of fortune deals out the prizes. For instance, Phil Scott, the heavyweight boxer, who entered the draw last year, won two tickets for a show in New York, whilst another passenger, residing in New York, won two tickets for a performance at the Grand Theatre pantomime in Southampton. Again, another passenger, residing in Newcastle, won half a ton of coal which required to be collected from a Southampton firm—a real case of "carrying coals to Newcastle." The passenger concerned sent his ticket back to the ship with a request that it be put back into the pool for redrawal. A passenger residing in Texas was the next to win that half-ton of coal.

A sailor's wife leads a lonely existence, for even with a ship of our quick service the men only see their womenfolk on an average of about four days per month. Rodgerson, the ship's writer, therefore, started a fund a few years ago, and from the money raised about fifty relatives of the crew were taken on a round trip to New York and back. Rodgerson accompanied this party on the *Franconia*, and we, the *Berengaria*, sailed out of Southampton just in front of the smaller ship. In mid-Atlantic we ran into a terrific hurricane, a real snorter, and the men on the *Berengaria* became a little anxious about their womenfolk on the smaller vessel, which was then somewhere astern of us. Consequently my crew wirelessed Rodgerson's party:

> "Sympathise hurricane experience. Trust you are all O.K."

The answer flashed back, signed by several of the seamen's wives, sent the crew of the *Berengaria* into hysterics. It read:

> "What hurricane? You landlubbers!"

One American passenger got hold of this message and at once wirelessed, altering a word in the opening chorus of a famous song:

> "Daughters of the Sea,
> All British born."

Mr. Waterman, of the Waterman Fountain Pen Company, was also on board, and he also wirelessed Rodgerson's party:

> "Brave ladies, I invite you to luncheon with me on your arrival in New York."

A few days later the entire party were entertained to a sumptuous luncheon at India House, Broadway, and Mr. Waterman presented each member with a valuable souvenir fountain-pen.

Rodgerson tells me that during the voyage, on the night of carnival, the ladies pinched all his clothes, leaving him to go down to breakfast next morning in evening dress. He tried to borrow a steward's rig-out, but owing to his corpulency found this impossible. The day following carnival was sports day as well, and as Rodgerson was in charge, he was obliged to conduct the sports' meeting in tails and a boiled shirt. It was late evening before the ladies disgorged the filched raiment.

We carried Carnera, the gigantic boxer, with us some years ago, and during that voyage we celebrated Christmas at sea.

At the crew's special Christmas dinner, which was held late in the evening, we generally stage a little ceremony. Very solemnly the Chief Steward, followed by a retinue of white-coated chefs, carries the turkey on a silver salver, round and round the table. On this occasion the crew smacked their lips in joyous anticipation, for the silver salver was of enormous dimensions. Here was a turkey indeed! Carefully the great dish was placed in position at the head of the table, then very slowly and reverently the cover was removed. The roar that followed must have been heard back at Southampton, for instead of a juicy turkey Carnera's size nineteen boots were tastefully arrayed on that dish.

On another occasion my crew staged a show which is still talked about on the Atlantic highways. But I will call upon Miss Edith Beggs, my head shop-lady, to tell this yarn, as she was one of the leading spirits behind the movement.

Miss Beggs says:

"The boys, or ought I to say men, of the ship's company, decided to run a pantomime, a burlesque of *Cinderella*, with an all-male cast, round about Christmas-time a year or two ago, and we girls of the ship agreed to rig them out. The fun began when the time came to fit the dresses on the men.

"For the skinny ones we had to use much gauze and cotton-wool as pads, but the job was fairly easy until we came to Rodgerson. You've heard of, or maybe some of you have seen, Rodgy? With his wonderful figure he had to have 'out-sizes' and then some. For him the dresses had to be cut open, and insertions made—in the front of course—but when we finally succeeded in rigging him out the result was charming.

"Well, the night of the 'panto' duly arrived, and the scene behind the stage was indescribable. Most of the boys had forgotten their lines, and half of them had lost their props, and it looked as if we girls would never get them rigged up for the show before about midnight. But we managed it somehow, and Rodgy, with his fair face, dark hair, painted cheeks and rouged lips looked really wicked as 'Stunk,' one of the ugly sisters in *Cinderella*. Later on, before the end of the first act, as he perspired freely, all the grease-paint ran down his face, and he looked like nothing on earth. He was very cheerful about it, however, giving his face an occasional wipe with a mop he had on the stage, which made matters worse, and the audience complimented him on having the finest pair of girl's legs seen on the stage.

" 'The Fairy Queen' was a thin fireman with a girlish figure and ugly, angular, hairy legs. Somebody suggested he ought to have his legs shaved before he went on, but he wouldn't agree, so I'm afraid the beautiful white dress we made for him was not effective.

"Every one of the ship's company had done their bit to make the show a success. Electricians, carpenters, joiners; in fact, everyone had assisted in preparing the stage, and the first-class dining saloon for the occasion. We had an audience of well over a thousand. The full band was in attendance, and the orchestral enclosure was a mass of flowers and fairy-lights. The stage also was beautifully rigged up, with the exception that boxes were utilized for the entrance and exits. In the second act 'Cinderella' had just retired gracefully from the stage when she put her foot through one of the steps, barking one of her bare, hairy shins rather badly. If you could have heard her remarks when this happened you would have hardly thought her the charming little character depicted in the real version of the story.

"The most humorous part of the performance, however, was the final denouement.

"All the characters being amateurs, and anxious not to forget their lines, were rigid teetotallers during the whole of the performance, content to wait until the end of the show before enjoying the bottled refreshment which the social club had laid aside for them. Some of the crew had broached these supplies, and delighted with the way their comrades were putting the show across, they proceeded to toast them at a distance. When finally the curtain was rung down on the last act, the hot and weary performers made a rush to get a drink, only to find 'returned empties.' Deprived of their beer, it was then that the bold, bad baron, and the two ugly sisters particularly, really excelled, finding impromptu, and most expressive lines to suit the occasion.

"Still, it was a good show, and I believe one of the most wonderful staged on the Atlantic."

Allow me to introduce the youngest member of my crew, my junior bell-boy.

"Carnera" Giles stands about four feet six inches in height, is not yet fifteen years of age, and at the time I write he has not yet completed his third voyage at sea.

I must tell you how he came by the name "Carnera."

We have some very fine boxing talent amongst the crew, and every voyage we stage a display for the benefit of the passengers. Therefore, during "Carnera" Giles' first voyage with us we persuaded him to enter the ring against one of the heavyweights. To lessen the little fellow's handicap, however, we rigged three life-belts around him. As he entered the ring, wearing an enormous pair of boxing-gloves, and draped in the life-belts, only the tip of his nose was showing. But the plucky wee fellow put up a good show. His head did not reach to the other fellow's waist, but he well battered the knees of his enormous opponent. For this effort he was rewarded with the sum of five shillings, and will be known throughout his seafaring career by the nickname of "Carnera."

Later that night I met him in the main square of the ship.

"Well, Carnera!" I greeted him. "What are you going to do with that five shillings you won to-day?"

It was the first time I had spoken to him, and the little chap was just a little nervous of his Commodore.

"I—I don't know, sir!" he stammered.

"You don't know!" said I. "Well, I hope you put it in the bank, my lad," I added.

"I'll bank half of it, sir."

"And what will you do with the other half," I asked him.

"Well, sir—I—I—this is my first voyage, sir, and—and when I get home to Southampton I'd like to give mother and my little brother a treat, sir."

"What sort of a treat, my lad?"

"Take them to the pictures, sir, in the afternoon, sir, and—and I might buy mother some chocolates."

"How much will that cost, Carnera?"

He did a little quick thinking. "Maybe, one-and-thrippence, sir—the pictures are cheaper in the afternoon."

"One shilling and threepence, eh! Well, if you bank

half of the five bob, and spend one shilling and threepence on your mother and brother, what are you going to do with the rest of the money?"

"I've got a—a friend, sir, and—and——"

"Ah! A sweetheart, eh?" I interrupted quickly.

Carnera snorted: "Nah! I don't believe in sweethearts, sir, she's just a pal."

"And you're going to share the rest of the dough with her, eh?"

"Yes, sir. I'll take her to the skating-rink at night, sir."

"How much will that cost?"

"Thrippence each, sir."

"Still another bob to blow-in. What will you do with that?"

"Well, sir, we might have some fish and chips when we come out of the rink, and share a bottle of pop."

"A real good day and all on half a crown. D'you think you can do it, Carnera?"

Again he did a little mental calculation:

"Yes, sir. I think we'll just manage it, sir."

Part of the duties of Webber, my deck steward, consists in collecting the accounts from passengers for the hire of deck chairs and rugs, and as we near port this job keeps him fully occupied. On a recent voyage he was standing on the promenade deck when one of his assistants handed him an envelope containing three one-pound notes. Webber's mind was on something else at the time, and somewhat absently he extracted the money and threw the envelope overboard. At least, he intended to throw the envelope overboard.

Off our starboard beam lay the Military Hospital at Netley, and as the ship passed in line with this building, an American lady approached Webber.

"Say, Steward!" said she. "What is that big place over there?"

"That," groaned Webber sadly, "is an asylum for deck stewards, Madam. I shall land there one day," he added with a louder groan.

She looked at him somewhat queerly.

"You're joking, of course," she said. "You don't seriously tell me that you expect to go mad one day."

Webber waved the empty envelope.

"Well, I'm on the right road, Madam. I've just chucked three quid overboard."

Mr. Chubb, my staff purser, was crossing on the ferry-boat from New Jersey to Manhattan one night and had rather a unique experience. Two gentlemen were standing close beside him at the rail of the ship and, as the ferry-boat approached New York, she passed quite close to where the *Berengaria* was berthed.

"Fine ship, that!" exclaimed one of the gentlemen, pointing towards my vessel.

It was then that the second fellow dropped a remark which made Chubb catch his breath.

"Yes, I happen to be Staff Purser aboard her," said the second fellow blandly.

Mr. Chubb awaited his opportunity, and then he approached the first speaker and asked if he could speak to him aside.

"Excuse me for butting in," whispered Mr. Chubb, "but that gentleman whom you are with has dropped a remark which I know to be a lie, and from the nature of it I judge that you are not very well acquainted. Is that so?"

"Right first time. That guy has been trailing me all day, for some reason best known to himself. But who are you? Are you a cop?"

"No, I'm not a cop," said Mr. Chubb. "I happen to be *the* Staff-Purser of the *Berengaria*."

The American let forth a loud roar of laughter.

"Say, this beats everything. Have you got a card on you?"

Mr. Chubb produced a card, and the American immediately marched over to his late companion and thrust the card in his hand.

"Say, you, Guy," growled the American, "fix yer lights on this card, will yuh! Then take the air, pronto!"

The bogus one gave a quick glance at the card then faded quickly away.

The world is indeed very small.

On one voyage we had Mr. Joseph Schincks, the film magnate, and his wife, Norma Talmadge, and when we reached New York a party of friends came aboard to meet them. Pearson, one of my bedroom stewards, who had attended to the Schincks, who had occupied the Prince of Wales' suite during the passage, was requested to show the visitors over the ship.

There was one extremely good-looking, chean-shaven gentleman amongst the party, and when they returned to the suite after the inspection, Schincks, turning to the former, said:

"I'll bet you a new hat Pearson has not recognized you."

The bet was accepted.

Schincks turned to Pearson. "You're an Englishman, aren't you, Pearson?"

"I'm a Cockney, sir!" said Pearson.

"A Londoner, good," said Schincks. He pointed towards the good-looking gentleman. "Take a look at this gentleman, Pearson. He is a world-famous Englishman, and at least half the world has seen his face."

Pearson took a good look.

"D'you recognize him, Pearson?" asked Schincks. "Have another look," he invited encouragingly.

Pearson had another look.

"No, sir," said Pearson, staring hard. "I don't know him from a crow.

Mr. Schincks slapped his leg delightedly.

"There you are, Charlie," he cried, addressing the

gentleman concerned; "without your whiskers, nobody believes you are yourself."

The good-looking gentleman was Charlie Chaplin.

Mr. Leonard Michils, the Director of the Travel Bureau aboard, comes up against a squall at times in the course of his duties. Incidentally, as this book of mine may prove of service to many potential ocean travellers, we will invite Michils to enumerate a few of the little jobs for which his department is responsible.

"As far as my duties are concerned," says Michils, "it seems sometimes as if I have to be able to answer every question under the sun. Passengers want to know how to get somewhere, which is the best way, how much will it cost, how long will it take to get there. Also, some may want to charter special aeroplanes to meet the ship, either for pleasure or to enable them to reach a destination quickly. Many may prefer a car, or a fleet of cars. It is my job to deliver the goods. Travelling towards England, I am the 'Imperial Airways,' westbound I act for the different American air lines. I also arrange the reservation of seats and special compartments on all trains meeting the ship, if requested, and in addition I attend to all passenger mail, parcels and telegrams.

"A few voyages back I was wading through a pile of letters and telegrams when a lady approached my counter. I had my back to her at the moment, and as I turned round, she said:

" 'Crookshank.'

"Now, I learnt later that this lady had just boarded the ship, and had approached me to enquire the number of her cabin. But concluding she was enquiring for letters, without looking up, I murmured: 'Mail?'

" 'No, female!' she snapped indignantly, and flounced off in high disdain.

"The words 'Information Bureau' inscribed above my office counter bring me a fair share of leg-pulling every voyage. 'Can you tell fortunes?' some bright young thing will ask. 'Do you read the Crystal?' others often enquire, or maybe a large open palm will be thrust under my nose with: 'Read my hand and tell me how many times I'm going to be married!'

"A gentleman, accompanied by his wife, was saunter-ing past my counter on a recent voyage when his eye caught the word 'Information.'

" 'Ah!' he said. 'You're the man I want to meet. "Information" is rather an expansive term. What can you tell me I do not know, young man?' he demanded lightly.

" 'You tell me what you know first,' I answered politely. 'Then I'll fill in the blanks.'

"His wife laughed loudly as she pulled him away.

" 'You asked for that,' she chuckled delightedly.

"On a recent world's cruise, passengers who wished to land at certain ports were issued with a form to fill up. The colour of these forms was pink. On one occasion I casually approached a lady whom I knew had been making enquiries about filling up this form, and said:

" 'May I have a look at your little pink form?'

" 'Oh! How dare you! How dare you!' she cried indignantly, and off she marched to the Purser and demanded my immediate annihilation, declaring I had indecently insulted her. The good lady was so upset that it was deemed advisable to alter the colour of the 'little pink forms' to blue.

"On our West-bound Track from Southampton to New York I receive frequent enquiries from European passengers as to the conditions of commercial air-travel in the U.S.A., and as I consider that sooner or later the world will become air-minded, perhaps the following may be of general interest:

"First of all, the tremendous speed at which the American commercial airplanes travel is an asset to the tourist passenger who wishes to see as much of the country as possible in a short space of time.

"If you can imagine attending the theatre in New York

City on your first night of arrival, then, after the show, motoring a few miles to an airport, being tucked into a comfortable airplane seat at midnight by an attractive stewardess, awakened at breakfast-time 1200 miles away from New York, followed later by a late luncheon on the Pacific Coast at Los Angeles, 2700 miles from New York, you can visualize the tremendous speed at which airplanes travel long distances in the Unites States.

"Or, if you choose another United Air Lines schedule, and are in a hurry to get to Australia, say, you can leave New York in the afternoon and be in Los Angeles or San Francisco or Seattle, the major seaports of the Pacific Coast in the United States, in time for breakfast the following morning.

"The United Air Lines fly machines of the twin-engined Boeings type, the same as Roscoe Turner and Clyde Pangborn flew with such distinction last October in the London-Melbourne race. These low-winged monoplanes, carrying 10 passengers, 2 pilots, and a stewardess, who serves meals aloft, have a top speed per hour of 202 miles, and a cruising speed of 189 miles per hour. Their most efficient altitude is about 10,000 feet because of their supercharged engines. The plane has a wing span of 74 feet and is 51 feet long. Fully loaded, it weighs approximately seven tons, and it can cruise 700 miles without refuelling.

"On the 2700-mile flight from New York to California the plane flies from sea level to 15,000 feet crossing the Rockies and the Sierras. On this 2700-mile flight, United planes stop at Cleveland, Chicago, Omaha, Cheyenne, and Salt Lake City. At each stopping-place a fresh crew takes charge.

"The scope of aviation in the United States is grasped when I say that United Air Lines alone flies 15,000,000 miles per year, requiring a fleet of fifty-five of these 200-mile-an-hour planes and a staff of 1400 employees.

"Because of this extensive flying, the pilots of these big transports have vast experience. One of the

stewardesses told me that of the 150 pilots employed by
United Air Lines on its coast-to-coast route, 50 of them
have flown a million miles each, and that the average
flying experience of all of the pilots was 7500 hours.

"The cost of flying is also much cheaper than in
England, the fare working out at about threepence per
mile, which is on a par with rail travel in the United
States.

"For long-distance night flying the American Government has lighted airways providing illuminated emergency
fields every thirty to fifty miles along the entire route and
a revolving 2,000,000-candle power beacon every 10
miles. To sit in a plane, flying at 3 miles a minute, and
look out and see the flashing beacons giving the pilot
just as sure a roadway as the motorist has on a lighted
boulevard, is indeed a thrilling experience.

"But that's not all! Airplane companies in the
United States have developed two-way radio communication to an exact science. All the way across America,
United Air Lines' pilots are in constant voice communication with ground stations spaced approximately 250
miles apart. The pilots of the plane in the cockpit wear
earphones. Through these they hear a steady hum
very much like the note of a dial telephone you hear
when you lift the receiver. That hum tells the pilots they
are flying directly on the sky highway. It comes from a
Government broadcasting station, one of the many
located along the route.

"Should the pilot veer to one side of the route, the
hum immediately changes to a dot-dash, and if the pilot
diverts to the other side, the hum changes to a dash-dot.
This sky highway which they travel is in truth fenced in
by radio, which even in fog makes flying possible and
safe.

"While the Americans have sacrificed part of the cabin
space that European travellers enjoy in order to provide
considerably more speed than Continental planes have,
the planes offer comforts which appeal to even the most

fastidious traveller. There are wide upholstered reclining
chairs in which one can get a good night's rest on long
flights, and letters may be written with ease, and meals
enjoyed in comfort. Surprisingly enough, Americans
spend most of the night on these long-distance hops
sound asleep, requiring to be aroused by the stewardess
at the infrequent landings. Delicious meals are provided
by the company free, and tipping is prohibited, which is
in line with the company's advertising, 'Your fare includes
everything.' A splendid chain of passenger depots dot
the airways.

"On the western trip you fly over the picturesque
Appalachians, look down on the huge industrial area
centring around the Great Lakes, with Chicago as the
hub city of the cross-country airways. Then the course
is over the great fertile plains called the 'bread basket'
of America until you reach the continental divide plateau
country, about 8000 feet above sea-level, with the
magnificent scenery around Salt Lake City; you continue westward over Salt Lake, the largest inland salt
sea in the world, and the desert, with a slight detour over
Boulder Dam, the mammoth lake constituting the greatest
engineering project in America. After a short flight over
the San Bernardino Mountains you suddenly glimpse
the great Los Angeles Valley and the remarkable city of
two million enterprising people. This is the terminus,
and, if you look at your watch, you will find that it has
required only a little over fourteen flying hours to fly
right across the mighty Continent of America; surely a
marvellous achievement."

So much for Mr. Michils, our Information man.

Now I must tell you a yarn in which I played a central
part only a few voyages back.

We were on our West-bound Track, *en route* for New
York, and quite early in the voyage Lady Broom,
Sir Ernest Bain, and Sir Hewitt Skinner and myself
made up a four at bridge. We played regularly after

dinner, for maybe a couple of hours during the first three nights at sea.

Then came carnival night, and the spirit of carnival was in the air when we sat down in the lounge for our usual game. Sir Ernest Bain and Sir Hewitt Skinner were partners and, at the end of one hand, which Sir Ernest had played, Sir Hewitt asked him:

"Why did you only call two tricks on that hand, Bain? Why not four, you could easily have got that number?"

"Why should I call four?" Sir Ernest retorted. "I called two, and if I get four, what difference does it make?"

Sir Hewitt didn't answer, we were getting ready to play another hand.

A few hands later Sir Ernest again had the call, and obtained five tricks over his contract.

"I say, Bain!" said Sir Hewitt earnestly, leaning over the table towards Sir Ernest. "Tell me, what game *are* you playing?"

"I'm playing bridge, of course," said Sir Ernest somewhat sharply. "What game d'you think I'm playing?"

"Yes, I know you're playing bridge, Bain, but what kind of bridge?"

"Auction bridge!" exclaimed Sir Ernest caustically.

We all laughed.

"I fail to see the joke!" said Sir Ernest, eyeing us severely.

Sir Hewitt again leaned towards him. "No, but we do," said Sir Hewitt suavely. "You see, Bain," he murmured quietly, "we happen to be playing *contract* bridge."

Sir Ernest jumped to his feet with a laugh.

"In that case I can go and dance," said he, "I don't even know the bally game. I've never played it in my life."

The next morning I chaffed him gently over this affair, but he had the last laugh.

"Well, at any rate, Commodore, you can't know so much about the game," he retorted. "You only found out by accident, after playing for three nights, that I was a dud," he added slyly.

Sir Ernest told me a couple of good yarns concerning a cruise which he made on the *Mauretania*. It was an exceptionally low-priced cruise, to Gibraltar and back for an inclusive sum of eight guineas, and I believe the first trip of the kind ever made by the famous vessel.

"When I got aboard, Commodore," Sir Ernest Bain told me, "I was surprised to find the ship crowded with Tynesiders.

"I approached one typical Geordie and I asked him: 'Why are there so many of your townies aboard, old chap?'

" 'Ay, lad,' he answered proudly, 'we built t'old ship, tha knows, an' it's first time we've ever been able tae afoord tae sail on her.'

"There were also several Lancashire men aboard her," Sir Ernest continued, "and I remember I was sitting next to one big fellow, who was slightly under the weather, when a steward approached and asked if he might bring him a bowl of soup and a few biscuits as he, the sick man, had had nothing to eat all day. No, the big fellow did not fancy either soup or biscuits.

" 'Is there anything at all that you fancy?' the sympathetic Steward enquired of him. 'We can supply you with anything you like on this ship,' the Steward added, somewhat proudly.

" 'Is that so, lad?' the big fellow murmured faintly.

" 'Yes, sir, anything, no matter what it is, I'll wager we have it aboard,' again declared the Steward.

"The big fellow pondered a minute, then:

" 'Aw reet, lad,' he said very gravely. 'Fetch me stick of Blackpool rock.' "

Mr. Duncan, my Chief Engineer, tells a good yarn about one of his junior engineers, which he swears is true. I'm not going to vouch for that, but still, it's a good yarn, especially when Duncan tells it in his own native Scotch.

Here it is:

"We named him 'Heather Jock,' Commodore, an mon, he was that Scotch ye cud see the heather growin' oot of his ears. But he was a braw engineer, tho', aye, he was that.

' In those days, Commodore, the engineers on the four to eight watch in the afternoon used to hae a meal o' sorts a'fore they went down inta the engine-room, an' I mind fine that was the first time I saw Heather Jock eatin'.

"Mon, he must hae come fresh frae the hills o' Scotland, for he had an appetite like a horse.

"I mind there was a big jar o' chutney left on the tea table frae dinner-time. I suppose the steward had forgotten to clear it awa'. At onyrate, Heather Jock got hold of it, sniffed at it suspeeciously for a second, and then he stuck his knife in the jar and commenced to spread it on his bread.

"We didna' take ower much notice of him to begin, but when furst one slice of bread and then another began to disappear, each slice covered thick wi' chutney, we cudna' help but stare at the laddie.

"After he'd feenished his tae, an' half the jar of chutney, I leaned over the table and said to him:

" 'Did you like that, Jock?'

"He gave his lips a bit lick wi' his tongue and did a gulp before he answered:

" 'Aye, it wasna' bad,' he said.

"Then he gave another big gulp and said, kinda confidential like:

" 'But, mon, dae ye ken (gulp), it's the hottest damned jam I've ever tasted in ma life.' "

During the present voyage, Mr. Allan K. Taylor, a Fleet Street scribe, promoted a short-story competition aboard, confined to members of the crew. He offered prizes for brief essays of either human or humorous interest, imposing the one restriction that the entries be yarns of the sea. The crew responded quite royally, but it is sad to relate that 99.9 per cent of the effusions sent in to Mr. Taylor were quite unfit for publication. There were a few gems, however, which contained a minimum of nautical expletive and invective, and Mr. Taylor, hearing that I was preparing this log, suggested that these might be included in this yarn.

I do so without apology, appending the entries verbatim, untouched by any other pen.

Mr. Rodgerson, the Ship's Writer, determined to win the first prize, sent in three efforts.

Here they are:

A Budding Financier

Some years ago, when small boys used to sell the daily papers outside the dining-room, a little lad, making his first voyage to sea, informed me that a gentleman had taken a paper at breakfast-time and had not paid him for it, and at dinner-time he pointed out the gentleman, and I told him to remind the purchaser at breakfast the following morning. Later that day I said to the lad: "Did you get paid for that paper?" and he replied: "I told the gentleman, and he gave me a shilling for myself —but *he did not offer to pay for the paper.*"

A Little Mixed

A small boy acting as telephone operator received a telephone message from the bridge that the Chief Officer would like to see the Surveyor. This occurred during the Board of Trade Survey, and, getting a little confused, you may imagine the perplexity caused when the following message was delivered: "The Chief Officer would like to see 'the survivors of the lifeboat on the bridge.'"

SIGNALS

Yet another small boy story. The lad was attending his first boat drill, and was asked by one of the Board of Trade officials what the ringing of the bell was the signal for. "Dinner, sir," was the prompt reply.

Webber, my deck steward, sent in two entries. One was most rudely censored by Mr. Taylor.

Here is the other:

HAUGHTY BILL

We had one Captain we named Haughty Bill. He was strutting up and down the promenade deck one day, all his gold braid and brass buttons and the four gold rings on his sleeves glittering in the sunlight, when a dear old lady, anxious to secure a chair, approached him and asked: "Are you the deck steward?"

Bill stared at her a moment then he asked:

"Do you really mistake me for the deck steward, Madam?" and before the lady could reply, Bill tapped his brass buttons, and waved one gold-braided cuff: "Then what the deuce d'you suppose the Captain looks like, Ma'am?" he demanded.

Dunsby, one of my bedroom stewards, sent in the following:

OVERHEARD WHILE SCRUBBING DECKS

Agitated old lady during fog:

"Steward, why do they keep blowing the whistle this morning?"

Harassed deck steward: "It's quite all right, Madam, we're only going under a tunnel."

OVERHEARD WHILE WASHING PAINTWORK

Deck-hand to mate after three tiring hours of washing paintwork:

"Don't you know any yarns, Mike?"

(Mike): "Why, sure, I'll tell you one.

"A few years ago I was on the . . ., a small passenger boat, and the only lady passenger on board would insist on leaning over the rail during a storm, and despite my warnings, she eventually got washed overboard."

"Really," said his mate (wide eyed).

"Sure," said Mike. "So I pulled off my belt, trousers, oilskins, deck boots, etc., and dived after her, but just as I reached her I espied a twenty-foot shark about to strike, so I immediately grabbed my knife from my belt."

"Hey! Hey!" said his mate, "you said just now you pulled all that off before you dived in."

"I see," said Mike, "you don't want to hear a yarn, all you want is a bluggy argument."

There are two gems from Charles Westbury, the second cook of the *Berengaria*.

THE FOUR-LEGGED GOOSE

On the *Lusitania* we used to give the firemen a whole goose between four men for their Christmas dinner. Some cooks chopped the wings off close, while others left the whole wings on, consequently some quartettes got a goose with big wings while others were not so fortunate. We sent the cooked birds down the lift from the galley to the men's mess-room, and suddenly a hoarse voice shouted from the depths below:

"Hi, cook—what's the (censored) game? Send down a goose with four legs same as the other sluggers have got."

A ROTTEN COOK

The new firemen's cook thought he'd give the men poached eggs instead of fried for a change.

The firemen's "Peggy" (the man who looks after their mess-room) saw the new cook preparing the eggs, and dashed back to the mess-room.

"What's up, mate?" all the men asked him in chorus.

"Coo, blimey!" gasped the agitated Peggy, jerking his thumb towards the galley. "He's some cook, he is—he's frying the (censored) eggs in water."

The next yarn comes from Hooper, another bedroom steward:

BLACKLISTED

We had a passenger who was barred from having drinks by the doctor for his health's sake—the passenger's health, I mean, not the doctor. . . .

Well, one day he (the passenger) was sitting very morose in the crowded smoke-room, sullenly watching others enjoying themselves. There were many drinks on the tables round about—gin, fizz, beer, whiskey, etc.—when suddenly whales were seen spouting in the water near the ship. Everybody made a dash for the port-holes, and when their backs were turned he (the passenger, not the doctor) made a dash for the drinks and swiped the lot.

The next entry comes from R. Fairminer, one of the engineers of the *Berengaria:*

THE TYRANT

There was once a senior engineer on board the *Mauretania* who was a strict disciplinarian, and consequently the junior engineers of his watch nicknamed him "The Tyrant."

He was an adept at finding hot jobs for his juniors, and it always seemed that the unfortunate who "went below" in a spotless overall was picked for the messiest jobs.

The juniors of this watch decided to give vent to their feelings by making an effigy, and calling it "The Tyrant." So at the end of a certain watch the juniors repaired to the overall locker, where lots of obsolete clothes, boots, caps, etc., accumulated.

There they made a faithful effigy, complete with mask, tow for hair, note-book in pocket, usual kerchief around neck, and a notice pinned on breast and in large letters was painted: "The Tyrant."

Highly satisfied with their efforts, they shouldered "The Tyrant" and slowly wended their way towards the ship's rail, chanting the while:

"One! Two!! Three!!! and over he goes!"

As "The Tyrant" struck the water the lads turned from the rail, and there, behold, was the tyrant himself.

He was doubled up with laughter.

The juniors didn't wait to explain.

One of the ship's waiters, F. Bahaire, supplies the next yarn.

OUR NAUTICAL SAILORS

It is customary upon the *Berengaria's* arrival at Cherbourg to drop anchor inside the Breakwater.

The following incident occurred on one such occasion.

It so happened that the carpenter, his mate and sailors were at their various stations, awaiting the commands of the Chief Officer for the operation in lowering the anchor.

"Avast heaving!" came the command of the Chief Officer to the carpenter, who in turn shouted the order, "Whoa!" to his mate manipulating the winch gears (the winch being operated on a lower deck).

The Chief Officer was heard to exclaim in the most pleasing manner: "All right you—you—ruddy agriculturist!"

Here is another entry by R. Fairminer, a ship's engineer:

THE HAUNTED SHIP

The following story concerns the *Mauretania*, and occurred in 1927.

The vessel was outward bound from Southampton to New York, and on the second day out a weird noise began to make itself manifest throughout the midship section of the ship. The noise was intermittent, and resembled a long-drawn wail, like some soul in torment. As the voyage progressed it grew worse; passengers shuddered and officers and crew were nonplussed.

Something had to be done. A general search in the engine department was ordered. Engineers and firemen were to be seen like bees, searching the boiler-rooms, trying valves, inspecting air-pipes from oil-fuel bunkers and double-bottom tanks, lashing and bolting every likely resonant fitting. There was excitement everywhere. Passengers bombarded the Purser for an explanation; none could be given. The groaning continued, and rewards were offered any person who could lay the "Menace," as it was called in the engine department.

New York was reached without having solved the mystery.

Homeward bound it recurred, and the staff became desperate.

It was evident, however, that the "Menace" was at its worst when the vessel rolled heavily; it was also evident that the ship had been thoroughly searched, it therefore left only the underwater hull to search.

On arrival in Southampton a diver was sent down to inspect the ship's bottom. He reported a portion of the bilge-keel carried away by some obstruction. The vessel was dry-docked. (The ship has a hollow bilge-keel made of teakwood, which runs down the port and starboard side of her bottom like fins.) A portion of the forepart of one side had carried away, allowing water to course into the hollow, between teak and ship's plates.

This was repaired, after which the "Menace" ceased its activities.

The following entry, which was awarded a prize, was sent in by a young assistant cook of the *Berengaria* named Edgar Hilton, who has not yet reached his twenty-third birthday.

It requires no comment.

Something Worth While

Amongst the criticisms of religion that I have heard is that it holds nothing for seamen, who are forced to work seven days a week, and who lose all contact with God. A few plain facts will soon prove this accusation false.

When I decided to give my life to Christ it was through the Oxford Group, and I soon realised from what I saw in them that if true Christianity means *anything* to a man it means *everything*, and people with whom one is in contact cannot fail to notice it and to be affected by it for the good.

I had long realised that there is in the hearts of men of every class a definite longing for and respect for God, an eternal reaching-up for the infinite, and that seamen are no exception to this. When it became known in the ship that I was studying for matriculation in my spare time at sea with a view to training for holy orders, men began to approach me and to confide in me, and I soon began to see under the tough hides of the men around me, and to see the gold hidden there and seldom seen by the casual observer. I was at first surprised to find that there was so much good lying dormant in them, due for the greater part to an inner religion that they were afraid or ashamed to admit to the outer world, for fear of being laughed at, but I realized that I could if I was willing, be useful to help them to bring out and develop it.

This, of course, was difficult. In the first place it meant keeping "up" to the scratch myself, for we were living together twenty-four hours a day and seven days a week throughout the greater part of the year, and the slightest fault soon showed up glaringly. Also the men were busy for many hours per day and, as I sleep in a twelve-berth room it is very difficult to get into intimate touch with men. I found, however, that men who were really sincere would be willing to go to any ends, stay up to any hour, or approach me in any circumstances in order to have a chat about the more serious things. The attraction was not, of course, me, but what I represent. One fellow whom I was teaching to play chess soon forgot the game in his eagerness to talk about more important things, and after several such talks he made a very definite decision for Christ.

One of the greatest points of contact is through my ability to distribute Bibles and Testaments given me by the New York Bible Society representative, and it is worth mentioning that although not all of the men will promise to read them themselves, most of them are eager to take them for their children and wives and for other relatives, and often to put me into close contact with them.

When other Oxford Groupers are travelling as passengers in the *Berengaria* I usually am able to get into touch with them and we are able to work together quietly amongst some of the men and even amongst the passengers. I have known a steward make a decision for Christ as a result of the Christian quality of life he saw carried out continually by the passengers on whom he waited. Another man told me that he never spent a happier trip than the one when he looked after "Hundred per cent Christians," and that they treated him so considerately he would be content to wait on them always. Such men are quite willing to accept for themselves what they see other people enjoying, but naturally enough they are not so ready to jump into a religion as drear and gloomy as many people interpret it.

We Christians are virtually responsible for much of the sin in this world, for we do not show in ourselves that Christ's Message really holds the answer to all the problems that beset us in this very earthly life. There is a Group of *three of us* at present in this ship who together are trying to do this. We meet almost every night to talk over any new problem that may occur and to compare notes on the day's portion of the Bible, to pray for anyone who needs help, or to discuss plans.

When ashore on either side of the water we regularly make many interesting contacts with other "teams." Although I regularly take complete charge of Church of England services in my home town (Cowes, Isle of Wight), I have never yet done so on the ship, but look forward to the day when there will be enough of us to hold a large voluntary service here.

This is by no means the only ship that has a religious party aboard. To mention a few, there are the *Majestic*, *Laconia* and *Ausonia*, and if one looks down the list of members of the Merchant Service Officers Christian Association one will see many more.

My "Parish" on the water does not include men alone, for there are among our contacts several women and also boys. The latter, however, are probably the most difficult to reach, for they are usually fresh from the Home atmosphere, and ready to enjoy their "fling," so that the least restraining influence is continually avoided. It needs a very great deal of tact for someone who has no definite authority over them to make any contact with the majority of them.

A really genuine representation of true Christianity cannot fail, however, to appeal to anyone, and if we can with God's Help prove our sincerity, we will increase daily and believe me, nothing is more vital or more worth while. It makes for a continual interest in life, and makes life worth living.

Since I began this another member of the crew has made a decision to throw in his lot with us, so we are now *four*.

CHAPTER XV

THE WONDERS OF THE BRIDGE

Aboard R.M.S. "Berengaria."
At Sea.

CAN you, my readers, wade through a comparatively dry chapter devoid of incident, that I
may describe some of the wonder mechanical
devices which are installed on the modern liner of
to-day? To ocean travellers, but more especially to those
who are somewhat timid of the sea, these devices should
be of first importance, for they have indeed reduced
ocean accident to a negligible quantity.

Space will allow me to deal only with a few.

First of all, then, we will describe the "Wireless or
Radio Direction Finder."

The transmission of wireless signals through hundreds
or thousands of miles of space is now so familiar to
most of us as to be taken for granted. That these same
signals, however, may be used to show the direction and
position of their origin, or conversely that of any station
receiving them, is not so widely known.

Most passenger ships nowadays carry a wireless
direction-finder or "radio compass," as it is sometimes
called. One of the most useful innovations since the
adoption of wireless as a safeguard to life and shipping
at sea, the direction-finder as a means of navigation is
comparatively new, even relatively to wireless itself.
It was used during the war for "spotting" (i.e. locating)
enemy submarines and warships, and its existence was

of necessity kept a secret, so that it was not introduced into the Merchant Service until after the war. Since then it has been greatly developed and is now in general use.

As its name implies, the direction-finder will indicate accurately the direction from which wireless waves are coming, that is to say, it can be made to point directly towards any wireless station which may be transmitting. By its use much of the danger accompanying fog is eliminated, since the exact position of the ship can be found when within a few hundred miles of land and, if necessary, the ship can be guided by it right to port through the thickest fog. It is also much used to locate nearby or approaching vessels in foggy weather, thus obviating the chances of collision.

In finding the position of the ship by wireless, two or three coastal wireless stations in known positions are selected, and by means of the direction-finder the bearings for angular directions (north being 0°, east 90°, and so on) of these stations from the ship are ascertained. The positions of the stations are marked on a chart, and then the bearings given by the direction-finder are laid off from their respective stations as straight lines. These lines should all cross at one point, which is the location of the ship on the chart. By taking a succession of bearings at intervals of say half an hour, the ship can be followed up on the chart accurately and so guided along even in dense fog.

It is not absolutely necessary, though extremely desirable in some cases, to have special sending stations for the purpose of fixing the ship's position, as any station which happens to be transmitting at the time may be used for this purpose ; if not transmitting, the station is called by the ship and asked to send signals for one minute for the ship to take bearings on it, and will always do so. The United States have given a lead, however, by equipping a number of the lightships and lighthouses round the coast with wireless sets, the sole purpose of which is to send signals to enable ships to take bearings on them in fog, and other countries are now following suit. It is probable that the establishment of wireless "fog-signals" will soon be standardised by international agreement.

All direction-finders as used at present utilise the receiving properties of a special form of aerial. This is the "loop," "frame" or "coil" aerial (to give it its various designations), the same as that with which many of the more elaborate broadcasting listening sets are equipped; indeed, any receiver of this type, suitably calibrated, is quite a useful direction-finder in itself.

The frame aerial possesses the property of receiving strongest signals if pointed towards the distant transmitting station, and when turned at right angles to this (i.e. to face the transmitting station) will give no signals at all. Such a loop (which is simply a coil of a few turns of wire), if pointed towards the transmitting station and then turned round slowly to face it, will give signals (via a suitably sensitive valve receiver) starting at maximum strength and dying away until they reach zero. If rotation is continued beyond this point, signals will reappear and rise to maximum strength again, when the loop has been turned through a half-circle. In practice the zero point is used since, when approaching this, signals die away very rapidly, making its position easy to determine. A pointer fixed to the axis of the coil turns round a scale marked in degrees and will, when zero point is found, indicate the direction of the transmitter.

All direction-finding is based upon the method outlined in the preceding paragraph, and many direction-finders use this actual procedure in practice. Most British ships use a modification of this "rotating loop" system, namely the "Bellini Tosi" or "crossed loop" direction-finder, named after its two Italian inventors. This employs two large loops crossing one another at right angles, which may be seen usually in the vicinity of the wireless room of the ship, either as very large single-turn loops (up to forty or fifty feet across) strung between upright posts, or in the later types as smaller loops of four or five turns inside a cage of wire. These loops are permanently fixed (i.e. they do not rotate), their function being to "collect" the wireless waves, so to speak, and reproduce them on a small scale inside a box about six inches square, by means of similar though very much smaller crossed loops inside this box, which forms part of the D.F. instrument in the wireless room. Inside this box is a tiny rotating loop a few inches across, with which the bearings are taken in the same way as with the large loop previously described, and read off on a small scale. One advantage of this is that the small loop is very light and easy to handle, but otherwise the two systems are identical in principle.

All large masses of metal have a deflecting effect upon wireless waves in their vicinity and so the ship tends to draw the waves along its length, and hence alter their apparent direction. This is corrected by suitable balancing or calibrating devices, which are adjusted for the particular errors when tests are made on fitting the direction-finder in the ship.

The rest of the instrument consists of an ordinary valve receiver, employing usually six to ten valves, for the receiving power of the loop aerials is very small, and it is necessary to use very high amplification of the signals to secure a direction-finding range of two to three hundred miles.

Another method of using direction-finding to find the position of the ship is the shore service, by means of which a ship not fitted for direction-finding may obtain her position from special direction-finding stations ashore. The procedure in this case is reversed, the ship sending the wireless signals and the stations ashore finding her direction. A large number of these are now in operation in nearly all countries, and are calibrated to a very high degree of accuracy. Sometimes both ways are used, one acting as a check to the other.

Next there is the Gyro Compass, and perhaps I should have given this wonder invention pride of place.

Look where you wish about the ship in which you may be travelling and it will be found that she generally represents a continuity of progress and constructive engineering. The hull is of steel, the propelling machinery may be Diesel; she is equipped with a most elaborate wireless plant and supplied with every conceivable device to give added comfort. Yet it remains a solid truth that the safety of the lives of the passengers and crew, and the care of the vast amount of wealth represented by the ship and cargo, ultimately depend on the application of the human mind to the direction given by the compass.

It is sometimes thought that wireless has revolutionized navigation. Its uncanniness fills one with awe. We see four or five masts in the vicinity of the operator's room —or perhaps a frame aerial—and we learn that it is the wireless direction-finder. Not unnaturally, we ask "What of the compass?" and it surprises us to find that the information obtained by wireless is only a direction with respect to the ship's line of progress which may be anywhere from the North to the South Pole. Consequently, as the art of navigation is primarily based on the knowledge of the direction of the magnetic or true meridians, the instrument which supplies that need is of paramount importance, since the accuracy of wireless bearings and everything else is subservient to it. Thus a ship cannot be up-to-date unless her first essential to safety—the compass—be in accordance with the most modern practice.

In retrospect it will be found that the compass has, until recently, utterly failed to march in time with improvements and changes made in every other branch of industry connected with ship construction and marine equipment. Every traveller is familiar with the magnetic compass—either in the form of a small pocket instrument or the 10-inch compass card which is found afloat. In both cases the principle is the same, so that either may have its north deflected from the magnetic meridian by means of a magnet, a pocket-knife, or any substance possessing even a small amount of magnetic energy. In this connection it is not generally realized that the process of riveting and hammering, which takes place during the period the ship is being built, actually induces magnetism into the hull, the funnel, ventilators and every piece of steel used in her construction; so that the whole vessel develops into a magnet of a complex nature and becomes a most disturbing factor to the mariner's compass.

To the late Lord Kelvin is due the respect of seamen for his labour in devising a scheme to eliminate, as far as possible, the errors arising from the iron and steel in the modern ship; so it happens that other magnets are employed in an artificial endeavour to compensate for the evil effects. It is true that by those means the errors are brought within manageable limits, but it remains a fact that whereas the magnetic compass was entirely suitable in the days of the "wooden walls of Old England," it is fundamentally wrong in principle for a vessel built of material which destroys and distorts the force by which it is expected to operate.

While it would be unjust to pass on to the subject of the gyro compass without giving recognition to the fact that the world has been discovered and charted by the aid of the magnetic compass, it is obvious that we cannot live on the past, but rather can we improve, and in that way have the scientist and engineer perfected a machine which gives to the sailor the direction of the true Pole by utilising forces which are entirely independent of the uncontrollable and varying magnetism inherent within the earth.

There are large and small gyroscopes, and the largest known to man is the earth on which we live. All gyroscopes are rotating bodies, and in the case of the earth, in addition to revolving about its axis, it also moves around the sun and describes a path known as its orbit. We know that during this bodily movement through space its axis continues to point in the same direction, for the reason that the North Star is always to be found over the North Pole. This can readily be seen by referring to an ordinary atlas, when, on looking at the map describing the solar system, it will be noticed that the angle of the earth's axis remains constant to the path traced by the movement of the earth round the sun.

This phenomenon is the first characteristic of the gyroscope, and in the case of the earth is responsible for the regulation of the seasons and the determination of the areas known as the tropics, the temperate and arctic zones. Its importance to us all will be appreciated, because any failure of this peculiar property of the earth would result in a mix-up of the seasons, when the frozen area of the polar regions might move round to Equatorial Africa. So, in order to prevent any such disturbing situation, it is necessary that the earth should keep on spinning and also that its axle should maintain its direction in space during its annual voyage round the sun. When this peculiarity of the earth is appreciated, it will be seen that since a compass is nothing more than an indicator of direction so the earth's axis becomes a compass; and it was left to Leon Foucault, in 1852, to reproduce these properties of the earth in the form of a model gyroscope.

It can well be imagined that many difficulties arose, and one of the principal factors to be taken into consideration was to arrange a wheel so that it could be free to move in space, irrespective of the stand which supported it. This was overcome by mounting the wheel in gimbal rings in a manner similar to the old-fashioned oil lamps used in ships, which permitted a vessel to roll and pitch while the upright position of the lamp was more or less maintained.

By the use of these gimbal rings the gyro wheel is free to turn about its own axle, free to move about both a vertical and horizontal axis, or, in other words, the wheel and the axle can be moved in any direction without disturbing its medium of support. Thus, if a properly balanced wheel is mounted in this way and set spinning with the axle pointing to, say, the bright star Sirius, it will continue to do so provided the rotation of the wheel is maintained. As the star approaches the zenith so the axle of the gyro wheel will tilt upwards with respect to the surface of the earth and in the direction of the star.

The model gyroscope instead of being supported is suspended, and the wheel is contained in a case. There is also added on each side a box containing mercury with a connecting pipe between them and an arm to the bottom of the case. It is the flow of mercury from one side to the other that is the controlling force which causes the axle of the wheel to take up a position in the same plane as the true meridian, and to point to the North Pole.

If this same model was set spinning in a room with the axle pointing to a clock on the mantelshelf the observer would find that six hours later it would be pointing to the ceiling; in another six hours to the door opposite to the clock, then to the floor, and at the end of twenty-four hours it would be back at its original starting position facing the clock. At first it would be thought that the gyro had moved, but that is not so, and the reason is apparent, because the room—being attached to the earth—revolves with the earth. Thus the French scientist bewildered all the members of the Royal Society when he demonstrated the rotation of the earth and the phenomenon of "rigidity in space" by the aid of his model gyro; and it became obvious that once a means was found to keep the gyro wheel spinning continuously the experimental model of Foucault would take practical form in the shape of a compass, depending for its direction-giving qualities on the rotation of the earth.

Something had to be done to make the gyro always seek

a definite direction because, as then constituted, it would continue to point in the direction in which it was set; and one's imagination does not have to be vivid to see that a force would disturb it, when a new direction would be maintained until such time as another force was applied.

This brings us to the second characteristic of the gyroscope, which is called "precession," and is the name given to the peculiar movement which takes place when a force is applied to it. It is readily explained by considering the case of a boy's hoop rolling rapidly along a straight path which, provided it is untouched, continues on a straight course when its imaginary axis more or less exhibits "rigidity in space." If the boy, running behind it, wishes to make the hoop go off to the left he does not push the front part from the right nor the back part from the left, but applies a force on the right at the top; that is to say, the hoop, instead of falling over as it would do if it were not rotating, turns at a right angle to the direction in which the force was applied. It is the same in the case of a man riding a bicycle; if the rider leans to the left the machine turns to the left, but does not fall over. This precessional movement is used for making the gyro axle turn into the true meridian.

Let us go back to Leon Foucault's model and put the wheel in a case, suspend it, and add a couple of little boxes—one on each side, connected by a pipe—and partially fill them with mercury. For purposes of explanation we will assume that the wheel is set spinning at sunrise, with its axle pointing to the sun so that it is horizontal with the earth's surface and pointing east. Under those conditions the mercury will be distributed equally in each box and nothing will happen. However, as the earth rotates so the sun will apparently rise above the horizon and our gyro axle—still pointing to the sun —will tilt upwards with respect to the earth. Now it will be seen that one mercury box is higher than the other, and the mercury, acting under the law of gravitation, will

flow from the high to the low side, which will result in a
force being applied to the gyro similar to the force
applied by the boy to the hoop, and the gyro instead of
falling in the direction in which the force is acting will
turn about its vertical axis. This movement will continue until the axle is horizontal again and the action of
gravity will cease, when it will be found that the axle is
in the same vertical plane as the earth's axis. Thus the
gyro axle will give a true north and south indication,
and although a disturbing force will cause it to leave the
true meridian temporarily the action of gravity will cause
it to return to its only resting position.

With the advance in science generally, and electricity
in particular, it happened a few years prior to the World
War that Anschutz and Sperry produced their first
electrically driven gyro compasses. Both based their
efforts on the discovery of the Frenchman and, although
the underlying principles were identical, the manner in
which each approached the subject resulted in two
entirely different pieces of apparatus. Anschutz used a
small wheel which was driven at the enormous speed of
30,000 revolutions per minute, while Sperry adopted the
wise course and utilized a heavier wheel weighing
approximately 50 lbs., which was rotated at a rational
speed of about 6000 revolutions per minute.

The practical gyro compass of to-day is nothing more
nor less than an accurate electrical machine designed to
give the direction of the geographical pole by utilizing
the rotation of the earth combined with the controlling
force of gravity. That part of the equipment is called
the master gyro compass, which is usually to be found
somewhere accessible to the navigating bridge, but not
in a position exposed to the weather. It may be regarded
in the same light as an electric master clock which
operates time dials in the lounges, smoke-rooms and
elsewhere, for the master compass controls repeater compasses on the bridge, in the captain's quarters, in the
wireless room, and such other positions as required.

The principal navies of the world started to adopt the gyro compass in 1912, but it was not until 1919 that the *Aquitania* led the way in the Merchant Service by being supplied with a Sperry gyro compass equipment. Since that time the number of ships using gyro compasses has steadily increased; and, as the real advantages of the true north compass become fully appreciated, there will be few shipowners who will fail to realize that the safety of a ship still depends more on the accuracy of the compass than anything else. There are no errors, it is unaffected by the movement of the ship, it has nothing to do with magnetism, and therefore is the only ideal compass for a modern steel ship.

The Sounding Machine is an instrument that enables the navigator literally to feel his way along the ocean floor, and is one of the most important aids to safe navigation that we possess. It consists of a drum holding 300 fathoms of very strong thin wire, which has a breaking strain of about one ton. The drum is fitted with a friction brake on the flat sides, which, when in the "off" position, allows the drum to revolve freely, thus unwinding the wire as the lead drops to the bottom. When bottom is reached the brake is applied, which clamps the drum to a cog-wheel, that is driven by a small electric motor for winding in. The wire is led from the drum out to the end of a spar about 25 feet long, called the sounding boom, the object of this being to prevent the lead and wire from getting foul of the ship's propeller. The "lead" itself weighs 28 lbs. and has a cavity in the bottom end about $1\frac{1}{2}$ inches in diameter. This cavity is filled to overflowing with a mixture of white lead and tallow, soap, or other sticky mass, the protruding part being smoothed and rounded off with the palm of the hand.

This is called "arming the lead," and the object of it is that when the lead hits the bottom a sample adheres to the arming and is brought to the surface.

Fastened to the wire, a few feet above the lead, is a brass cylinder about 2 feet long with a detachable cap at the top end. This cylinder is perforated to allow free access of sea water, and it is purely a protecting case for the glass tube that fits into it. This hollow glass tube is 2 feet long, sealed at one end, and has a bore of one-eighth of an inch. The inside of it is coated with chromate of silver, giving it a reddish-brown colour. Every time a sounding is to be taken a new tube is inserted in the cylinder, which is carried down to the bottom with the lead.

The deeper it goes, the greater the pressure of the water that forces its way into the tube, and in so doing the chemical action of the sea water on the chromate of silver turns it white as it creeps up the tube. When bottom is found the lead and tube are hove up to the surface, and the tube is laid on a boxwood scale marked in fathoms. This shows immediately, at the cut between the red and the white, how many fathoms deep the lead has been. The amount of wire that runs out when taking a cast of the lead has nothing to do with ascertaining the depth, and of course it varies according to the speed of the ship. There is a dial on top of the machine that indicates how much wire is out, but this is merely to prevent the officer from letting it all run off the drum and so lose the whole contraption. The speed of the ship and the weight of the lead cause the wire to be fairly taut as it runs out, and the officer who is taking the cast feels the wire for bottom with a metal hook called a "Feeler" by resting it with a slight pressure on the wire as it runs out. When the lead hits the bottom the wire slackens momentarily, and he knows he has got bottom. He then applies the brake gently, turns on the "juice," and heaves in.

When it reaches the surface the Quartermaster pulls it in from the end of the boom, removes the tube carefully from the case, slices off the bottom of the arming, and takes them up to the bridge for the Captain's inspection.

With this machine it is possible to get a sounding at a depth of 100 fathoms with a ship going 20 knots, and the whole operation can be done by two men in less than five minutes. What a difference to the old sailing-ship days, when it took the whole of the watch on deck, say seven or eight men, half an hour at least, and they had to stop the ship to do it. In those days they used small hemp line instead of wire and they had no patent glass tube to show the depth. Instead, the line was marked every 10 fathoms by bits of spun yarn with knots in them, and the depth was measured by the amount of line that was out. First of all the ship was stopped by means of backing the main yards, then the lead and line would be passed forward on the weather side and each man of the watch would stand at intervals along the rail with a coil of a few fathoms of line in his hand. The Mate would be on the poop with the line in hand a little short of the anticipated depth, and at the order "Heave!" from him the man forward would cast the lead into the sea. As the lead sank each man would, in turn, allow his coil to slip through his fingers, feeling at the same time for possible bottom, and as his coil was about gone he would call in a peculiar sing-song voice: "Watch, there, watch," as a signal to the next man to take up the sounding. Finally it would come along to the Mate, who would allow the remaining line to run out till he felt bottom, when he would jig it about up and down to make sure and then give the order to hoist away, having first noted the depth by the nearest mark on the line. It was then put in a block and the watch would tail on and pull it in hand over hand. On a dirty cold night, with numbed fingers, and the water from the dripping line trickling down your sleeves, this was the sort of job that made you wonder why in the world you ever went to sea.

But to return to modern methods, let us examine for a few moments the use the captain makes of his soundings. First of all it should be explained that all charts, and especially those showing the approach to land and har-

bours, are covered with small figures showing the depth
in fathoms at low water, and also here and there letters
or groups of letters showing the nature of the bottom.
It may be gravel, small stones, shells, mud, yellow or
grey sand, sand with black specks, and so on. All these
soundings and information are obtained by Government
surveys. In clear weather, steaming along the coast, the
captain can always keep track of his ship's position by
means of bearings and angles of the various points of
land and lighthouses he passes, and so make allowance
for any abnormal set of tide or current that may place his
ship in danger. In thick weather he is deprived of these
aids and so commences sounding at short intervals,
usually every half-hour or hour, as prudence demands.
A course line is then drawn on a piece of tracing paper
and the depths, etc., as obtained, are marked on it at the
correct distance apart in accordance with the scale of
the chart in use. When several have been plotted in this
way the tracing paper is laid over the area on the chart
where the ship is supposed to be, and a little juggling
about with it amongst the corresponding figures on the
chart will soon indicate whether the ship is being
set inshore or off shore, or whether she is ahead or astern
of reckoning. This method is termed using a "line of
soundings." In very shallow water, when the ship is
going slow, such as approaching an anchorage, the hand
lead and line is used. The leadsman stands on a small
projecting platform called the "chains," below the bridge.
The lead weighs 7 lbs. and is swung backwards and
forwards several times in order to cast it as far as possible
in the direction in which the ship is moving, so that by
the time it reaches bottom the line is vertical and a good
up and down cast is obtained. The line is marked at
2, 3, 5, 7, 10, 13, 15, 17 and 20 fathoms in such a way
that the leadsman can tell the depth by feeling the mark
on a dark night. If he gets a sounding of seven fathoms
he sings out to the bridge: "By the mark seven." If he
gets a sounding by eight, where the line is not marked,

he sings out: "By the deep eight." It was this method of reporting soundings that prompted Samuel Clemens to adopt his ever-famous pen name "Mark Twain."

The greatest contribution to the art of navigation which has been presented to the maritime world during the past decade is the Submarine Signal Fathometer, a depth-measuring apparatus developed and manufactured by the Submarine Signal Corporation, of Boston, Massachusetts. The invention of the fathometer by Professor R. A. Fessenden, of the Submarine Signal Corporation, was based upon experiments conducted by him on board the United States revenue cutter *Miami* during International Ice Patrol duty in 1914. The vital importance of an efficient sounding apparatus, and the necessity for its use when "on soundings," can hardly be exaggerated, and the increasing size and speed of modern vessels demanded something more rapid and accurate than the sounding machine just described. The evidence of the need for improvement in the methods of safeguarding navigation to prevent strandings is shown in the records of marine disasters. During 1926 *Lloyd's Register of Shipping* reports that 146 ships of approximately 234,000 tons gross, conservatively estimated at a value of £5,000,000 exclusive of cargoes, were total losses due to stranding. It will therefore be realized that it is the continuous desire of all navigators to obtain the most efficient means of keeping themselves informed at all times of the depth of water under the keel of the ship, and thereby determine their position or bearing in relation to the course which is being followed on the chart.

The fathometer amply fulfils this urgent need. The apparatus consists of three distinct parts: a fathometer indicator with an accompanying amplifier, an oscillator (sound producer), and a hydrophone (sound receiver). The fathometer indicator controls the emission of sounds from the oscillator, receives the electrical impulses produced by the impact of the returning sound echo upon the hydrophone, and translates the time interval between the emission of the sound and the reception of the echo into an indication of depth, by means of flashes of light on the fathometer dial. The amplifier is essentially a relay, which transforms the sound echoes transmitted by the hydrophone into electrical impulses of sufficient strength to cause flashes in the neon tube, which acts as a luminous pointer, indicating the depth on the dial. The above-mentioned apparatus is situated in some convenient position on the bridge of the vessel. The oscillator is situated in the bottom of the ship, and in contact with the shell plating. It delivers loud, short sounds of great intensity, usually one every three seconds. The sounds travel to the ocean bottom beneath the ship, and are reflected upwards, striking the hull of the vessel and being caught by the hydrophone, from whence they travel up to the amplifier. The performance of the apparatus is based on the fact that sound travels through water at the rate of 4800 feet, or 800 fathoms, per second. A stop-watch, started at the instant a sound is made under water and stopped at the instant the sound echo is received, would in a quarter of a second indicate that the sound had travelled 200 fathoms. This, however, would only indicate a depth of 100 fathoms, as it must be borne in mind that the sound travels there and back in the time given. The type of fathometer that is installed in all the great passenger vessels is capable of indicating depths of from 5 to 130 fathoms. It can be set in operation by simply turning a switch, and will continue to give accurate soundings every three seconds for as long as may be desired, regardless of the speed of the vessel, the nature of the bottom, or weather conditions. It seems unquestionable that the fathometer is destined to save countless lives and hundreds of valuable ships.

In addition to the wonder devices described above there are a thousand-and-one other gadgets too numerous to detail. For instance, there are fire-alarm bells at practically every few yards throughout the ship and, in the rare event of fire, each separate alarm independently rings a loud gong on the bridge, and an indicator shows the exact location where the alarm has originated. The organization for dealing with fire can be set in motion almost instantaneously with the ringing of the alarm. In case of collision an electric device operated from the bridge closes instantly all watertight doors throughout the vessel. Telephones communicate with all parts of the ship, operated through a central exchange.

In conclusion it may be said that the bridge is the nerve centre of the vessel, and the officer on watch, with his finger constantly on the pulse, is in touch with everything that matters for the safety and comfort of the passengers.

CHAPTER XVI

A FLOATING PALACE

Aboard R.M.S. "Berengaria."
At Sea.

YOU, my readers, have heard much of the *Berengaria* in this long yarn of mine, and yet, although my story draws to a close, I have not yet thought fit to describe the Big Girl in any sort of detail. Allow me to do so without further delay. Let me show you a glimpse of the wonder ship which it is my privilege to command, and at the end of the visit maybe we shall find time to describe life aboard during an ordinary mail and passenger voyage from Southampton to Cherbourg, and New York and back.

Permission can always be obtained from the Cunard White Star to inspect the *Berengaria*; and at Southampton, prior to every voyage, parties of visitors are regularly conducted over the vessel. I should imagine that the expectant visitor gets the first thrill on beholding the wonderful square on "E" Deck, exposing to view as it does the great width of the ship, its alcove facing the twin lifts, and its beauty of decoration. That thrill must turn to amazement on entering the Swimming Pool on this deck. The effect of many softly shaded lights sparkling on the water, the dainty dressing rooms, the shower baths, and the mosaic decorations, are enchantingly inviting and very beautiful.

Wending your way down the steps to the water-level and passing beneath an entrance way, hidden wonders are discovered—Turkish Baths, Electric Sea Baths, Rest Rooms, Massage Rooms, all on a sumptuous scale.

Emerging from the Swimming Pool and crossing the Square, one enters the Main Dining Saloon (first class). On approaching the far end one sees the Balcony Section above, and with the beautiful dome overhead, a comprehensive view of its size is obtained. Even then one does not realize that no less than 815 first-class passengers can be seated at once.

Passing up the Main Companionway or Staircase a veritable galaxy of floral decorations strikes the eye, while the staircase itself is reminiscent of the old ancestral halls of England. As we traverse its beautifully carpeted steps the ship's offices come into view—the Purser's and Chief Steward's staffs always busy at work, and the Passenger Office and Information Bureau, prepared to deal with every kind of query.

We reach the Upper Promenade Deck and visit the ideal Ball Room, which, combined with the Palm Court, is one of the most exquisite of recreation rooms. Here, amid an atmosphere of palms, the orchestra performs for the benefit of the ever-ready crowd of happy dancers.

Reaching the Boat Deck we climb to the Sun Deck, where deck games are such a prominent feature of the daily round of enjoyment in the life of a passenger. Here famous athletes like Helen Wills, Gertrude Ederle and Jack Dempsey have kept themselves fit with general sports, the conditions being ideally run in combination with the Gymnasium just below, another feature of the ship, and fitted with every kind of device for the training of the athlete. The massive funnels are a source of wonderment to the visitor, who eagerly searches for a comparison with a smaller ship.

Whilst on the Boat Deck the magnitude of the lifeboats and their number is invariably commented upon, and many are the questions asked. The guide explains the life-saving system, and points out how every member of the crew is detailed to a boat, the routine to be followed, the regular drills, and the wonderful percentage of holders of lifeboat efficiency certificates; a tribute to the instruction

THE SWIMMING POOL

THE PALM COURT
R.M.S. *BERENGARIA*

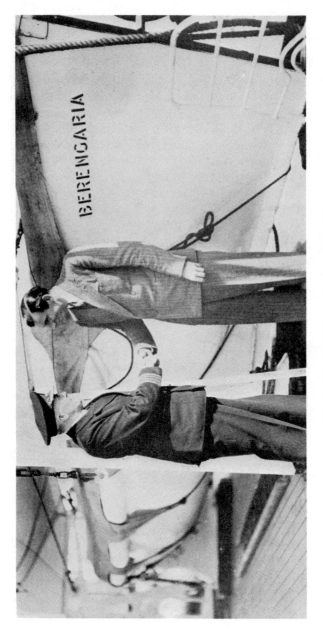

SIR EDGAR BRITTEN AND FRED PERRY

"Good luck, Fred. I hope you win the championship again this year."

imparted to all with a certain period of service by the navigating officers of the ship, who help the men to pass the necessary Board of Trade examinations.

Passing forward, we enter the Smoke Room, a perfect example of English architecture of the Tudor period, the furniture all covered with tapestry, the big open fireplace, the old-fashioned system of lighting, the magnificent decorative work on the panels, the distorting glass in the thousands of miniature panes (originally used before curtains came into vogue so that privacy could be obtained from the inquisitive.) All lend an air of peacefulness and perfect taste.

Outside the Smoke Room one peers over the balustrade of the forward staircase to a depth of six decks, and visualising her eleven decks sees approximately half the depth of the ship, an awe-inspiring spectacle.

Arriving back on the Promenade Deck there is from this location a perfect view of the amazing promenade, exactly five times round to the mile, and sufficient to provide exercise for the most energetic.

We then enter the Library and Reading Room, softly lighted and richly furnished, well stocked with the latest books and magazines, and enter the Main Lounge, one of the finest rooms on any ship in the world, with a magnificent dome. The most wonderful thing in the room—to use an Irishism—is the entire absence of any pillar support, the complete open space making the enormous size of the room the more noticeable. Filled with little tables and easy chairs, with beautiful tapestries on the wall, the room is replete with every conceivable charm, and the photo of the Prince of Wales which adorns the highly decorative panelling at one end is a souvenir of the wonderful trip His Royal Highness made aboard the *Berengaria* in 1924.

At the other end of the Lounge we have a splendid orchestral platform surrounded by flowers—a gardener is kept on board specially for the floral work—and on this platform nearly all the leading artists of the world have given their services and talent for the benefit of seamen's charities.

Adjacent to the Lounge is a Kiosk for the sale of cigars, chocolates and books, and opposite one sees the shields and trophies held by the Club and its members in the athletic world, for their prowess in which they are justly celebrated.

Descending to "A" Deck we view the two Imperial suites, representing the last word in luxury, each containing an open veranda, two bedrooms, two sitting-rooms, private bathrooms and its own pantries. To-day these suites are popular with prominent people in the business world, and particularly those in the film industry, and they are seldom unoccupied.

Apart from these suites there are many smaller ones, all full of infinite charm, while the spaciousness of the state rooms is a feature of the *Berengaria*. Over four hundred rooms have hot running water in addition to the cold supply.

Wending our way through the Balcony of the Dining-Room, which we have already seen from below, we enter the second-class accommodation; and ascending to "B" Deck we find ourselves in the Annexe to the Lounge. Here dancing takes place nightly to the music of their own orchestra. The Lounge itself is a great surprise to visitors, for it ranks with first-class accommodation in many ships. At each side of the far end are little writing-rooms, and there is a splendid library for the use of passengers.

Across the passage is another wonderful room, the Smoke Room, replete with its own bar and every comfort. Leaving the second-class accommodation for the moment, we survey the tourist and third-class rooms, each with its own conveniences for washing. The deck space is very ample, there are a ladies' dainty retiring-room, smoking-room; and the dining-room, with its floral decorations and settees, is most inviting. The kitchen and pantry in this class are inspected, and we cross the deck.   After an inspection of second-class state rooms, which bear comparison with anything on the high seas, we delve into the second-class dining-room just below and see a splendid saloon, with accommodation for 350. People find it difficult to believe it is second class and not first.

We journey past the second-class kitchen and pantry, all gleaming with polished covers and stoves, and return through the first-class kitchens.   On the way we see the butcher's shop, the confectioners' shop, and the bakery with its electric ovens, store-rooms for glassware, the ice-cream plant (always an item of interest), the salad and fruit rooms, and the immense kitchen which can cope with over eight hundred orders at once.   The pantry, with its special divisions for coffee and tea service; a still-room for milk, butter, cheese, etc., and its ice boxes, and the hot presses from which everything is served direct to the passenger in the dining saloon; are always a source of delight to the lady visitor.

The first-class accommodation is over 850, with 750 second class and 1500 tourist and third class, plus a crew of 1000 hands, and you will find that, on occasion, there are sometimes more than 3000 souls aboard.

So much for the vessel.

At sea there is never a dull moment aboard.   Games of all kinds, dances, fancy-dress balls, organized lotteries and cinema and concert shows, make the trip one continuous round of enjoyment.   For those who want rest and quiet there are the smoke room, the library, and a thousand and one secluded nooks where absolute peace may be secured.   It is part of the executive officer's duties —the Staff Captain—the Purser and the Chief Steward among others, to organize little cocktail parties and other functions for the purpose of drawing happy groups of passengers together, so that the least timid or shy may not feel out of the fun.   Refreshments of all kinds may be obtained at all hours of the day and night.

The fancy-dress ball is probably the most popular

feature on board ship, and one or two prizes are always given for the most original costumes concocted on board. Although the event has been advertised for days beforehand, the choice of a costume is usually left till shortly before dinner on the stated night, when the ship suddenly becomes alive with excited people wondering what they shall wear. This belated activity might be termed the "carnival spirit" in more senses than one. To give a list of costumes that can be devised on board would be to spoil the fun of the fair, but a list of helpful articles that can be obtained on every ship, and the most likely people to obtain them from, is given below, and from it you may hit on an idea which, with the aid of a little ingenuity, may prove a winner.

From the Officers: Flags, strips of red, white, blue and yellow bunting; coloured thread and needles for sewing same; oilskin coats; sou'westers; seaboots; white duck suits; brass buttons; uniform caps; telescope; whistles; revolvers.

From the Purser: Coloured inks; cardboard; twine; printed notices; paste; glue; paper fasteners; crayons; baggage labels.

From the Doctor: Cotton wool; adhesive tape; Red Cross badge; nurse's cap.

From the Chief Steward: Linen; towels; curtains; table covers; trays; empty bottles; bottle straws; brushes; ship's biscuits; goblets; curtain rings.

From the Boatswain: Rope yarns (for combing into wigs, beards, etc.); lanterns; canvas; broom handles; lifebuoys; burlap; jerseys; knives; sailor's caps; thin wire for stiffening; silver and other paints.

From the Barber: Fancy coloured paper; hair ornaments; jewellery; slippers; hats; walking sticks; bathing costumes; pipes.

Note.—A lady's black silk stocking pulled on the head and twisted makes a good Chinese pigtail. Burnt cork is a good method of blacking one's face and is easily washed off. A round tray covered with a flag makes an excellent shield. Curtain rings make splendid Oriental earrings. Wonders can be worked out of cardboard and paper fasteners.

Every day the ship covers a certain number of miles, and the Auction Pool, which is based on the ship's run, is a great event in the daily round.

The method of running this pool is as follows: Twenty passengers form themselves into a committee and pay one pound, or five dollars into the pool. Twenty numbers are selected, allowing ten each side of what the probable run of the ship is expected to be. For an expected run of 575 miles the numbers selected would run consecutively from 565 to 584. These numbers are then written on slips of paper, rolled up and drawn from a hat or box, each member getting one number. At night, after dinner, when the bidding is likely to be fast and furious, all these numbers are put up for auction, anybody being allowed to bid, whether they are members or not, but a member has this privilege: that if he bids, say, £30 for a certain number and it is knocked down to him, he gets a rebate of half that sum from the pool. A non-member would have to pay the full price, £30. After the twenty numbers have been auctioned, if any members have not secured numbers, they automatically drop out of the committee and those non-members who have bought numbers and, incidentally, paid full price for them, take their places and enjoy the privileges of the rebates on the next day's pool. In addition to the twenty numbers two other chances are sold, viz. "high field" and "low field." In this instance, if the ship ran anything over 584, "high field" would win, and if she did anything below 565 "low field" would win. Everybody has to pay full price for either of the "fields." Should the ship run into dense fog, "low field" stands a good chance of winning. It is always a popular chance off the Banks of Newfoundland. On the other hand a good Gulf Stream with the ship bound east and "high field" stands a good chance. A good auctioneer with a glib tongue and a few choice nautical expressions can usually boost the pool up to several hundreds of pounds and it has been known to touch a thousand.

In addition to the Auction Pool, small groups of passengers band together and form what is termed a Decimal Pool. This is a simple pool that can be quietly arranged amongst ten people who do not care for the excitement of the smoking-room auction. Ten numbers are drawn for—o to 9—and whoever holds the number corresponding to the last figure in the day's run is the winner.

The day's run is decided each day at noon by the Captain as soon as the noon position is obtained. In clear weather this is done by means of observations of the heavenly bodies, in which case it is called the "observed position." In thick weather when observations cannot be taken the position is calculated as nearly as possible by using the total number of revolutions of the ship's propeller since the previous noon and allowing for "slip," or using the distance run by patent log, or by soundings if in shallow water. A position obtained in any of these ways is termed "dead reckoning." Therefore, supposing the day's run should be 584, the person holding the unit 4 would win the Decimal Pool.

Then we have another sport at sea which may surprise those who have never made an ocean voyage. This is no other than horse racing, and the ever-increasing popularity of these meetings shows in no small degree that the "sport of kings" has lost little of its magnetism. Oceanic races are very simple to run, and the enthusiasm of those attending amply repays for any time or trouble expended upon them.

The following rules will give a general idea of the way marine horse-racing is conducted :

1. There are six horses in each race.
2. Horses are numbered from 1 to 6.
3. Winners will be paid on the pari-mutuel system,

after 10 per cent has been deducted for seamen's charities.

4. If your horse wins, proceed to the cashier, who will pay you your winnings.

5. Tickets are sold for one shilling or 25 cents each.

6. Tickets for each race are of a different colour.

7. Two dice are used for flat racing and three for hurdle racing.

General Method.

The course is chalked out on the open deck (very often the sun or boat-deck), and is in most cases of a circular or horse-shoe shape. It is divided into 25 or more sections. Six wooden horses are placed on the first section in readiness for the race to begin, and the deck sailor is generally appointed to move the horses along the course. The Purser selects a lady to come forward to throw the dice, the method of throwing being from a container into a megaphone on to a table, to ensure an accurate casting.

Time is up and the bookmakers, usually ladies, are requested to cash in their money and tickets to the cashier, who, while the race is in progress, is busy checking tickets and money and calculating the odds on each horse in the race—ready to "pay out" immediately the race is concluded.

As soon as the bookmakers have left the course, the bell rings and the dice are thrown. Upon lifting the megaphone, numbers 5 and 2 are shown. "Five and two" cries the Purser, and a cheer is raised by those holding tickets for these horses, and so on until the race is over.

The difference between flat racing and hurdle racing is that three dice are used for the latter, and when a horse is on the section immediately preceding a hurdle, two dice showing its number must be thrown to allow it to get over the fence. Great excitement prevails when an apparently winning horse is checked at a fence and an "also ran" moves slowly up to an even place.

Given a pleasant day and a good quota of people, horse-racing is unanimously declared to be the "king of sports" on shipboard as it is the "sport of kings" ashore.

Pari-mutuel (Fr.), or mutual betting, is the system adopted on shipboard at race meetings. It is sometimes styled the totalization system, and is very simple to understand.

We will suppose that there are six horses in the race and each bookmaker has one hundred and fifty tickets to sell for the horse she is boosting. When the bell rings the bookmakers take their tickets to the cashier, and the result may be as follows:

No. 1 Horse	70	tickets sold
No. 2 Horse	80	,,
No. 3 Horse	40	,,
No. 4 Horse	65	,,
No. 5 Horse	105	,,
No. 6 Horse	85	,,
Total	445	
10% deduction for seamen's charities	45	
No. 2 Horse wins	80)400(5	
	400	
	. . .	

Therefore, backers of No. 2 horse receive five shillings for each ticket they have purchased.

Next there is deck tennis, and as this is by far the most popular game and form of recreation aboard, for the benefit of those contemplating a sea voyage, I will describe it at length. Those of my readers not interested are advised to skip a few pages.

The ideal dimensions of a deck tennis court are 34 feet long, 14 feet wide for the doubles court, and 12 feet

wide for the singles court. Deck space rarely permits of
this ideal, but an excellent game is possible with courts
only 30 feet long and 14 feet wide. In trying to obtain
the maximum of space there is no valid reason against
the base or side lines running up alongside the bulkheads or other deck impediments, these latter in no way
interfere with the character of the game and are indeed
sometimes an advantage in arresting erratic flights of
the quoit.

The court consists of service courts and inside courts.
The former lie between the service lines and the base
lines. The latter between the service line and the net.

The service lines run parallel to the base lines at a
distance of five feet from the net.

There is a right service court and a left service court,
obtained by a line running midway between the side
lines from the service lines to the base lines.

The singles court, where the court is of full size, is
obtained by running lines two feet within, and parallel
to each of the side lines. The inside lines must be dis-
regarded in a doubles game. This does not mean that
the doubles game cannot be played on a court of singles
dimensions.

The top of the net should be 4 feet 9 inches above the
deck, and its depth should be at least 2 feet. A rope
is not advisable since it is almost impossible sometimes
to decide whether the quoit has gone over or under the
rope, if the players stand as they must sometimes at
the back of the court.

Badminton posts and nets are adequate and are
frequently used for deck tennis. If these are not available
then the net should be taut and should be attached to
firmly secured standards or posts.

The deck quoits are about $6\frac{1}{2}$ inches in diameter and
about $1\frac{1}{2}$ inches thick, and are usually made of tarred
hemp with a covering of some soft material and an outer
cover of tough material like canvas. A softer and more
pliable quoit may be kept for initiation into the game,

but should be discarded as soon as possible. A solid rubber quoit has now also been adopted.

The scoring follows that of lawn tennis and the games and sets are, unless otherwise determined, 'vantage.

The players take their turn, as in lawn tennis, at serving and receiving. The server begins with one foot on the base line at the right side of the middle line and serves the quoit into the opposite diagonal service court, after that point is secured one way or another, he goes along the base line to the other side of the middle line and serves to the other service court and so on. The quoit is a fault if it falls anywhere outside the particular service court in play. It is no fault, however, if the quoit is touched either by the receiver or his partner, even if it is flying outside and even though "OUTSIDE" is shouted before it is touched. This latter rule is of very great importance in deck tennis because a very large number of throws may be obviously going outside, but the game is so fast and furious that it requires the greatest self-control not to take sometimes an obvious flyer. A player in fact occasionally tempts his opponent with a fast one and it is the latter's lookout if he attempts to take it.

The server may have a second service, as in lawn tennis, if his first be a fault, and he may repeat his service if he serves a let. A let can be claimed only if the quoit touches the top of the net and drops into the service court or is touched before dropping, by either receiver or his partner.

Each of the partners opposing the server becomes successively the receiver. The receiver, for the time being, must stand within the service court, if he steps forward into the inside court on receiving or returning a service he loses the point.

The receiver's partner waits until the receiver has returned or missed the service before he takes part in the game, so touches the quoit or takes a service meant for his partner at the risk of losing the point.

In service, the quoit should not be twisted, except in its own axis, otherwise a let may be claimed.

After the service, the eccentric twist may be imparted to the quoit as desired.

The play is called open immediately the service has been returned, and the whole court, inside as well as service courts, is now also open.

A quoit before it is returned must be caught cleanly; fumbling, ringing the quoit over the wrist, or pausing in the act of returning the quoit, renders it a foul catch with the loss of the point. It is obvious from this that no feinting with the quoit is permissible. The quoit moreover cannot be hit back.

A quoit in its delivery must not be thrown, nor lifted, above the level of the chin in service or open play.

The quoit must touch only the hand of the player; any other part of his person, his partner or the deck touched by the quoit renders it a foul, with the loss of the point.

A player may not touch, by accident, his partner's hand or lower arm, if the latter is securing a catch. The hand returning the quoit must neither touch nor pass over the top of the net.

It is a foul to serve or return a quoit with both feet off the ground, i.e., while in the act of jumping.

A quoit falling on the base or side lines must be considered "in."

If the base or side lines run alongside impediments a quoit must be considered "out" if it touches the latter in the course of play before happening by deflection to drop on the line or within the court.

There is so much scope for latitude in playing deck tennis, that it becomes of utmost importance to preserve a bona fide.

The players must themselves acknowledge the fouls they may commit and must not leave this matter entirely to the umpire.

It is sometimes almost impossible for umpires to detect

fouls quite obvious to the players and so the players themselves volunteer information to the umpire or in the absence of umpire to their opponents.

When, for instance, a quoit in being caught and returned touches the clothing or any part of the rest of the person, or when a quoit flying outside is touched or, again, when the player's arm, hand or quoit is touched accidentally by his partner, and, again, when the quoit is hurled above the level of the chin: these are occasions for good faith, and the participants must make their acknowledgments.

It is remarked, too, that in the heat of a fast rally, the players themselves seem quite unaware of such fouls. Observance and acknowledgment of such are possible only by rigid attention to these matters and by an intense desire for fair play.

CHAPTER XVII

TO THE RESCUE OF THE *SAXILBY*

Aboard R.M.S. "Berengaria."
At Sea.

FOR years I have made it a practice, immediately after the Church service on Sunday mornings, to invite my senior officers to my cabin. This is the one short hour during the busy week when we have the opportunity to get together. My Staff Captain, Captain Bate, and my Purser, Mr. Owen, are invariably able to attend, and sometimes my Chief Engineer, Mr. Duncan, if he is not too busy, and on rarer occasions, for the same reason, Doctor O'Brien. When the five of us are together our combined sea service exceeds two hundred years. This is always a contented hour, and as my readers might like to listen-in to the yarns of a few old salts for an hour, let me draw a pen picture of my cabin that I may give some idea of the atmosphere in which we are gathered.

My suite faces directly for'ard, high up beneath the bridge, and my sitting-room, in which we are gathered, is a spacious one, luxuriously furnished. On a large settee, on the port side, Mr. Duncan and Doctor O'Brien are comfortably perched. These two are fast friends but chaff each other unmercifully. Across my dining table, which is situated in the centre of the room, Mr. Owen and Captain Bate sit facing each other, whilst I am perched on my desk chair on the starboard side of my cabin, lazily watching the men who share my responsibility through the blue haze of smoke set up by their pipes.

The atmosphere is one of restfulness, of quiet contentment, and this feeling is further enhanced by the unspoken
thought in all our minds that we are Homeward Bound.

Duncan rises and walks towards a port-hole. He gazes
pensively for'ard for a moment contentedly puffing his
pipe, the sun-rays lighting his strong, rugged face.

"G-r-rrand mor-r-ning!" he remarks, rolling his "r's"
with that enchanting Scotch "burr" of his. "A g-r-rand
mor-r-ning," he repeats absently. But no one answers;
only the gentle swish of the swirling waters outside, and
the faint, pulsating throb of the great engines far beneath
our feet, disturb the contented silence. The Doctor
suddenly leans forward from his perch on the settee.
His keen grey eyes are riveted on the Purser.

"You look tired, Owen," says O'Brien. "Had a
hectic night?" he asks.

The Purser smiles whimsically.

"Not exactly a—ahum—hectic night, Doc," Owen
answers. "But I've certainly had—ahum—an extremely
hectic morning," he adds.

Duncan walks quickly back to his seat. The Purser
tells a good yarn once he gets off the mark.

"What happened, Mr. Owen?" I ask him quietly.

"Oh—ahum—nothing *very* unusual, sir; just a slight
misunderstanding between a passenger and his wife."

"Well, let's hear the yarn, Mr. Owen," I invite.

Owen clears his throat and sits back in his chair.

"Well, sir," the Purser begins. "About half-past one
this morning Hughes, the chief Master-at-Arms, came
to my room and informed me that a male passenger was
sitting down fast asleep outside the door of a cabin in
'B' deck alleyway.

" 'I've woke him up, sir,' said Hughes, 'but I can't get
any sense out of him.'

" 'Is he sober, Hughes?' I asked. 'And have you
found out where he lives?' I added.

" 'He's had a few, sir,' Hughes answered. 'He says
he's forgotten the number of his cabin.'

" 'All right, Hughes, go back to him. I'll be with you in a moment,' I instructed.

"As soon as Hughes had disappeared," Owen went on, "I jumped out of bed, slipped on a dressing gown and slippers, and thus attired I hurried to 'B' deck alleyway. The passenger was still sitting on the deck when I arrived, but Hughes and I at once assisted him to his feet.

" 'Belay there, avast heaving,' he growled belligerently, shaking free from our grasp, and swaying like a reed in the wind.

" 'Steady, old man, steady,' I counselled. 'Pull yourself together, there's a good chap.'

" 'Pull your—hic—darned ship together,' he muttered thickly, clutching wildly at the hand-rail in the alleyway. 'This ish the—hic—whorst she boat I've—hic—ever been on in my life.' "

Owen shook his head despairingly, looking in my direction.

"The ship was as steady as a rock, sir."

I nodded sympathetically.

The Purser continued: " 'Where'd you live, old man? I next asked him. 'What is the number of your cabin?'

" 'I've—hic—forgotten,' he muttered.

" 'It's on your passage ticket. Search your pockets and try and find it,' I pleaded.

" 'I've—hic—losht it.'

" 'Then please tell me your name, then. I can find out the number of your cabin for you,' I coaxed.

" 'I've forgotten my—hic—name. Anyway, who the —hic—blazes are you?' he demanded.

" 'I'm the Purser, old man. It's my job to find out where you live. You can't stay here all night, you know.'

" 'Can't I?' he roared, flopping down on the deck again. 'Who the—hic—shays I can't?' "

Owen sighed deeply, and again caught my eye.

"D'you know," sir, he said sadly, "it took me nearly two hours before I could wheedle his name out of him.

He offered to fight both Hughes and me separately, and then collectively, and at the finish he demanded that Hughes should kiss him before he would divulge his name.

"As soon as he told me his name," continued Owen, "I hurried to my office, quickly scanned the passenger list, obtained the number of his cabin—we'll say it is B 13—and returned to where I had left him with Hughes. Incidentally, I discovered that his wife is travelling with him, sharing the same cabin.

"Would you believe it, sir?" said Owen, again turning to me. "All the time we were arguing with that fellow, trying our utmost to find out where he lived, we were actually standing outside the door of his own cabin, B 13.

"'Why, man,' I said to him, somewhat annoyed, and pointing to the door opposite us. 'This is your cabin.'

"He lurched towards the door until his eyelashes were brushing the number plate.

"'Ish it, Pursher?' he hiccoughed in mock amazement. 'Why sho it ish! How the—hic—hell—did it get here?'"

Owen again sighed deeply.

"I tried the handle of the door, sir, but it was locked. Then I knocked, and from inside the cabin I heard the faint creaking of a bed-spring.

"'Madam!' I called softly, gently knocking a second time. 'Madam! Please open the door, your husband wishes to come in.'

"'He can't come in,' a distant feminine voice snapped, and for a moment there was silence. Then I heard the bed creak again.

"I knocked a third time: 'But Madam,' I said. 'You must please open this door, your husband has nowhere to sleep.'

"The bed gave a louder creak, and presently I heard the sound of heavy obstacles being banged against the inside of the door. She was evidently barricading herself against forcible entry by means of the room furniture and cabin trunks.

" 'Madam!' I pleaded, knocking for a fourth time. 'Do please open this door?'

"An irate feminine voice hissed through the key-hole: 'I don't care who you are, but if you don't go away from my door I shall scream the ship down.'

" 'But, Madam!' I cried in despair. 'What am I to do with your husband?'

" 'Where is the top deck on this ship?' she demanded fiercely, still through the key-hole.

" 'The where, Madam?' I asked in surprise.

" 'You heard me,' she snapped. 'Where is the top deck on this ship?' she repeated.

" 'The boat deck, Madam,' I answered.

" 'Then take him up there,' she hissed viciously. 'And drop him overboard.' "

"Delightful person!" murmured the Doctor.

"What happened then, Owen?" asked Mr. Duncan. "Ye didna' drap him overboard, did ye?"

The Purser waved his hands despairingly. "No, I didn't follow the lady's instructions, Chief," he answered with a sigh. " But I spent another abortive hour arguing with her. She flatly refused to open the door, and in the end Hughes and I made the husband a shake-down in the Lounge."

"One of the Purser's joy nights," laughed Captain Bate.

Owen smiled wanly. "I saw them go hand in hand into the dining-room this morning," the Purser concluded, "so I suppose they've both forgiven me for keeping *me* out of my bed last night."

My crowd were silent for a moment, after the Purser had finished his yarn. Then Duncan broke the stillness.

"Wummen are funny craters," began Duncan, musingly, puffing his pipe. No one answered.

"Aw the same, mind ye," the Chief continued, "we folk wud be in a bad way without the wummen."

The Doc made to interrupt, but I signed to him to be silent. It's not often we can persuade the Chief to open out, and his yarns are too good to miss.

"I was on holiday wi' the wife an' family no lang ago," went on the Chief. " 'Alex,' says she to me one night when we were having dinner in a hotel. 'Alex,' she says, 'I never enjoy a holiday unless you're with me.'

" 'I should hope not,' I telt her, trying to look indignant-like.

" 'No, no, Alex,' she says. 'I dinna mean it that way. But when I go anywhere alone, or with the children, it seems so difficult to get what you want. I can't seem to get the same service as you get. But you, Alex,' she said, 'why, as soon as you lift your little finger everybody runs to serve you.' "

Duncan paused and gave vent to one of his rare smiles before he continued.

"Thinking I was getting one in," he went on, "I said to her: 'If you use your brains, my dear, you can get onything you like in this wor-rld.'

"That did it. 'Brains!' she retorted, fire in her eyes. 'Don't you talk to me about brains,' she wagged an indignant finger at me. 'What would you be to-day, if it hadn't been for me? Who looks after your interests when you're away at sea? Who looks after your soiled linen, gets everything spick and span for you, sews on your buttons, darns your socks? Where would you go during your few hours ashore if you hadn't a nice home to come to? Answer me these questions, Alex Duncan,' she says. Then she wags her finger again. 'A woman has more to do with a man's efficiency, Alex Duncan,' she says, 'than ever the world gives her credit for.' "

Duncan wagged his ponderous head.

"I didna' agree wi' her at the time," said the Chief thoughtfully. "But, mon, there's a lot of truth in what she said." He leaned forward on the settee, his manner earnest, tense. "Take a single man, with no home ties, an' we've plenty o' them," continued Duncan. "He gets back at the end of a voyage wi' all his clothes dirty, perhaps the ship is making a quick turn about, and he has only a few hours ashore—sometimes only one or two during the busy season—what happens? He goes straight to the nearest pub, and sits there drinking until its time to go aboard again. Mind you, I don't say all the single fellows do that, but some do, and I know it."

Again the Chief paused: then he waved his great hands appealingly.

"Mon, isn't it nice to go to your drawer an' find all your clothes nice and clean—all beautifully ironed—everything ready to your hand? But what about the single fellow who has nobody to look after him? His turn comes to go on watch, an' there's his clothes all filthy an' dirty, just as he left them."

The Chief wagged the stem of his pipe at O'Brien.

"You, Doctor-r-r," he demanded. "Will you tell me that that single man in his uncomfortable clothes is as efficient as his mates who have wives to look after them?"

"There's plenty of laundries ashore, Chief," said O'Brien for the sake of argument. "He needn't be married to have his clothes washed."

Duncan snorted disgustedly. "An' when we've only a few hours ashore, how many will trouble to take their clothes to a laundry?" he demanded. "Damned few," he added, answering his own question.

"Then, again," continued the Chief, "there's the letter from home. Immediately the ship reaches port abroad the first thing we look for is a letter from the wife," Duncan lowered his voice. "Oh, mon," he said emotionally, "if there's no letter, doesn't it make you unhappy?" The Chief raised his voice. "What about the poor fellow that never gets a letter, the man who hasn't a soul in the wor-r-rld that cares for him? Has he the same incentive for work as the married man. Will he work as cheerfully? Is he really as happy? I say, an' I speak from experience, that he is not."

The Doctor interrupted. "I suppose, Chief," said

O'Brien, "that this little lecture of yours simply means that you contend that all sea-going men ought to get married as early as possible?"

Duncan edged quite close to O'Brien. "Listen, Doctor-r-r," he said earnestly. "In my younger days I sailed out of Liverpool wi' the sweepin's of hell in my stoke-hold." The Chief waved a clenched fist under O'Brien's nose. "This was the only thing to enforce discipline in those days, O'Brien, especially during the first few hours at sea." Duncan lowered his fist. "Do you know why, Doctor-r-r?" he demanded. "Because the majority of men in those days were single, that's why," said the Chief. "Now-a-days," he went on, "they're mostly married, and as docile as lambs."

We all laughed. "The wives have tamed them," jeered O'Brien cheerfully.

"Laugh as much as you like," retorted Duncan. "But let me tell you this," he concluded emphatically. "The Cunard White Star, or any other shipping company for that matter, would be in a bad way if it wasn't for the wives of their men."

The Doctor again gently chaffed Duncan, but as he concluded his peroration, in our hearts we knew there was wisdom profound and deep in the Chief Engineer's philosophy.

"Your turn for a yarn, Doc," I murmured, addressing O'Brien. He reached lazily for a cigarette.

"What must I talk about, sir?" he asked.

"Tell us about your early experience in India, Doc," invited Captain Bate.

"Not much to tell about that," said O'Brien modestly. "My work out in India was mostly concerned with tropical disease and rough-and-ready surgery. Operations had to be performed under the crudest conditions, under trees, on the open road, in mud-huts, and sometimes in the depths of the jungle. This, of course, was before the war, when we were chiefly combating cholera, famine and smallpox."

O'Brien paused, a grim smile playing about his face.

"Fighting smallpox was our greatest problem," continued O'Brien. "Simply because we were handicapped by the Indians themselves. They regarded the victims of this dreadful disease as some form of offering to the goddess Martha Devi, to whom it is dedicated. Why, it was quite common, when passing through villages, to see vendors in the scabbing stages of smallpox serving out foodstuffs and groceries to their fellow Indians. They knew they were doing wrong, and if they saw us coming they would make a bolt for it. The scabbing stage is, of course, the most dangerous; as the scabs fall off they are scattered by the wind, and infection spreads rapidly."

The Purser shuddered: "I say, Doc," he said quietly. "Do you mind—ahum—changing the subject?"

"I should think so, too," growled Duncan. "Tell us some of those monkey yarns of yours," he added.

O'Brien glanced at the clock above my head.

"Not much time left to tell you about your early ancestors, Chief," he chuckled. "However——

"During my early years in India I made a close study of the habits of monkeys and their extraordinary intelligence rather amazed me. I quickly discovered that not only do they possess the faculty of reasoning and thinking to a high degree—not much lower than many human beings whom I've met—but they also have a sense of humour, a conscious sense of being able to appreciate a joke, if I might put it like that. For instance, I have seen a little black-faced grey monkey playing a game which you would hardly think could be played by any but humans.

"A crowd of these little beggars, perhaps about twenty of them, will sit in a large circle tossing a wood-apple round and round to each other. The wood-apple is about the size of an egg, and they toss this to each other at amazing speed. In the course of the game, if one monkey fails to catch the ball, the others jump on him in a body and there is a rare scrum. After having thoroughly rubbed the victim's nose in the dust and spanked him good and hard, the circle is re-formed and the game starts afresh. Owing to their natural agility and dexterity, and the fact that they exercise exceeding care not to miss the ball, the game sometimes becomes monotonous. It is at this stage that one realizes that monkeys do see the point of a joke. There are always one or two wise old fellows in the crowd who are determined not to be baulked of their fun. These wily ones wait their opportunity, and just as a young monkey throws out a hand to catch the ball an older fellow will pull the arm down, causing the youngster to miss the ball. The young monkey will send up a wail, which is unmistakably a protest that he has been fouled, but this is drowned by the chattering glee of the remainder as they promptly proceed to jump on him."

The Doctor paused, and reached for another cigarette.

"Have you actually seen the monkeys playing that game, Doctor?" Owen asked quietly.

"Why, of course I have, hundreds of times," O'Brien answered emphatically.

"Extraordinary! Extraordinary!" muttered Duncan in an undertone.

"It is, rather," O'Brien agreed.

The Chief coughed dryly: "I wasna' thinkin' aboot the monkeys, Doctor-r-r," said Duncan acidly. "It's your imagination I hae in mind."

O'Brien shrugged his broad shoulders.

"All right, Chief," said he. "Maybe you'll believe this yarn: At one hospital at which I was stationed in India the approach to the main drive was lined with overhanging trees, the latter occupied by a colony of monkeys. Whenever a new patient approached, one of the monkeys would swoop down out of the trees and collar the man's hat, then the animal would dart aloft again with the prize. Itinerant sweet-sellers, knowing the playful habits of the monkeys, used to take up their position just inside the front gates of the Hospital under the trees. The outraged patient would at once commence to stone the raiding monkey, but all in vain.

"'Buy him some sweets, sahib; then he bring your hat back,' a sweet-seller would advise."

O'Brien laughed. "Believe it or not," chuckled the Doctor, "I saw those hold-ups practised many times daily for months. As soon as the patient purchased the sweets the monkey would scamper down, gingerly stretch out a hand for the sweets, and hand over the hat with the other. The monkey never attempted to obtain the sweets and retain the cap, he always strictly adhered to a code of honour. But the most extraordinary part of this game was that the trick was never attempted against an old in-patient. If a person had paid toll once he was immune, but unerringly the new patient was singled out, and as we had hundreds of old and new patients calling daily, how on earth the monkeys were able to single out the strangers is quite beyond my imagination to explain.

"I have also seen monkeys kill snakes," O'Brien continued. "For hours the monkey will watch at a snake-hole, generally as an act of revenge if one of a tribe has been killed by a snake. They grab the snake by the back of the head as it emerges from its lair, but the stroke must be lightning quick. The monkey generally arms itself with a piece of flint, and once the grip is secure, and the monkey doesn't mind the snake coiling around him, it proceeds to rub the snake's head away, spitting on the flint at intervals to make moisture. Only when the head has been rubbed to a mass of unrecognizable pulp does the monkey toss his victim aside and walks calmly off, wiping his hands on its fur as much as to say: 'That's a good job done.'

"One of the most wonderful sights imaginable," continued O'Brien, "is to see an army of monkeys on the move. There are hundreds of different species of monkey in India, and if two different tribes get into the same region one must move. I have seen thousands of them on a country road so dense that all traffic was held up. The monkey is, of course, sacred in India and free from human molestation, and while they are trekking I have seen a long line of carriages, carts and cars all lined up at the side of the roadways patiently waiting for the strange monkey army to pass.

"In Muttra," went on the Doctor, "as in all other Indian cities, there are the usual 'ghats' or temples, where the bodies of Hindus are cremated. There is a god, Hunnaman, the Hindu Monkey God.

"The River Jumke flows through Muttra, and the shadow of Hunnaman falls aslant the river.

"Along the river banks the Hindu populace gather daily and feed the monkeys with grain or chunna. The river teems with turtle . . . turtle varying in size from a man's thumb to about four feet in diameter. The turtle lurk at the water edge and grab their share of the chunna. They, too, are immune from harm as all life is sacred to the Hindu."

The Doctor paused, again glancing at the clock. Our hour is nearly spent.

"Will I have time to finish my yarn, sir?" he asks, addressing me.

I nod assent.

"Well, one day," continued O'Brien. "I was walking along the banks of the Jumke when I saw a Hindu sprinkle a few grains of chunna at the feet of a mother monkey who was carrying a baby monkey in her arms. Like a flash a huge turtle leapt from the water, grabbed the baby's leg and pulled it into the water. In a moment there was a scene of indescribable pandemonium and uproar. Shrieking, swearing and chattering, thousands of the big monkeys at once plunged into the river, and there commenced a terrific struggle between them and the turtle. The monkeys could not hurt the turtle in the water, so four of them would grab a turtle, drag it up the steps to the bank of the river, turn it on its back, bite its stomach to pieces, and then dive back into the

AMBITION!
SIR EDGAR BRITTEN ON THE *BERENGARIA*

THE PROUDEST MOMENT OF HIS LIFE
THE R.M.S. *QUEEN MARY* STARTING HER MAIDEN VOYAGE

water for another victim. In this manner they slaughtered thousands of turtle, and certainly avenged the stricken mother monkey."

Again the Doctor was silent, his eyes pensive, and there was just the slightest trace of emotion in his voice when he spoke again.

"One last monkey yarn, before we break up, sir," he continued, quietly.

"I had an old brown monkey, a dear little fellow I had had for years. He accompanied me on all my travels, riding on the pommel of my saddle. Passing through the villages he would ignore the grain shops of any place which we had previously visited, but if we called at a strange place, he would look out until he saw the man in charge of a shop go inside the back premises, then he would dart off the saddle, dash into the shop, grab a couple of handsful of grain and be back on the saddle again within the space of a second. I used to cuff him for this, much to his surprise and indignation, for he always gravely offered me a share of the loot, but I could never cure him.

"One day," went on O'Brien sadly, "I left him behind, and in my absence he raided the dispensary, devoured a bottle of quinine tablets and washed these down with a copious draught of red ink from my writing-desk. When I returned he was stone deaf from the effects of the quinine, full of red ink and was suffering from syncona poisoning. It took me weeks to get him better, but he eventually recovered. The next time I left him he got hold of a bottle of number nine pills—the powerful laxative of army fame—and swallowed the lot. When I returned he was passing out with violent diarrhœa and vomiting. I gave him several injections of strychnine and did everything possible for him. I can still remember his brown eyes gazing into mine pleading for me to save his life. But it was no good, the little fellow died and . . ."

Above our heads the bridge bell clanged. We all stood up.

"I had had him so long that I greatly missed him," concluded O'Brien sadly.

The hands of my cabin clock stand at noon.

"Eight bells, gentlemen!"

A minute later I am alone; our short hour has passed. Slowly I walk to a cabin porthole, and idly gaze for'ard on the placid water. As I gaze my mind goes back to another voyage, still very vivid in my memory. Thus musing, the scene before me changes; the blue skies give place to dark, lowering clouds, the quiet waters to great, green walls of thundering combers, the soft moan of the wind to the frenzied howl of the tempest.

At 9.30 a.m. November 15th, 1933, the bridge telephone bell tinkled sharply and a second later I was in communication with my Chief Wireless Officer, Duncan Cragg.

"S O S from the Steamer *Saxilby*, sir, asking for immediate assistance."

A few minutes later the written message was in my hands, giving the exact position of the stricken vessel.

The *Berengaria* was then 300 miles west of Ireland, homeward bound on our Eastern Track, the *Saxilby* some 200 miles from us on the Western Track.

"Wireless all ships, Mr. Cragg, and find out if any are any nearer than we are," I instructed.

Many ships were much nearer than we were, but back came the message from various vessels:

"Hove to! . . ."

"Hove to! . . ."

"Hove to! . . ."

"Cannot make headway! . . ."

"Impossible to reach her! . . ."

Tremendous seas were running at the time, lashed to fury by a hurricane wind, and we were running before the gale.

"Stand by, all hands!"

It was a ticklish job turning the towering sides of

the Big Girl broadside on to those crashing seas, but bravely she responded and slowly the great bows swung round, and her nose was pointing for her small, disabled sister.

That job safely accomplished, quickly I entered the chart-room and with the aid of my officers we worked out the exact bearing and distance between the two vessels.

"Received your message, *Saxilby*. Proceeding to your position maximum speed. Expect to reach you by midnight."

That message of hope, flashed by the powerful wireless installation of the *Berengaria*, reached the world and soon every paper in Fleet Street was phoning me craving for fuller details. One paper offered a fortune for a 500-word story of the rescue. All day long these messages reached me, but at one time I had a brief respite, for my radio telephone wires carried away. My wireless staff had to clamber aloft in the teeth of the howling gale to fix the wires, and no sooner was this job completed than the New York papers joined the chorus of their English confrères.

Down below, my passengers were seething with excitement. Shielded by the safe screen of the promenade deck, their eager voices reached me on the bridge. Their one cry was:

"Will we be in time?"

Will we be in time! As I watched the great, green walls of water rushing to meet us I had grave, grave doubts. Heaven help the crippled vessel at the mercy of those terrible seas.

Towards noon Mr. Duncan stamped on to the bridge, his face oil-grimed and pouring sweat.

"How's things below, Chief?" I asked him.

"Wor-r-rking smooth as butter-r-r, Skipper-r-r. She's giving all she has."

She was giving all she had! Maybe the Big Girl knew that on her speed depended the fate of the little vessel being slowly battered to pieces by the pounding seas.

From the bridge it was an awe-inspiring sight watching her ceaseless battle with the mountainous waves, rolling in an endless stream towards her razor-edged bows. Only a ship of her great size could have fought through those mighty seas. At intervals, a gigantic comber, its white-crested ridge forty feet high, would crash aboard, splashing the spume and spindrift high o'er the bridge, shaking the ship from stem to stern. For a moment she would seem to hesitate, as if weary of the fight, then she would toss her great head and sweep ahead again, proudly defiant of the mighty onslaught.

As the grey day waned and darkness fell the storm increased, but we were still many miles from the unfortunate ship.

Then we received a last message of despair.

"Our hatches stove-in. Cannot last much longer."

We could do no more than we were doing, but I wirelessed back:

"Hang on, *Saxilby*, we are not far away now."

Every available officer was on the bridge, all hands were standing by. Down below Dr. O'Brien was all prepared to receive the rescued men.

Pray God we would still be in time.

But even if we were in time, how, in the darkness, in the face of these raging seas, could we transfer the men from the storm-wrecked ship.

"Call for volunteers for the life-boat crews!" I ordered.

In the face of almost certain death, I am proud to say that every man of my crew offered himself for service.

About ten o'clock, Cragg, my wireless officer, appeared on the bridge.

"I'm afraid, sir, we're too late!" he said, with a catch in his voice.

"Too late?"

"Yes, sir! I've just picked up another message from the *Saxilby*, sir. It was broken off almost as soon as I received it, as if her operator tried to wireless just as she was going down."

Cragg handed me the message, it contained only two letters: GO . . .

Go . . . Good-bye!

Two hours later I arrived at her last wirelessed position at midnight exactly.

With every searchlight ablaze, slowly I circled and zig-zagged for miles around.

Of ship or men there was no sign. Nothing but the lonely, angry seas.

All the long night I searched and only when the grey dawn broke on the empty wastes did I turn my ship once more towards England.

There is nothing more to tell.

Even as I write, two flashes from the Bishop's Rock tell me I am nearly home. To-morrow at dawn we reach Cherbourg, and a few hours later Southampton. But in those busy waters my place is on the bridge, so to-night I close this log and wish my readers good-bye.

Good-bye!

EPILOGUE

FOR many long years it has been customary to regard a popular passenger ship and her commander as just two parts of one whole; so that you often hear regular ocean travellers remark: "I always prefer to cross with Captain So-and-so in the S.S. *Nonesuch*. I should never think of doing otherwise."

Now it would be difficult to find a more complete unity and perfect identity of steamer with her Master than in the association of Sir Edgar Britten with the *Queen Mary*. During the first few months of the latter's existence, and the final chapter of the former's career, it was impossible to think of the one without regard to the other. All the Commodore's long and varied experience afloat in every kind of vessel and weather; all his voyages backwards and forwards over the merciless Atlantic; all those unexpected difficulties and sudden situations were but the preliminary training to fit him for the most responsible task which ever an officer in the Merchant Navy was called upon to perform. In the preceding chapters the reader will have seen for himself the kind of routine lived by the Captain of the *Berengaria*, yet the lessons acquired in commanding such a large vessel were essential before undertaking the pioneer duty of handling the *Queen Mary*. It was like beginning a seafarer's life over again, but with a different set of problems.

One sometimes hears it bewailed that as a result of the present age, which has brought about such amazing invention and construction, the machine has already begun to dominate the man which brought it to perfection; that the modern liner, for example, has become altogether too big for human control. During the period when *Queen Mary* was being completed on the Clyde, many a Master Mariner of ripe service and accustomed to taking great liners over the ocean, was heard to exclaim: "Well, I don't envy the Captain, whoever he may be. There's enough worry in a ship of 20,000 or 35,000 tons. But the *Queen Mary?* No. Not even if she was offered me." Yet Britten just took over this immense job with that quiet confidence and disciplined optimism which had always marked his career. One who had known him for years, and been to sea with him, prophesied at the time of Sir Edgar's appointment: "Oh! The *Queen Mary* won't frighten him. Nothing ever ruffles Britten. Calm, cool, collected— that's his nature."

And so it turned out. This distinguished sailor with the modest manner, the sensitive and retiring character, but the tremendous ability for handling ships and men owed his success to that self-restraint acquired in a hard school of seafaring. Nothing could have been further from his qualities than those of the old-time blustering, bullying skipper; for Britten was essentially a lovable being. His officers and men held him in respectful affection; both the *Berengaria* and *Queen Mary* were known as "happy ships"; he himself loved both vessels ardently, though his pride in the newer ship knew no bounds. He who had been brought up in sail, who had graduated in the largest, fastest and most deep-draught Atlantic mail-carriers, never had the slightest doubt about the *Queen Mary*. On the contrary, when once she had been brought out of the Clyde for her trials in the open sea, he was not long in affirming that never had he known a ship so amenable, so responsive, so sweet-tempered. Thus, from first to last, by a fortunate set of circumstances the most wonderful ship in the world had been placed in the hands of the faultless commanding officer.

For several months he was a central figure in the daily

news, and his name on the lips of everyone. Millions
of people all over the globe listened-in to the departure
of his ship from Southampton on her maiden voyage:
the sailing was regarded as a national event. Never
in the Merchant Navy's long history had such royal
patronage been bestowed. This was the great liner that
had been launched in the presence of King George and
Queen Mary, and aboard which King Edward had
lunched a day or two before the final departure for
America. The ovation which sped the tall black vessel
down Southampton Water—the cheers of myriads, the
shrieking of syrens, the fluttering of bunting—had their
counterpart a few days later on the Hudson. The
pandemonium of New York's wild reception was enough
to unnerve the most unemotional, yet Commodore
Britten all the while stood on his lofty bridge perfectly
poised, immune to the din, his entire attention confined
to the safe handling of the tall black ship with the scarlet
funnels.

And when once she had been nursed safely out of the
strong tide alongside the dock, the first anxious voyage
finished, he sought immediate privacy in his cabin high
up above the acclamation that was going on outside.
"That's that," he sighed with relief. "And now for
some sleep."

That first voyage had begun on May 27th, 1936,
and during the summer he kept his ship running to
schedule without a hitch, taking her in and out of
harbour without a scratch. A new steamship needs some
time before she reaches her prime, and engines have
settled down to smooth running. For many years the
"Blue Riband" of the Atlantic had been the Cunard
Company's proud possession unchallenged: then, after
the War, the record for speed had passed to other
nations, but at last the *Queen Mary* re-won this during
the summer. It was a fitting climax to Edgar Britten's
fine sea service. In a few months he was to leave the
Atlantic, the *Queen Mary*, and cease to be a public figure.

He had taken a house in Blundellsands; the rest of his days would be spent with his wife and daughter, cultivating his garden, enjoying a well earned rest after millions of miles navigating.

But that repose following a strenuous life, that quiet haven after much voyaging, was denied him. Five months after he had first taken the *Queen Mary* from her Southampton berth, she was again lying at the same quay and about to proceed. The time of her departure should have been 9 a.m., but at 7 a.m. the Commodore's personal steward on entering the cabin found his master in great affliction. A sudden stroke had cut short a brilliant and adventurous pursuit of duty: the *Queen Mary's* first skipper was carried ashore to die within a few hours. He who had spent so much of his life afloat could not be tied to the land for long.

"He was the kind of man that our people most hold in honour," spoke the Dean of Winchester at the funeral service held in St. Mary's Church, Southampton. "He was one who faced all weathers with an equal calmness of mind, who rose to the top of his profession by his merits. The sorrow and pride that we feel is felt throughout the whole nation and on every sea where the British flag is flown, and above all, through all ranks of the Merchant Navy."

That fairly summed up the combination of quiet simplicity, kindliness, devotion to duty and straightforwardness which composed Edgar Britten's character. It might have been said of him as Nelson said of those who served under the British Admiral on a certain historic occasion: he had "the happiness to command a Band of Brothers." Never did a ship's officers display more loyal and affectionate regard for their Captain than in the *Berengaria* and *Queen Mary*. Rarely, if ever, has the great Brotherhood of the Sea in all its branches been so meticulous in paying its final homage to a splendid seaman and navigator.

It was blowing the usual autumn gale on October 31st,

whilst the *Queen Mary* was rushing westwards across the Atlantic, and at Southampton the first portion of a sad ceremony took place in the presence of many who bore her original commander in such high esteem. Fitting, indeed, was the tribute paid from the Board of Admiralty represented by Vice-Admiral H. J. S. Brownrigg (Admiral Commanding Reserves); Vice-Admiral G. C. Dickens and other naval officers; whilst the Cunard White Star Company were headed by the Chairman, Sir Percy Bates, Sir Thomas Royden, in addition to former captains of that fleet, and some of Sir Edgar's passengers who had been wont to sail with the Commodore.

From the *Queen Mary's* customary berth the body of a tired mariner was taken by the tender *Calshot* down Southampton Water, past the Isle of Wight, and out to sea beyond the Needles. His daughter, his old steward who had served him to the end, and an assistant chaplain who had once been an officer in the Cunard White Star Line, went out in the *Calshot* for the final rites. In those waters, through which Commodore Britten had so often taken the big ships, his body now rests. So little of his life had been spent ashore, so intimate an association had ever existed between him and the sea, that it was well he should go back to where he belonged. He had spent the whole of his physical strength, the whole of his conscientious energy in maritime endeavour; and to the English Channel his ultimate voyage was made.

THE END